The Art of Raising Multilingual Children

Full details of all our publications can be found on https://www.multilingual-matters.com, or by writing to Multilingual Matters, BLOCK, The Fairfax, Pithay Court, Bristol, BS1 3BN, UK.

The Art of Raising Multilingual Children

Xiao-lei Wang

MULTILINGUAL MATTERS
Bristol • Jackson

DOI https://doi.org/10.21832/9781836684497
Library of Congress Cataloging in Publication Data

Library of Congress Control Number: 2026016792
A catalog record for this book is available from the Library of Congress.

British Library Cataloguing in Publication Data
A catalogue entry for this book is available from the British Library.

ISBN-13: 978-1-83668-446-6 (hbk)
ISBN-13: 978-1-83668-447-3 (pbk)

Multilingual Matters
UK: BLOCK, The Fairfax, Pithay Court, Bristol, BS1 3BN, UK.
USA: Ingram, Jackson, TN, USA.
Authorised Representative: Easy Access System Europe - Mustamäe tee 50, 10621 Tallinn, Estonia, gpsr.requests@easproject.com.

Website: https://www.multilingual-matters.com
Bluesky: @multi-ling-mat.bsky.social
X: Multi_Ling_Mat
Facebook: https://www.facebook.com/multilingualmatters
Blog: https://www.channelviewpublications.wordpress.com

The policy of Multilingual Matters/Channel View Publications is to use papers that are natural, renewable and recyclable products, made from wood grown in sustainable forests.

Typeset by Nova Techset India(P) Ltd, Bangalore and Chennai, India.

Contents

This book is dedicated to my late father, Zhong-luo Wang, whose steadfast belief in the power of learning first kindled my love for languages. When I was young, he taught me a few English phrases he had learned in Catholic school before 1949 and showed me the words printed on foreign currencies. His cherished collection of magazines from around the world opened windows to distant lands, and I would lose myself in their pages for hours. Though he himself spoke only Chinese, as his times offered few opportunities to learn other languages, he encouraged me to explore other tongues and worlds beyond our own. His faith in the beauty of language and culture has shaped my life in countless ways, and it is because of this priceless gift that I have devoted myself to raising my own children as multilinguals. His spirit lives on in every page of this book.

Preface

How time flies! Eighteen years have passed since I first shared our two children's multilingual journey in *Growing up with Three Languages: Birth to Eleven*, followed eight years later by its sequel, *Maintaining Three Languages: The Teenage Years*, which chronicled their continued linguistic and personal development through teenage years.

Today, our sons (Léandre and Dominique) continue to grow in their multilingualism as they chart their own paths in life. Born into a world shaped by three languages, they have matured not only as multilingual individuals but also as cultural navigators, adapting and connecting across communities in ways that remind us daily of the enduring value of multilingualism.

Léandre now works in the fintech sector, specializing in machine learning. Multilingual from birth, he was exposed to French, Chinese and English simultaneously, and has since added German, Spanish, Russian, Italian and others, along with some knowledge of Greek, Georgian and Portuguese. He attended school in the United States from preschool through college, where he quadruple-majored in economics, mathematics, international studies and German. During his undergraduate years, he studied abroad in Berlin, Germany, before completing a graduate degree in statistics in Zurich, Switzerland. A passionate problem-solver, he enjoys math as a hobby and is remarkably handy – often dismantling and rebuilding electronics, from cell phones to computers to Tesla components. A curious and adventurous traveler, he blends his love of languages, technology and global discovery in both his professional and personal life.

However, like anyone else, he also has his shortcomings, chief among them being a confident belief in the art of procrastination. Travel preparation is a perfect example: He often packs his bags at the very last minute, smiling as he insists that this is simply the most efficient time to get things done. Whenever he is asked to do something, he begins by saying, 'I'll do it tomorrow' or 'later,' earning him the nickname Monsieur Demain ('Mr Tomorrow') or Monsieur Plus Tard ('Mr Later'). When we tease him about his habit, he defends it with surprising conviction, even citing research on 'active procrastination,' which describes people who intentionally delay tasks yet still perform effectively under pressure. Really? Just recently, because he packed at the last minute and couldn't find his Global Entry card, all of us had to wait for him in the regular line when returning from Montréal instead of using fast entry.

Dominique is currently in the field of computer science, specializing in cybersecurity. Like his brother, he was raised with French, Chinese and English from birth and has since added German, Spanish, Italian and several others to his linguistic repertoire. He completed his education from preschool through college in the United States, majoring in international studies as an undergraduate. He subsequently earned a graduate degree in environmental policy in Paris, France, and later returned to the US during the COVID-19 pandemic to complete a second graduate degree in computer science.

A versatile and creative individual, Dominique has explored a wide range of interests, from soccer and modeling to music production and songwriting. He is also a deeply engaged reader with broad intellectual curiosity. Each morning begins with philosophy, and his recent readings include works by Wittgenstein. He now enjoys playing the piano daily, a pursuit he once resisted as a child. At one point, he even ran for local office in a Swiss village, reflecting his early interest in civic life and global issues.

Dominique's talents are accompanied by a deeply kind heart. For example, during a trip through Basel, Switzerland, he noticed a traveler who lacked the money to purchase a train ticket to Zürich and was about to be removed from the carriage; without hesitation, Dominique bought the ticket for him. In college, he often brought apples and food to people experiencing homelessness, and during one of my visits, several greeted him warmly as we walked by, calling out, 'Here comes our Dom!'

Conversations with him are rich and wide-ranging, his breadth of knowledge always expressed with thoughtfulness and humility. His talents, curiosity and compassion continue to grow and evolve.

Of course, he also has his less-than-perfect side. His meticulous nature sometimes turns into perfectionism, leading him to spend excessive time refining his work. For instance, when preparing a presentation, he might spend days fine-tuning every detail, from the font on the slides to the cadence of each sentence, determined to make it flawless. Recently, while helping Léandre paint the French door of his new apartment, Dominique spent an entire day carefully taping each frame, another day meticulously applying the paint and a third day removing the tape, yet the work was still not complete. We couldn't help but laugh and ask if he was painting a door or restoring a masterpiece!

Though their paths have taken different directions, Léandre and Dominique share a deep connection shaped by their multilingual upbringing. Their languages have not only expanded their ability to communicate but have also deepened their capacity to see the world through multiple lenses, to adapt to new environments and to approach life with empathy and curiosity. Their strengths and even their quirks reflect the richness of growing up among languages and cultures, and how flexibility, persistence and creativity emerge through a lifetime of navigating words and worlds.

As parents, my husband (Philippe) and I are grateful to have given them something more enduring than material possessions: The gift of languages, a legacy that continues to unfold. This book is a tribute to Léandre, Dominique and to all families committed to preserving their heritage languages. May our story inspire you to cultivate the art of raising multilingual children and pass on this priceless gift: The world of words, connection and belonging that multilingualism makes possible.

1 Introduction

In today's interconnected world, families are being formed across borders and cultures like never before. People relocate for work, study, adventure or necessity, building relationships that span linguistic and cultural boundaries. As a result, many children are growing up in homes where multiple languages coexist. For these families, passing on a **heritage language** (a language from a family's origin, usually different from the mainstream language of the surrounding community) is both an opportunity and a challenge.

Yet despite the growing interest in maintaining linguistic and cultural roots, many parents find themselves navigating this path alone. Even with abundant research and good intentions, there is still a striking lack of social infrastructure to support families who hope to preserve a heritage language (American Academy of Arts and Sciences, 2017). Parents often face deeply personal high-stakes decisions with few clear examples to follow and limited communities to lean on.

One father's heartfelt message to me captures this struggle (see Box 1.1). He writes with worry and urgency, torn between the desire to preserve his family's linguistic heritage and the practical limits of life in a place where that language is nearly invisible. His story is poignant and familiar, echoing the deep desire many parents feel to pass on their heritage language and the loneliness that often comes when trying to keep it alive.

Box 1.1 A father's struggle

Professor Wang,

We do not know each other, but I know of your work and I am writing to thank you – because it has made an impact on my life and given me guidance on how to raise my own children as trilinguals.

I first came across your book, *Growing Up with Three Languages*, prior to my elder child being born. I have since re-read certain parts of your book several times, and my elder child is now 4 years old, the younger one now 2 years old. I am ABC from New York Chinatown, my wife is Japanese, both my children were born in Japan, and the elder child is now enrolled in kindergarten at the Yokohama Overseas Chinese School in Yokohama.

> The added complication for myself is that I am American-Born Chinese and grew up speaking Cantonese at home, but almost all formal school instruction in Chinese these days is in Mandarin. As you are likely thinking, my grasp of Cantonese is functional enough for home use, but not enough to properly teach a child as a parent. So I speak only English to my child, and my wife speaks Japanese to her. Unfortunately, there are virtually no Cantonese speaking people where we are, and in those rare instances where we do have family gatherings – the kids get together and play in Japanese. Finally, I saw it coming that my children would not be able to converse with my parents (whom are still in New York) in Cantonese, but now that the 4 year old is capable of proper conversations, it aches my heart even more so that she cannot talk to my mom and dad, since my parent's English are poor, and their Mandarin is not great (neither is my child).
>
> Especially because our 2-year-old is just starting to talk now. Do you have any thoughts, advice, stories or online discussion threads you know of where I can get a sense of what I can do with my child with respect to Cantonese?
>
> - Try exposing them to more Cantonese (cartoons, movies, overseas trips, people)?
> - Stray from the strict One-Parent One-Language rule that we have been practicing since the birth of our children?
> - Give up Cantonese for Mandarin?
>
> I apologize as you must be busy, but this is first and foremost meant as a thank you for sharing your story.
>
> Thank you (and stay safe in these strange times)!
>
> XXXX

This father is not alone. Around the world, parents wrestle with similar dilemmas: Which language should we speak to our children? Can we support more than one heritage language without overwhelming them? Should we be strict in our approach or flexible? And what happens when our children resist or when we ourselves feel insecure in the very language we hope to pass on?

These were the questions my husband (Philippe) and I faced over 30 years ago when we were expecting our first child, Léandre. We were determined to raise him with our heritage languages, French and Chinese, alongside English. Determination, however, did not erase the uncertainty. Would we be consistent enough? Would our child embrace all three languages? Would our efforts matter in the long run?

Looking back now, we feel incredibly fortunate. Through years of **intentional strategies** (grounded in research, cultural values and daily practice), our two sons, Léandre and Dominique, have grown into multilingual adults. More than that, they are curious, thoughtful, open-minded, creative and full of life. Every conversation with them is lively and surprising, often weaving together ideas and perspectives from multiple worlds. Their multilingual upbringing has shaped not only how they speak but also how they see and engage with the world.

This book is for families like ours: Families navigating the complex and sometimes challenging but ultimately rewarding journey of raising multilingual children, especially in their heritage language. Whether you are wondering how to begin, feeling isolated in your efforts or simply looking for inspiration, you are not alone. There is no single formula for success, but there are insights to share, beginning with the lived experiences of families who have walked this path.

What This Book Is About

Drawing on over three decades of my experience as a researcher, parent and educator, this book is especially written for families who wish to pass on their heritage language(s) but feel uncertain about how to begin and how to sustain the effort. Rooted in research and informed by my own family's long-term journey, it offers tested strategies to support **typically developing children** (those without intellectual and linguistic disabilities[1]) in becoming multilingual, particularly in heritage languages, while growing holistically across the physical, cognitive, emotional, social and identity dimensions.

Spanning from birth through the late teen years, the book addresses the real-life complexities families face when navigating multiple linguistic and cultural legacies. Whether you and your partner speak different languages or are striving to maintain ancestral ties across generations, this book encourages thoughtful decision-making that honors each family's unique situation.

Rather than prescribing a one-size-fits-all approach to multilingual childrearing, it invites you to reflect, adapt and build language-rich home environments where multilingualism and the identities it shapes can thrive. Ultimately, it is a book about possibility: how families with diverse heritage languages can raise confident, connected and resilient children in a multilingual world.

What This Book Is Not About

This book is not about multilingual privilege, idealization and superiority. Nor is it about coaching you to produce genius children who speak many 'perfect' languages (in fact, nobody really speaks a language perfectly). While there are numerous advantages to being multilingual (see Chapter 2), the ability to speak multiple languages does not guarantee super-intelligence. Furthermore, this book is not a field guide that provides a magic formula for bringing up multilingual children. It does not propose one only way of raising multilingual children either. Like any other practice in childrearing, approaches to raising multilingual children vary from one family to another, and it is a process of exploration, negotiation, reflection and adjustment. In fact, Dr Ilze Ieviņa expressed this so well in her comment on my previous book,

Growing up with Three Languages: Birth to Eleven (Wang, 2008), which I believe still rings true for this book as well (see Box 1.2).

Box 1.2 A comment from a reader

If you're looking for a foolproof guide for raising your kids in three languages this book is NOT for you. Rather, it is suited for what Xiao-lei calls 'reflective parenting': it brings to the forefront issues that you might want to consider and gives plenty of examples and strategies. It is up to you to decide whether these issues and strategies fit your situation and whether they are something that you want to implement. 'Growing Up With Three Languages' can help parents who want to raise their children with three languages to reflect about their situation and gives ideas for specific methods and practices that can be adapted to their particular situation (Ievina, 2014).

Moreover, to contextualize the strategies in this book, I draw on examples from my two multilingual children, Léandre and Dominique, who have been participants in my longitudinal research. Their examples are not shared to boast but because following the same children for three decades has given me rare, firsthand insight into multilingual development. Much like watching a tree grow from seed to maturity, observing their journey has shown how multilingual abilities take root, branch out and adjust to the changing seasons. Their experiences help illuminate what works, what doesn't and why, adding depth to the strategies presented in this book.

Why This Book Now?

In recent years, there has been a noticeable surge in publications and online resources dedicated to raising multilingual children, including heritage language development within the family environment. This growing interest reflects how common multilingualism has become and highlights the need for support. You may wonder why another book on this topic is needed. There are several reasons I felt compelled to write this one.

Multilingual childrearing is more than simple recipes

There is a tendency in some current parenting materials, including those on multilingual childrearing, to present advice almost like a recipe. The idea is that if parents follow a few simple steps, everything else will fall into place. Simple advice can certainly be useful, especially when life feels busy and overwhelming. But simple does not mean simplistic. Even with a recipe, a dish rarely turns out exactly as written. In the same way, raising children in more than one language is rarely as easy as choosing a method from the 'menu' and trusting that the outcome will take care of itself. For families with limited input in a heritage language, the process is often far more complex.

Raising a child is not like assembling a machine where you follow instructions and end up with a finished product. Children are living, growing and ever-changing. Multilingual childrearing requires flexibility, patience and a deeper understanding of why it matters. Without that 'why,' surface-level advice such as 'just speak the language at home' can feel discouraging when the results do not match expectations.

A more helpful way to think about raising multilingual children is to see it as tending a garden, as bilingualism expert Colin Baker (2014) famously put it. You cannot drop a seed into the soil and expect it to grow on its own. Plants need water, sunlight and care through the changing seasons. Sometimes growth is quick and visible, like a flower blooming in spring; at other times, it is slow and hidden, like roots forming underground. Weeds may appear, storms may come, and the gardener must keep adjusting, protecting and nurturing. Each plant has its own needs, and the gardener responds thoughtfully, knowing that time and steady care will bring results. In the same way, children need consistent input, encouragement and cultural connections to thrive in multiple languages.

This is one of the reasons I wrote this book. As a parent, you deserve more than quick-fix recipes; this book offers research-informed ways to understand not only what to do but also why it works, grounded in real experiences. Just as important, you need space to reflect on your choices and understand what helps or hinders your child's growth. With mindful approaches, your child's heritage language can flourish and become a lasting gift. Like a gardener learning through each season, you are invited to observe, adjust and trust the process. This book offers ways to tend that garden and encourages you to reflect, adapt with care and make the journey your own.

The gap between research and parenting practice

Though research on multilingual acquisition and heritage language development has generated a wealth of information in recent decades, this knowledge has not effectively reached the general public. We now know that the human brain is naturally equipped for multilingualism, and with adequate exposure, children can acquire more than one first language without cognitive detriment (Rochanavibhata & Atagi, 2025). However, this understanding has not been widely shared beyond academic circles. Misconceptions and myths about multilingualism continue to circulate, creating unnecessary anxiety and confusion. Consequently, many parents who aim to raise their children with their heritage language(s), as illustrated in Box 1.3, find themselves searching for reassurance and direction.

Box 1.3 Parental uncertainty

Dear Dr Wang,

My name is XXXX and I would like to write you with a request of your opinion and help if you won't mind and if you will have a bit of time.

We bought your book (Growing up with three languages) and were very happy to have it!

With my husband we are expecting our first baby, a girl, that is going to be borne by the end of April. Being each of us of different nationality with read your book to prepare ourselves for how to speak to her.

My husband is Romanian and speaks fluently 4 languages (Romanian, English, German, Spanish) and average French. He works as a scientific researcher at XXXX. Myself, I am Slovak, with mother tongue being Slovak, and consider speaking rather fluently English, French, German and have some basic knowledge of Spanish. I work as a physician in local cantonal hospital.

We live since 4 years in French-speaking part of Switzerland. Our common language is English since we knew each other in English and our relationship was entirely built in this language. We only use French at work and in communication with the others in everyday life (shops, medical appointments, etc.).

For this reason, we feel natural that at least one of us would speak to her in English even though it is not our mother tongue. I had initially the idea of speaking in Slovak because my mother (her future grandmother) only speaks Slovak. All other members of the family speak and understand reasonably well English. Since our desire is to stay settled in Switzerland, the baby will be supposed to learn at least French (eventually German later on) in kindergarten and school. That means that she will have to be exposed to 3 languages from the very beginning (English, Slovak and French).

However, we start to have some doubts if this is a correct way of proceeding. From what you explain in your book, the child associates the language to a person. Which means that even though I might speak in Slovak, she will witness me speaking English to her father and French outside our home. My husband's parents might wish to speak Romanian with her.

Do you think that a child can deal with 3 languages? The daily exposure to our non ideal English and potentially 4th language: Romanian would be too much? Should we rather encourage the Romanian side grandparents speak in an average English to her? Or encourage them to speak Romanian and maybe risk to overwhelm her?

We would be very thankful to you for your point of view and answer.

Kind regards,
XXXX

The value of preserving a family's heritage language

For many immigrant parents, speaking their heritage language to their children is not just practical; it is deeply tied to identity. Author Sasha Vasilyuk captures this sentiment:

> When I became a parent... my obsessive goal was to teach my son Russian... because Russian forms such a deep-rooted part of my immigrant identity that I couldn't imagine talking to my child in another language. (Vasilyuk, 2024)

I feel the same. I cannot imagine speaking to my children in anything other than Chinese, which reflects my upbringing, cultural identity and the values that shaped me.

Research affirms the importance of this emotional connection. Multilingual expert Jean-Marc Dewaele's research shows that multilinguals often experience their earliest-learned and heritage languages as more emotionally resonant, shaping intimacy, identity and parent–child bonding (Dewaele, 2010). A recent policy brief from the Harvard Graduate School of Education similarly notes that children who maintain their heritage language tend to form stronger relationships with parents and extended family (Aguilar *et al.*, 2024).

Passing on a heritage language, therefore, reaches far beyond vocabulary. It links children to their cultural roots, family histories and intergenerational wisdom, nurturing a deep sense of belonging. As children explore their cultural legacy through their heritage language, they strengthen familial connections, broaden their worldview and carry forward an identity that endures across generations.

Some may wonder whether heritage language learning is still necessary in an age of advanced artificial intelligence (AI) translation technology, which can now provide impressive real-time translation. Yet these tools cannot replicate the profound benefits of true language acquisition. Actively learning a language shapes a child's developing brain, enhancing cognitive flexibility, problem-solving skills and executive function in ways that passive translation never can.

This is precisely why my book is needed. Parents often know the value of preserving their heritage language but struggle with how to do it when daily life is dominated by the majority language. Many parents feel isolated in this effort or worry that their attempts will not succeed, as shown in the emails I share in Boxes 1.1 and 1.3. By sharing lived examples from my own family alongside decades of research and stories from other multilingual households, this book seeks to empower parents to act with confidence and creativity. It demonstrates that while preserving a heritage language is challenging, it is also deeply possible and profoundly rewarding when approached with thoughtfulness and intentional strategies.

Unique challenges of heritage language acquisition and development

Contrary to the common assumption, children born and raised in families where parents speak a heritage language do not automatically learn it (Montrul, 2010). Both research and everyday observations suggest that exposure to a multilingual environment does not guarantee that a child will become plurilingual (Yamamoto, 2002). This is because the process of a child becoming multilingual is complex and demanding (Paradowski & Bator, 2018). The challenging conditions of heritage language acquisition manifest in at least two major ways, as shown below.

Input constraints

Children who live in a household with one (or more than one) heritage language that is different from the mainstream language outside home have more than one first language. A **first language** (often known as the **native language**) is the language that a child learns from birth or early on in life. The development of a first language is of utmost importance for a child's overall growth and wellbeing, including communication, cognitive development, cultural identity, educational achievement, language learning and emotional expression.

Children who have only one first language generally benefit from consistent input and a wide range of resources (such as parents, extended family, the surrounding community, peers and school), giving them an advantage in their language acquisition. However, children who grow up in families with more than one language often encounter limitations in terms of language exposure to each of the languages. This is particularly challenging when raising children with a heritage language in a non-heritage language country or region, as parents are usually the only or major source of heritage language **input** (exposure). The situation becomes even more complex when both parents have different heritage languages. Parents in these families literally must live up to the responsibility of representing a linguistic community (Wang, 2008). For instance, in my family, my husband speaks French to our children as his heritage language, and I speak Mandarin Chinese to them as my heritage language. However, we live in the United States, where English is the dominant community language. Therefore, our children potentially face a disadvantage in terms of both their heritage language input in French and Chinese and their community language input in English, compared with children who are only exposed to French or Chinese, or to English both inside and outside their homes. This input limitation poses challenges to the acquisition and development of each of their ambient first languages.

Inhomogeneity of the family linguistic constellation

Moreover, the configuration of heritage and community languages can differ greatly from one family to another. For instance, in Family A, the combination may consist of Chinese, German and Thai, but in Family B, it could be French, Italian and Spanish. Even though a typically developing child has the capacity to acquire any language in the world, a child in Family A is likely to face more difficulties in acquiring all three languages because of their significant differences. Conversely, a child in Family B may have a comparatively easier time acquiring the languages, given the greater linguistic similarities. Hence, when a child's ambient languages are disparate, his/her parents must use strategies tailored to the child's distinctive linguistic environment to facilitate the successful acquisition of multiple first languages, particularly the heritage language.

Given the complex conditions of heritage language acquisition, many parents either give up or never attempt to pass their heritage language to their children, even when they deeply wish to do so. A video clip I once saw on YouTube captures this common regret shared by many immigrant families. In it, a Chinese American YouTuber spoke with emotion about how his older son refused to speak Chinese with him and called him 'Dad' instead of '*Baba*/爸爸.' He described the sadness he felt while walking through the alleys of his hometown in Beijing, hearing other children call out '*Baba*/爸爸' to their fathers, and lamented that he had raised an American son rather than a Chinese son.

This sentiment is also echoed by many immigrant adult children who wish their parents had taught them their heritage language(s) while they were growing up. Lost opportunities often feel heart-wrenching for these families. As writer Mithu Sanyal (2023) expressed, 'I still feel the pain of not being able to read the books my father loved when he was a child.' The hope of this book is to help families avoid such regret by offering strategies and encouragement to keep heritage languages alive across generations.

Impact of my past work

As previously mentioned, I have documented the multilingual development of my two children and published my longitudinal observations from their birth to the teenage years. Over the years, I have received positive feedback from readers who have shared that my work has given them hope and opened possibilities for their own families in raising multilingual children. It is comforting to know that other families, like mine, face similar challenges (see Box 1.4). Most importantly, many parents have told me that my work has strengthened their convictions and empowered them to raise multilingual children with greater confidence (see Box 1.5). In their emails, I see reflections of their multilingual backgrounds, their desire to pass on a heritage language, and their determination to succeed. My books have played a small but meaningful role in helping them value their own decisions and reflect on their practices.

Box 1.4 Hope and encouragement for parents

Dear Dr. Wang,

Thank you so much for writing your book *Growing up with Three Languages*. Over the last few years, your stories and guidance have been a source of hope and inspiration for me and I wanted to thank you for that. I feel so grateful that you have shared your experience with so many hopeful parents like me.

I have long had a deep desire to teach my children Gujarati and Tamil, the languages of our families from India. But I know mostly of initial efforts that failed over time from parents in our community. I felt hopeless before I came across your book when I was pregnant with my son. After reading your book I have taken on this fun and challenging journey with conviction. No other advice I have come across in my research has been so specific, intentional and thorough. I am so thankful to have your wise voice in my head telling me that, though this is hard, it can be done.

My son XXXX is now 2 and we are amazed at how much he understands. My husband speaks to XXXX in only Tamil and I speak to Ishaan in only Gujarati. Though he's still learning which words to associate with which parent, we feel we are on the right track!

As I continue this journey and face new challenges, I would love to tap into additional resources. Do you have recommendations on other resources or communities that could be helpful? (I have your second book as well, though haven't read it yet.)

Thank you so much for what you have done. I'm eternally grateful.

XXXX

Box 1.5 Successful following of *Growing up with Three Languages*

Dear Professor Wang,

I hope you are enjoying the holidays and don't mind me writing directly to you. More than seven years ago I bought your book 'Growing up with Three Languages', one of the best decisions I ever made. I have since lent the book, and just reordered it for further advice. Your book inspired my husband and me, and we now have two sons, seven and four, who both speak four languages. As I had a moment I wanted to thank you profusely for your research and insights, and the clarity with which you wrote your book.

My family is Indian, my parents grew up very naturally trilingual, Sindhi at home (we are originally from Sindh, a region now in Pakistan), Hindi with friends and English at school – as well as Marathi as they grew up in the state of Maharashtra. When they tried to replicate this with my brother (born in Ghana), they found they were not succeeding. Their paediatrician at the time suggested sticking to one language, and they chose English thinking it would be most practical. They did the same with my sister and I (both born in Brazil). We ended up going to an English school in Chile, and were naturally bilingual Spanish–English, while our Hindi and Sindhi are not as strong, which is a regret.

When I was first pregnant, my husband and I started to think about languages. He is German, grew up only speaking German and later learnt English in school, exchange programmes and then studied and worked for around ten years in the US. To date, he works mostly in English and we speak English to each other. His parents only speak German, so he felt strongly about speaking German to our children.

> I wasn't sure whether to speak to the children in English or Spanish. For me, the language 'at home' has always been English. However, when we decided on English schooling for our sons, I thought I would try talking to them in Spanish, so that they could have this wonderful language, too. To add to the mix, we live in Geneva. So we had both boys do French preschool for three years the older and two the younger, and at the age of four move to the English school. The school still has an hour of French a day, which we supplement with extra-curricular activities in French.
>
> The boys now speak English, Spanish, German and French, with no accent in the other language. If you're ever on this side of the world, I'd love for you to meet them. They surely have an innate talent, but I credit your advice immensely.
>
> Best regards,
>
> XXXX

Motivated by this positive impact, I have been inspired to write the present book. My aim is to support you in raising your child to be multilingual. Whether you are navigating challenges, embracing joys or building a strong foundation for both language acquisition and overall development, this book offers strategies to help you move forward with confidence. You are certainly not alone in this endeavor. Together, we can embrace the beauty of multilingualism and nurture our children as whole individuals.

Since the publication of my previous books, I have received a growing number of emails from parents, particularly those who are just beginning their journey. Many express concerns about the challenges of raising children with heritage languages alongside a dominant mainstream language. As my professional responsibilities continue to expand, it has become increasingly difficult to respond personally to each inquiry. Moreover, the questions raised are often complex and highly context-specific, which makes it difficult to offer meaningful answers without understanding each family's unique circumstances. This book is my way of responding more thoughtfully to the questions I have received. By integrating extensive research with my family's lived experiences, I aim to offer a holistic understanding of the multilingual childrearing process and to share adaptable strategies that support families in navigating this journey with resilience and confidence.

Overall, this book is not just another addition to the growing literature on multilingual parenting. It is a response to real needs voiced by real families. By combining research, lived experience and intentional strategies, I aim to provide a resource that helps parents nurture their heritage languages in ways that are both realistic and deeply meaningful. My hope is that families from diverse backgrounds will feel empowered to give their children the priceless gift of multilingualism and cultural continuity.

The Meaning Behind the Book's Title

I considered many titles before settling on *The Art of Raising Multilingual Children*. I chose this title deliberately because 'art' best captures the depth, complexity and spirit of nurturing a child in more than one language. Multilingual parenting is not a technical manual to be followed or a set of mechanics to be applied. It is a relational, creative and deeply human practice that unfolds slowly and intentionally over time.

Like any form of artistry, raising multilingual children calls for attentiveness, flexibility and intuition. There is no fixed formula and no single approach that fits every family. Instead, it is a responsive craft. Just as a painter adjusts each brushstroke to the texture of the canvas, parents respond to the shifting contours of a child's personality, emotions and developmental needs. We make countless small, intentional choices, adjusting our language use, refining our expectations and reimagining our strategies as our children grow.

This artistry matters because language is never a neutral tool. It is a living part of human experience. Supporting multiple languages is not simply about achieving proficiency. It is the work of creating spaces where a language can live, where motivation can be sustained and where the emotional dimensions of communication are honored. Multilingual parenting adapts across stages of development and family life, recognizing that language is deeply tied to identity, belonging and relationships.

The title also reflects the significance of passing languages and cultures across generations. Language carries memory, values and ways of seeing the world. When we transmit a heritage language, we are doing more than teaching words or grammar. We are offering our children a connection to family history, cultural roots and multiple ways of understanding themselves and others.

Research shows that multilingualism is associated with measurable advantages in executive function and attentional control (Bialystok, 2015). However, its deepest impact often lies beyond what can be measured: In a grounded sense of belonging, in the ability to move between worlds with ease and in the experience of knowing oneself through more than one linguistic lens.

As parents who raised two sons multilingually, my husband and I have witnessed this process unfold over time. It was a deeply rewarding and enduring act of love that required patience and trust in a long-term journey whose results were not always immediately visible. Looking back, we see that what we offered our children through language was more than a skill. It was a priceless and lasting gift of connection, identity and possibility.

The Art of Raising Multilingual Children is not a task to complete but a relationship to nurture. It is about more than strategies or techniques. It is an evolving practice in which the art and the gift are inseparable. The art takes shape through daily, intuitive and intentional choices made with care and trust in the long view. The gift is the confident, connected life that unfolds from those choices, allowing a child to feel at home in more than one world.

Novel Approaches of the Book

In contrast to the parenting advice books currently available on the market, this book offers several unique approaches that distinguish it from the others.

Insights from multilinguals

One of the most distinctive aspects of this book lies in its incorporation of contributions from my two adult children, who have been active participants in my longitudinal studies since birth. Their invaluable insights shed light on the strategies used during their upbringing. Viewed through the lens of adulthood, their reflections now serve as a vital feedback loop for me as a researcher, a parent and an educator.

Drawing from their responses to a survey (see Chapter 6), I was able to delve deeper into the lasting impact of their multilingual upbringing on their self-awareness, identity, multilingual competence, attitudes toward multilingualism and perspectives on the strategies we used as parents. This approach offers a unique examination of multilingual childrearing, weaving together empirical research, personal experiences and reflective insights from both the author and the research participants. To my knowledge, no previous work has engaged with the same children over such an extensive period, making the intentional strategies discussed particularly valuable and credible.

Promoting parental agency

Another defining feature of this book is its advocacy for **parental agency** (the ability to critically engage with childrearing information and make informed decisions). Instead of passively accepting expert advice, parents can benefit from exploring research and evidence-based information for themselves. This challenges the conventional approach found in much parenting literature, including works on multilingual childrearing, which often adopt an author-centered model. In such books, the experts dispense advice and expect the readers to follow their instructions without understanding the reasoning behind them. A key problem with this traditional approach is its omission of original sources supporting the author's recommendations and its avoidance of common technical terms (jargon) used in the research literature.

Although the intention of omitting original literature and avoiding technical terms to make material more accessible is good, this practice can inadvertently limit parents' intellectual engagement. In this book, I intentionally include the original research that supports the strategies I propose, in case you want to explore it further. My experience confirms the value of this approach, as many readers of my previous work have reached out, requesting more direct resources on multilingual childrearing (see Box 1.6 for an example).

Box 1.6 I want to read more information on raising multilingual children

Dear Professor Wang,

I hope this message finds you well. I wanted to express my sincere appreciation for your incredibly informative book *Growing Up with Three Languages*. It has been an invaluable resource for me.

Having gained a solid foundation of knowledge from your book, I am now eager to delve deeper into the subject of multilingual family cohesion and parent–child interaction. I believe that these aspects play a vital role in creating a nurturing environment for language development and cultural preservation.

Could you kindly provide me with more information or recommended readings specifically focused on these topics? I am keen to explore strategies and insights that can help strengthen the bond within multilingual families and enhance the interactions between parents and their multilingual children.

Thank you once again for your exceptional work and for considering my request. I greatly value your expertise and guidance.

Warm regards,

XXXX

Further, in this book, I intentionally include some technical terms that frequently appear in the research literature to increase your accessibility to the original studies. For example, the technical term **theory of mind** (the ability to understand that others have thoughts, beliefs and perspectives different from one's own) is often used in research on children's cognitive and language development. Although such terminology may sound intimidating at first, when paired with a clear explanation, it opens a door for parents to connect with a wider body of research.

This approach to promoting parental agency moves beyond simple **knowledge transmission**, where information is merely presented, toward a **reader transaction**, in which parents actively integrate insights into their own family contexts, and ultimately toward **reader transformation**, in which sustained engagement with research helps refine parenting strategies over time. This book is intended to serve as a springboard, encouraging you to continue exploring, questioning and learning beyond its pages. The more you engage directly with the research literature, the better equipped you are to choose timely strategies that support your child's multilingual development without having to rely solely on experts' interpretation. With research literature now widely accessible through AI and digital resources, you can remain informed and pursue lines of inquiry that extend far beyond any single book.

Advocating for the parent as researcher

This book introduces the idea of the **parent as researcher**, a perspective that invites you to approach multilingual childrearing as a reflective and evolving practice. Although the word 'researcher' may sound intimidating, it is, in reality, something many parents already do instinctively. When you seek information, observe your child closely, notice patterns and adjust your approach according to what you see, you are engaging in a thoughtful and systematic form of inquiry.

The concept of parent as researcher draws inspiration from the well-established **teacher as researcher** tradition, which emphasizes that those closest to the learners are uniquely positioned to understand and support their development (Cochran-Smith & Lytle, 2009; Stenhouse, 1975). Applied to the home, this perspective shifts parenting away from the passive application of prescribed techniques and toward a process of discovery. Rather than relying solely on external experts, parents learn to value the insights that arise from their deep, everyday involvement in their child's life, which has been described as 'complete membership' (Adler & Adler, 1987). This proximity allows parents to perceive aspects of multilingual development that are often invisible in formal assessments, including the emotional dimensions of language use (Dewaele, 2010), as well as naturalistic interactional dynamics that highly structured, positivistic methods fail to capture (Poveda, 2009).

Engaging in parent as researcher involves three interconnected habits:

- **Inquiry:** Seeking out research and credible information on language development and multilingualism.
- **Observation:** Attending carefully to subtle shifts in your child's language use, preferences and challenges.
- **Reflective action:** Using these insights to make intentional and responsive decisions in daily interactions.

By embracing the role of parent as researcher, you move away from rigid formulas and toward a practice that is both informed by research and guided by your own observations and interactions. In doing so, multilingual parenting becomes a craft, grounded in evidence yet responsive to the unique rhythms, relationships and possibilities of your own family.

To ease any lingering worries and help you embrace the idea of the parent as researcher, I share below an example of what this looks like in everyday life, an approach you will have opportunities to practice throughout the book.

Example of the Parent as Researcher in Action

For one week, choose a small, everyday moment of your child's multilingual life to observe, such as storytime, mealtime conversations or play with siblings. Each day, jot down a few notes about the following:

- **Language choice:** Which language does your child use most at that moment?

- **Triggers:** What prompts the switch to one language or another (for example, a toy, a question or who they are speaking with)?
- **Your response:** How did you react? Did you continue in the same language, encourage the heritage language or switch yourself?

At the end of the week, take 10 minutes to review your notes. Ask yourself the following. What patterns do I notice? When is my child most likely to use the heritage language? Are there small changes I could make, such as adjusting my own response, that might encourage more heritage language use?

Then take your reflection a step further. Search for and read a study or article on a related topic and compare your observations with what the research reveals. What similarities or differences do you notice? How might these insights refine your approach at home?

This sample activity captures the core of research: Searching, reading, observing, reflecting, concluding and acting with intention. By turning everyday moments into learning opportunities and connecting them with existing knowledge, you'll see that 'doing research' is really about curiosity and discovery. It transforms parenting into an active process of exploration, where you gain confidence in making informed choices that support your child's multilingual development.

Emphasizing intentional strategies

Another distinctive feature of this book is its emphasis on **intentional strategies** (purposeful actions grounded in research and evidence-based parental practices). Though instinct and trial-and-error are natural parts of parenting, they may not be enough when navigating the complexities of multilingual development. The good news is that raising children with more than one first language does not automatically place them at a disadvantage. With appropriate exposure and support, children can achieve strong proficiency in multiple languages.

Unlike instinctive reactions, intentional strategies are applied with clear goals in mind and are designed to address specific challenges and foster multilingual growth. They involve deliberate planning and thoughtful adaptation, drawing on evidence about how children acquire and maintain multiple languages. Importantly, intentional strategies help counteract the input limitations that children often face when learning heritage languages alongside the dominant language.

Intentional strategies matter because they are supported by empirical research, giving you a reliable foundation to build on. They have also been tested and refined through more than 30 years of longitudinal observation, making them both practical and field-tested. Just as importantly, they are inclusive and adaptable, applying across languages with very different structures, vocabularies and phonetics, so you can tailor them to your child's unique linguistic environment.

At the same time, intentional strategies are not about rigid rules but about cultivating curiosity and reflection. By observing, questioning and drawing conclusions from everyday experiences, much like researchers do, parents transform ordinary moments into opportunities for discovery. This reflective approach not only minimizes the frustrations and detours often encountered in the heritage language journey but also empowers you to make informed, responsive choices. In doing so, you provide your child with greater consistency, clarity and long-term success in their multilingual development.

Prioritizing family wellbeing and foregrounding parental differences

This book distinguishes itself from other parenting guides by offering practical strategies to support family wellbeing in multilingual households, an aspect that is often overlooked in the existing literature on multilingual childrearing. Multilingual families frequently consist of parents from diverse cultural backgrounds, each with unique beliefs about childrearing. These differences can influence family dynamics in ways that are distinct from monolingual or culturally homogenous families, sometimes posing challenges to family cohesion.

This book provides strategies to help parents recognize and reconcile these differences, fostering a supportive environment where children can develop not only multilingual skills but also cross-cultural understanding. By implementing these approaches, parents can nurture their children's linguistic and cultural competencies while strengthening family bonds, fostering a deeper awareness of family dynamics and taking meaningful steps to enhance overall cohesion and harmony (Wang, 2013).

Situating multilingual childrearing in the process of childrearing

This book invites you to see multilingual childrearing not as a separate task but as an integral part of raising a whole child. Everyday interactions in the heritage language naturally support children's cognitive, emotional, physical and cultural development, weaving language into the broader process of childrearing rather than treating it as an isolated goal.

Cognitively, using multiple languages strengthens memory, attention and flexible thinking, allowing children to approach problems from multiple perspectives. Emotionally, navigating languages fosters empathy, resilience and confidence as children learn to express themselves across cultural contexts. Physically, language learning engages the body through sound, rhythm, gesture and movement, reinforcing learning through multisensory experience.

At a deeper level, multilingualism supports a strong sense of belonging. Each language connects children to family, culture and history while preparing them to engage confidently with a wider world. By situating heritage language use within holistic childrearing, you offer your children not only linguistic skills but also a richer, more grounded way of understanding and participating in the world.

Uncovering overlooked topics in previous parenting literature

This book also explores topics that are less examined in current multilingual parenting, such as the distinctive **discourse styles** of multilingual children (including how they mix, shift and creatively repurpose elements from different languages to suit various communicative situations) and their use of **language play** (the intentional and playful manipulation of linguistic features across languages to express ideas, entertain or reduce tension). These topics offer valuable insight into the rich and dynamic nature of multilingual communication and the expressive potential of multilingual children.

Focusing on multiple angles

Finally, this book recommends strategies informed by multiple perspectives: Research literature, the lived experience of raising simultaneous multilingual children, reflective analysis of our family's strategies through a longitudinal lens, and feedback from my now-adult children. This multiangle approach allows for a more comprehensive understanding of what works, why it works and under what conditions. By combining research-based, experiential and reflective viewpoints, this approach invites you to critically evaluate the suggested strategies and consider how they might apply to your own family's multilingual journey.

My Unique Advantages as the Author

The combination of my roles as a parent-researcher makes this book more insightful. These roles have at least three major advantages when exploring children's multilingual development longitudinally, despite potential biases that may exist in a parent-researcher approach.

First, as a parent-researcher, I recognize that an **emic** (insider's) perspective carries the possibility of bias, yet it also offers an in-depth understanding of what it means to raise children with multiple languages, especially heritage languages. With careful reflection and intentional handling, this perspective allows rich insights while helping minimize the influence of bias. I also have had the unique opportunity to observe my children's multilingual development daily, in contrast to typical research that often relies on limited observational sessions with young children. This ongoing, everyday access has enabled me to evaluate parental strategies and their impact on multilingual outcomes through a **longitudinal** (long-term) lens, sharing both successes and mistakes so that you can avoid potential pitfalls.

Second, the advantage of serving as parent-researcher can better understand the **underdeterminacy**[2] (Everett, 2017), which refers to situations where it is challenging to determine the specific source or cause of a language-related phenomenon or outcome, and which may be difficult for an outsider to grasp. For instance, consider the example I mentioned elsewhere (Wang, 2008) when Léandre used the term 大便-ing (having a bowel movement). An external researcher may not fully understand the genuine context and could misinterpret it as language mixing (mixing Chinese 大便 with the English ending -ing) caused by insufficiencies in Chinese, thus missing the deliberate use by Léandre as a form of language play and his knowledge as a young child on adding the -ing form to the Chinese verb 大便.

Third, my advantage as a parent-researcher allows me to reflect on my children's multilingual development. The observations made at a particular developmental stage can be revisited and analyzed over time. This also pertains to the intentional strategies I used, and I can observe how they have influenced my children's language development over an extended period. This **retrospective reflection** (looking back or thinking about past events, experiences or actions and considering their long-term impact) offers valuable insights into the evolution of multilingual development and the long-term impact of intentional strategies on heritage language development. In addition, such retrospective reflection can offer my insight on the lessons learned in my own multilingual childrearing process and can help you avoid unnecessary missteps and enhance the successful strategies. For example, in my early studies of my older son Léandre, I was convinced that he was fully confident in using his mainstream language, English. However, his later reflection (see Chapter 6) reveals that he sometimes questioned his English word choices at school. This underscores the value of retrospective reflection drawn from emic observations, which an outside researcher would not be able to access.

Notes on Terminology

To ensure a clear understanding of the terminology used in this book, I will clarify the definitions of some key terms. Though these terms may carry different meanings in other contexts or be subject to debate among researchers, the definitions provided here reflect how they are used within the scope of this book.

Home language and heritage language

There is no universal agreement on the definitions of home language and heritage language. Generally, **home language** refers to the language primarily spoken within the home during a child's early years, typically acquired naturally through daily interaction with her/his caregivers. **Heritage language**, by contrast, is often defined as a language connected to a family's cultural or ancestral background. It may not be the dominant language in the community and is sometimes one that children seek to retain, relearn or strengthen over time. Some scholars also extend the definition to include broader cultural and generational dimensions (Montrul, 2010).

In reality, however, the boundary between these terms can be fluid. For example, in my own family, I use Chinese at home with my children, a variety that may differ in certain aspects, such as accent and vocabulary, from the Chinese used in schools and the media. For me, this is a heritage language, rooted in my cultural identity. For my children, it functions as a home language, which shaped their earliest language experiences.

Given this overlap, I use 'home language' and 'heritage language' interchangeably throughout this book, focusing on the language(s) spoken at home from birth. The goal is not to draw strict distinctions but to explore how parents can support these languages in everyday family life, recognizing that what is a heritage language for the parent often becomes a home language for the child.

In line with this overlap, several other terms are also used interchangeably in this book, including **chosen language**, **designated language**, **target language**, **family language** and **ambient language**. Though each may carry specific meanings in different fields, they are used here more broadly to refer to the language(s) that parents intentionally expose their children to at home.

Bilingualism, trilingualism and multilingualism

Traditionally, linguistic labels have functioned like a headcount. Individuals speaking two languages are called **bilingual** and those speaking three are **trilingual.** However, contemporary research favors the inclusive term **multilingual** to describe anyone using more than one language (Cenoz, 2013). This shift reflects a move away from seeing languages as separate units toward viewing them as a fluid, dynamic spectrum.

The term **multilingual** captures how people actually use their languages as an integrated repertoire. This perspective, known as **translanguaging,** posits that children do not operate two or three distinct engines. Instead, they draw from a single, complex system of grammatical and cultural knowledge to navigate their world (Otheguy *et al.*, 2015).

Dynamic systems theory suggests further that language development is non-linear and constantly evolving depending on the social context (Herdina & Jessner, 2002). Whereas adding a third or fourth language certainly introduces unique cognitive and social variables, the fundamental process of managing multiple systems remains the core experience. Multilingual competence is therefore best understood as an integrated and adaptive system rather than a collection of separate skills (Cenoz & Gorter, 2011).

In this book, **multilingual** refers to all individuals who communicate in more than one language. Using this term does not erase the distinct differences between acquiring two languages versus three or more. Instead, it acknowledges the shared reality of living with multiple languages. Though I use 'bilingual' or 'trilingual' when specific numeric data is required, I primarily use 'multilingual' to focus on the common processes of identity and communication that define the experience of growing up with more than one language.

Gender pronouns and possessives

To promote gender inclusivity while maintaining readability, this book alternates the use of traditional gendered pronouns. In some sections, she/her/hers is used but he/him/his in others to acknowledge the diversity of readers' preferences and experiences. Where appropriate, gender-neutral language is also used.

How This Book Can be Used

This book considers multilingual development within a broad developmental context, from prenatal preparation to adolescence. Ideally, you will read it in sequence, whether you are planning to raise a multilingual child or your child is already in early childhood (birth-5 years), middle childhood (ages 6–12) or adolescence (ages 13–19). Each stage builds on the one before it, so understanding earlier foundations can clarify later behaviors, and learning about later stages can help you anticipate what lies ahead.

Research in developmental psychology supports this broader perspective, emphasizing that learning occurs within a continuous developmental process (Darling-Hammond *et al.*, 2019) and that a child's growth must be understood within the context and time (Bronfenbrenner, 1979). Reading sequentially helps you view multilingualism not as isolated milestones but as an evolving, lifelong journey that connects language, culture and identity.

Decision on Reference Inclusion

Because of space limitations, I will not include a separate recommended reading list or a single reference section at the end of the book. Instead, each chapter will contain its own reference list. These references can also serve as suggested readings. If you wish to explore the topics further, you may use these lists to locate additional sources. In selecting citations, I follow two guiding principles: To include the most relevant works and to credit original contributions. As a result, some references may appear 'dated', but they remain foundational to the field. I recognize that any selection involves difficult choices, and I extend my apologies to authors whose important work could not be included.

Overview of Each Chapter

This book includes a preface and seven chapters.

Preface

As you read in the preface, I provide a brief update on our two children, Léandre and Dominique, who were featured in my research and previous books on their multilingual upbringing longitudinally. This update helps orient readers who may be familiar with their stories and reintroduces them for those encountering them here, offering continuity with the longitudinal work presented in my previous publications.

Chapter 1: Introduction

The chapter you have just completed discusses the need to support the growing number of families in which parents come from different linguistic and cultural backgrounds in passing on their heritage languages. It clarifies what the book is and is not about, and explains why such a book is necessary. It also explains the choice of title, outlines the features that set it apart from other works and identifies the author's unique vantage as both a parent and a researcher. In addition, the chapter clarifies key terms used throughout, offers suggestions on how the book can be used and concludes with a brief preview of each chapter.

Chapter 2: Preparing for the Journey: Family Language Planning

Chapter 2 prepares you for the journey of raising your child with more than one language. It begins by dispelling common myths and misconceptions that often discourage families from pursuing multilingual childrearing. Next, it highlights the many benefits of raising children with a heritage language and nurturing multilingualism, especially those less commonly discussed, with the aim of inspiring you to invest in your child's linguistic growth. The chapter then identifies critical areas that require attention as you prepare for this journey. Drawing on research literature and successful practices, it emphasizes the importance of crafting a well-thought-out family language plan to overcome potential obstacles and support your success.

Chapter 3: The Multilingual Formative Years (Birth to Age 5): Building the Foundation

This chapter emphasizes the critical importance of early childhood and its impact on multilingual development. You will find practical ways to create a warm, language-rich home where all languages, especially the heritage language, can thrive. Through simple daily activities and routines, the chapter offers strategies to support joyful communication while nurturing your child's confidence and connection to her languages and cultures. You are also encouraged to take on the role of parent as researcher in action, observing and reflecting on your child's progress so your strategies can evolve with their growing needs.

Chapter 4: The Multilingual Testing Years (Ages 6–12): Sustaining a Shifting Linguistic Landscape

Chapter 4 focuses on middle childhood (ages 6–12), a critical stage when the mainstream language often becomes dominant and everyday opportunities to use the heritage language can slip away. For many families, this period becomes the real test of whether the heritage language will thrive or begin to fade. The chapter highlights common challenges that emerge as children's social worlds expand and offers intentional, developmentally attuned strategies to keep the heritage language active and meaningful. It also presents simple, research-informed ways to track your child's progress using clear developmental milestones and the parent as researcher approach. Ultimately, Chapter 4 helps you support your child through this shifting linguistic landscape so she can remain connected to her heritage language while continuing to grow as a multilingual individual.

Chapter 5: The Multilingual Negotiation Years (Ages 13–19): Making Multilingualism Last

Chapter 5 explores the teenage years, when your teen's proficiency in the mainstream school and community language often exceeds the heritage language. As academic demands rise and the language of schooling becomes dominant, the gap between home and school language may widen. This chapter provides strategies for weaving the heritage language into your teen's academic and social life, along with practical measures to track progress, reduce attrition and link home use with school-based language through the parent as researcher approach. It also shows how teens' growing metacognition and self-reflection can strengthen their identity and deepen their connection to the heritage language, helping them carry it forward with confidence.

Chapter 6: In Their Own Words: Perspectives from Multilinguals

This chapter presents the voices of Léandre and Dominique, siblings raised with the one parent–one language approach and followed over time. Now young adults, they reflect on how growing up with multiple languages shaped their self-awareness, identity and views about language. Through their personal narratives, gathered through a reflective survey, you gain a first-hand perspective on what multilingualism feels like from the inside. They also offer insights on their parents' childrearing strategies, noting what supported their growth and what posed challenges. Their stories provide an authentic picture of how multilingual practices are lived and remembered, and the chapter concludes with my reflections on the key insights their experiences reveal.

Chapter 7: All Things Considered: Closing Thoughts

The final chapter brings together the core messages of *The Art of Raising Multilingual Children* through a **middle voice framework**, which views parenting as a collaborative process in which parents and children shape each other's growth. It underscores that multilingual childrearing is a dynamic journey where both grow together. The chapter offers strategies to reduce common frustrations, navigate challenges and support overall family wellbeing, including cohesion and communication. It also briefly addresses topics beyond the book's main focus, such as raising multilingual children with neurodivergence. Ultimately, it invites you to view multilingualism not just as a linguistic goal but as a meaningful, identity-rich way of life.

Notes

(1) Because multilingual development in typically developing children is already complex, extending this discussion to neurodivergent populations, whose profiles and needs vary widely, would require a level of depth and specificity beyond the scope of this book. Nevertheless, Chapter 7 includes a brief section on supporting heritage language learning for children with neurodivergence.

(2) Linguist Daniel Everett, in *How Language Began* (p. 4), discusses the concept of **underdeterminacy**, which refers to situations where the available information is insufficient to determine a single, definite outcome. Multiple interpretations or solutions can arise from the same data. In everyday communication, each utterance carries implicit knowledge, values, roles and emotions, a kind of contextual 'dark matter' that is not fully expressed. Understanding language depends on a shared, internalized framework of social norms, values and knowledge; without this shared background, full comprehension is impossible.

References

Adler, P.A. and Adler, P. (1987) *Membership Roles in Field Research*. Sage.

Aguilar, G.M., Vázquez, M.Á. and Fitzpatrick, I. (2024) *Why Heritage Language Is Important for Immigrant Origin Children's Development and Learning*. Immigration Initiative at Harvard, Harvard Graduate School of Education. Available at: https://immigrationinitiative.harvard.edu/brief/why-heritage-language-is-important-for-immigrant-origin-childrens-development-learning/

American Academy of Arts and Sciences (2017) *America's Languages: Investing in Language Education for the 21st Century*. American Academy of Arts and Sciences.

Baker, C. (2014) *A Parents' and Teachers' Guide to Bilingualism* (4th edn). Multilingual Matters.

Bialystok, E. (2015) Bilingualism and the development of executive function: The role of attention. *Child Development Perspectives* 9 (2), 117–121. https://doi.org/10.1111/cdep.12116

Bronfenbrenner, U. (1979) *The Ecology of Human Development: Experiments by Nature and Design*. Harvard University Press.

Cenoz, J. (2013) Defining multilingualism. *Annual Review of Applied Linguistics* 33, 3–18. https://doi.org/10.1017/S026719051300007X

Cenoz, J. and Gorter, D. (eds) (2011) *Multilingual Education: Between Language Learning and Translanguaging*. Cambridge University Press.

Cochran-Smith, M. and Lytle, S.L. (2009) *Inquiry as Stance: Practitioner Research in the Next Generation*. Teachers College Press.

Darling-Hammond, L., Flook, L., Cook-Harvey, C., Barron, B. and Osher, D. (2019) Implications for educational practice of the science of learning and development. *Applied Developmental Science* 24 (2), 97–140. https://doi.org/10.1080/10888691.2018.1537791

Dewaele, J.-M. (2010) *Emotions in Multiple Languages*. Palgrave Macmillan.

Everett, D. (2017) *How Language Began: The Story of Humanity's Greatest Invention (Page 4)*. W. W. Norton & Company.

Herdina, P. and Jessner, U. (2002) *A Dynamic Model of Multilingualism: Perspectives of Change in Psycholinguistics*. Multilingual Matters.

Ievina, I. (2014) Book review: 'Growing up with three languages' by Xiao-lei Wang. *Let the Journey Begin*. Available at: https://www.letthejourneybegin.eu/book-review-growing-up-with-three-languages-by-xiao-lei-wang/

Montrul, S. (2010) Current issues in heritage language acquisition. *Annual Review of Applied Linguistics* 30, 3–23. https://doi.org/10.1017/S0267190510000103

Otheguy, R., García, O. and Reid, W. (2015) Clarifying translanguaging and deconstructing named languages: A perspective from linguistics. *Applied Linguistics Review* 6 (3), 281–307. https://doi.org/10.1515/applirev-2015-0014

Paradowski, M.B. and Bator, A. (2018) Perceived effectiveness of language acquisition strategies among adult multilinguals. *International Journal of Bilingual Education and Bilingualism* 21 (6), 647–665. https://doi.org/10.1080/13670050.2016.1203858

Poveda, D. (2009) Parent and ethnographer of other children. *Anthropology Matters* 11 (1), 1–10. https://doi.org/10.22582/am.v11i1.26

Rochanavibhata, S. and Atagi, N. (2025) Broadening horizons: 25 years of advancing cognitive development research through linguistic and cultural diversity. *Frontiers in Developmental Psychology* 3, 1605723. https://doi.org/10.3389/fdpys.2025.1605723

Sanyal, M. (2023) 'I can't say my own name': The pain of language loss in families. *BBC Future*, 26 June. Available at: https://www.bbc.co.uk/future/article/20230608-what-happens-when-you-cant-speak-your-parents-native-language

Stenhouse, L. (1975) *An Introduction to Curriculum Research and Development*. Heinemann.

Vasilyuk, S. (2024) 'How do I talk to my son about a war I don't understand?'. *The New York Times*, 15 April. Available at: https://www.nytimes.com/2024/04/25/opinion/russia-ukraine-war-mother.html

Wang, X.-L. (2008) *Growing up with Three Languages: Birth to Eleven*. Multilingual Matters.

Wang, X.-L. (2013) Multilingualism and family welfare. In T.K. Bhatia and W.C. Ritchie (eds) *The Handbook of Bilingualism and Multilingualism* (pp. 542–562). Wiley-Blackwell. https://doi.org/10.1002/9781118332382.ch22

Yamamoto, M. (2002) Language use in families with parents of different native languages: An investigation of Japanese–non-English and Japanese–English families. *Journal of Multilingual and Multicultural Development* 23 (6), 531–554. https://doi.org/10.1080/01434630208666484

2 Preparing for the Journey: Family Language Planning

You are expecting, filled with both excitement and uncertainty. Your heart overflows with dreams for the child you are waiting to meet: Her first smile, her infectious laughter and the sound of her voice. But your dreams go deeper. You imagine her chatting with grandparents, switching playfully between languages with friends and moving through life with the confidence of someone who belongs to more than one world.

This is more than parenting; it is a sacred promise. A promise to pass on not just your love but the very essence of who you are through language. The lullabies your mother sang to you, the bedtime stories your father whispered and the playful idioms that make your family's speech unique all have the potential to become your child's inheritance.

Beneath the excitement, however, questions often arise:

- Will our future embrace all of her languages?
- Can I really give her this gift while living in a linguistic community different from my own heritage language?
- How can I keep my heritage language alive when I am the only one speaking it at home?
- Will she ever feel truly connected to my culture if she grows up far from it?

These questions are part of your preparation for the journey in these precious months of waiting for your baby's arrival. Everything you do to support her multilingual future is already shaping her path. You are not only getting ready to meet your baby; you are preparing to welcome a little citizen of the world who will carry the richness of your voices, cultures and languages as part of her birthright.

For families whose home language matches the dominant language of their community, this process often happens naturally. Daily conversations, school environments and social interactions provide steady support for language development. But when a family's language differs from that of the broader society, particularly in households where each parent speaks a different language, thoughtful planning becomes not just helpful but essential to ensure that heritage languages have a real chance to thrive.

This is a reality my husband and I know firsthand. I am a native Chinese speaker, he is a native French speaker and we raised our children in the United States, where English surrounded us at every turn. Over 30 years ago, as expectant parents, we were both excited and uncertain about raising multilingual children. The challenge of supporting three distinct languages felt overwhelming. Yet having a language plan in place gave us clarity and direction and it ultimately played a key role in our children's multilingual success.

In this chapter, I will begin by debunking some common myths and misconceptions that might discourage you from pursuing multilingual childrearing, offering reassurance in their place. I will then highlight the many benefits of raising children with a heritage language and multilingualism, benefits that can inspire and strengthen your commitment. Most importantly, I will walk you through key considerations and practical steps for preparing your own multilingual parenting journey, helping you create a language plan that supports your goals while reflecting your family's unique strengths and circumstances.

Common Myths and Misconceptions

Parents often encounter myths and misconceptions that hinder their efforts to raise multilingual children. These misunderstandings can create unnecessary concerns and discourage families from pursuing multilingual childrearing. Despite research dispelling many of these myths, they continue to circulate in public discourse.

Myth 1: Multilingualism takes time away from the majority language

A common concern is whether prioritizing the dominant societal language, such as English in the US is more practical for a child's academic success. Some parents stop speaking their home language, fearing it might interfere with learning the majority language. However, research has consistently shown that maintaining a home language does not hinder acquiring another language. In fact, it can strengthen family communication, reinforce cultural identity and even enhance cognitive flexibility (Cummins, 2001). Supporting multiple languages offers children a broader foundation for growth.

Myth 2: True multilinguals have equal, perfect mastery of all languages

An outdated belief is that true multilingualism means equal fluency in all languages. As a result, multilinguals' language skills are often undervalued. In reality, most multilinguals use their languages for different purposes – home, school, work or community – so proficiency naturally varies. **Code-switching** (alternating between languages in conversation) and varying proficiency levels are typical and do not indicate confusion or 'linguistic contamination' (Garcia & Li, 2014). Multilingualism is functional rather than perfectly balanced, which means that individuals draw on whichever language best fits the situation, maximizing each to meet specific communication needs. Anyone who speaks more than one language knows it is nearly impossible to have exactly the same level of proficiency across all the languages one uses. Insisting on perfection in every language spoken is unrealistic. It is like a gardener expecting every flower in the garden to bloom at the same time and with the same intensity. Languages, like flowers, thrive differently depending on the soil and season, and that variation is what gives the garden its richness.

Myth 3: Multilingualism causes language delays or cognitive deficits

Some worry that introducing multiple languages may slow speech development or cause language delays, especially in children with existing speech concerns. However, research confirms that multilingualism does not cause language disorders (Paradis, 2021). In fact, multilingual children with specific language impairments sometimes match or outperform their monolingual counterparts in certain areas (Tsimpli *et al.*, 2016). Although multilingual children may initially have a smaller vocabulary in each language, their total vocabulary across languages is often larger (De Houwer *et al.*, 2014). Delayed word retrieval or complex sentence structure mastery is temporary and resolves over time (Ivanova & Costa, 2008). The cognitive and social benefits of multilingualism far outweigh these temporary variations in development (Luk *et al.*, 2011).

Assessing multilingual development using monolingual norms is misleading. These children navigate multiple linguistic systems, each with distinct rules, which may extend the learning process. Instead of being 'behind,' they follow a different developmental trajectory, with one language sometimes temporarily dominating, depending on exposure (De Houwer, 2007).

Myth 4: Children must learn multiple languages from birth to become truly multilingual

Many believe multilingualism must start in infancy to be achieved. Though early exposure has advantages, particularly in pronunciation, research shows that consistent exposure and meaningful interaction are what truly matter (Byers-Heinlein & Lew-Williams, 2013). Older children and even adults can attain high proficiency, though they may retain accents or non-conventional grammar (Paradowski, 2013). Even children raised multilingually from birth may end up dominant in one language; about 25% of them do (De Houwer, 1999). Language development is dynamic, shaped by usage, social context and communicative needs, not just age of first exposure (Hoff, 2006).

Pause and Reflect

Myth 1: Multilingualism Takes Time Away from the Majority Language

Reflect: Do you worry that speaking your heritage language might hold your child back in school? Where does this worry come from?

- Concern 1: ____________________
  Source: ____________________
- Concern 2: ____________________
  Source: ____________________
- Concern 3: ____________________
  Source: ____________________
- Concern 4: ____________________
  Source: ____________________

Parent as researcher in action: Explore what research says about these concerns.
Notes: ____________________

Myth 2: True Multilinguals Have Equal, Perfect Mastery of All Languages

Reflect: Think about the contexts in which you use each of your languages. Rate your comfort in each from 1 to 5 (1 = beginning comfort, 2 = somewhat comfortable in limited situations, 3 = comfortable in familiar contexts, 4 = mostly comfortable across contexts and 5 = very comfortable and confident across contexts).

- Language A: ____________ Rating (1–5): ____________
- Language B: ____________ Rating (1–5): ____________
- Language C: ____________ Rating (1–5): ____________

Look at your ratings of each of your languages. Do they function in the same way? What might this suggest when you later evaluate your child's multilingual proficiency?

Parent as researcher in action: What does 'success' mean for you? Is it equal fluency in all languages or effective use across the contexts that matter?

- **My definition of success:** ____________________
- **Is this definition realistic in your family context?** ☐ Yes ☐ No
  Why or why not: ____________________
- **One mini research step I will take this week:** ____________________
  (For example, evaluate my family situation and list elements that will support my child's heritage language success, scan two credible sources and note one insight from each, identify three local or online resources and record contacts, interview one multilingual family and write three takeaways.)
- **Notes:** ____________________

Myth 3: Multilingualism Causes Language Delays or Cognitive Deficits

Reflect: What do you think now about the myth that multilingualism can cause language delay or disability? Has your understanding changed? Write a few sentences about how you would respond to another parent who still believes this myth.

Parent as researcher in action: Imagine a friend asks you whether learning more than one language might confuse a child or cause speech problems. Take this as your opportunity to do a little research. Use Google Scholar or another source to find one or two credible studies showing that multilingualism does **not** cause disability or delay. Summarize what you find in your own words and share this evidence as if you were explaining it to your friend.

Notes: ______________________________

Myth 4: Children Must Learn Multiple Languages from Birth to Become Truly Multilingual

Reflect: Do you ever feel it's 'too late' to learn a new language? What makes you feel that way?

My thought: ______________________________

Action step (this month):
One thing I will do to begin learning a new language (maybe my spouse's language):

____

Start date: __________ Frequency per week: ____ Resource(s): ______________

End-of-month reflection:
What worked: ______________________________
What was hard: ______________________________
What I will change next month: ______________________________
What this taught me about learning a new language later in life: ______________
How this insight helps me support my child in case she starts a language later in her life: ______________________________

____

Parent as researcher in action: Find examples of children or adults who learned a language later. What helped them succeed?
Notes: ______________________________

Now that we have set aside some of the common myths, I hope you feel reassured and encouraged in your choice to raise your child with more than one language, even if you are starting later in your child's life. With a little intentional support, multilingualism can become a powerful gift that shapes your child's life in meaningful and lasting ways. In the next section, we will explore the many cognitive, social and cultural benefits that make this journey not only worthwhile but also deeply rewarding.

Benefits of Multilingualism

Raising multilingual children with your heritage language is a meaningful commitment, and the fact that you have chosen to read this book already reflects that dedication. Before you begin this journey, it is worthwhile to take a moment to explore the benefits of multilingualism. Doing so can strengthen your conviction and reassure you that the rewards far exceed the effort you will invest.

This is not a business transaction where you calculate how much you invest and how much you gain in return. It is about recognizing that your efforts lead to outcomes that cannot be measured in simple terms. The true rewards of raising a multilingual child often unfold in subtle and unexpected ways, enriching not only your child's life but also your own.

I can personally attest that the time and energy my husband and I devoted to raising our children with multiple languages has been profoundly worthwhile. Not only have we raised two multilingual children, but we have also nurtured two well-rounded, curious individuals. Their multilingual upbringing has given them unique talents and a broader, more nuanced worldview. At the same time, in the process of raising them multilingual, my husband and I have also grown. We have rediscovered our own languages, deepened our appreciation of our cultural roots and learned to see the world through their evolving perspectives. The journey has shaped not only who they have become but also who we are as parents.

I invite you now to explore these benefits more deeply, beginning with an overview in Table 2.1. They may affirm what you already believe or open new ways of seeing the value of what you are undertaking.

I now highlight the key benefits of multilingualism, including some that have received limited attention in research. Together, they show that multilingualism extends beyond language, enriching understanding, connection and lasting family belonging.

Novel concepts combination

One of the most fascinating benefits of growing up with more than one language is the ability to combine ideas from different worlds. The example in Box 2.1 shows how my younger son, Dominique, brings his multilingual background to life through music, one of his favorite creative pursuits. In his song *After Five*, he weaves together Chinese, English, French, Spanish and Russian. Each language contributes its own tone and emotion: English conveys his outward, everyday self, French expresses rebellion and freedom, Spanish adds rhythm and warmth, and the brief Chinese and Russian phrases provide sound effects, texture and playfulness. Through this creative process, he explores the contrast between day and night, and public life and private identity, showing how languages can work together to express complex layers of experience. This is something a monolingual speaker may find difficult to accomplish.

Table 2.1 Overview of multilingual benefits

Age group	Key cognitive benefits	Key social benefits	Key cultural/identity benefits
Birth to 6 years	Early exposure to multiple languages sharpens executive function, including attention control, task-switching and inhibition (Bialystok, 2001). Infants maintain the ability to discriminate a wide range of speech sounds, show neural sensitivity to new languages and develop enhanced brain plasticity (Werker & Byers-Heinlein, 2008).	Improved communication with parents and caregivers across languages. Early awareness of referential intent, including the ability to interpret pointing, gaze and tone of voice more accurately than monolingual peers (Yow & Markman, 2011).	Strong bonds to family heritage and traditions. Early foundation for multicultural identity formation (Grosjean, 2010).
6 to 12 years	Growth in metalinguistic awareness, stronger problem-solving skills and flexible rule-switching. Children perform better on tasks that involve conflict resolution and selective attention (Bialystok & Martin, 2004).	Improved peer communication, better use of humor and linguistic play across languages and stronger skills in navigating school and home language contexts (Wang, 2022a).	Multilingual children strengthen their identity through literacy in multiple languages and by valuing family language practices alongside school language (Bialystok, 2001).
12 to 19 years	Greater cognitive flexibility in problem-solving, stronger working memory and creativity. Adolescents are more likely to generate multiple strategies for academic tasks, including math and reading comprehension (Adesope *et al.*, 2010).	Deeper peer relationships across diverse groups, adaptability in social settings and strategic code-switching for conflict resolution or identity negotiation (Krashan, 1982).	Resilience in identity development. Adolescents draw on multiple cultural frameworks to navigate school, family and peer expectations (Yeager & Dweck, 2012).
Adults (20+)	Lifelong cognitive reserve that delays age-related decline and dementia (Alladi *et al.*, 2013). Advanced reasoning, abstract thinking and perspective-taking skills (Bialystok *et al.*, 2012).	Broader professional networks, cross-cultural collaboration and career advancement in global contexts (Saiz & Zoido, 2005).	A deeper global citizenship identity, with the capacity to integrate multiple cultural perspectives and act as a cultural mediator (Kramsch, 2011).

Box 2.1 Example of a novel concept combination in Dominique's lyrics

<u>After Five</u>

Saudi, 阿拉伯 (Saudi Arabia; no literal meaning, just for sound effects)
Bueno, vamos (Well, let's go)
Cada noche (Every night)
Salgo (I go out)
En el día (In the day)
Finjo (I pretend)
Para no ser
Encontrado (So as not to be found)
Walk into the scene I'm not

sorry
Feeling McFly just like
Marty
If you come with me don't get
Bodied
But you're sweating like I'm your search history
In the day
Do what they say
But that's just a disguise
And in the night
On the dark side
I live my private life
When I'm coming through
Slide
When I'm in the room
Rise
You know what to do
To survive (yeah)
I got all the moves
After five
Don't act so surprised
I know you wanna try
'Cause he who knows not vice
Doesn't really know what's right
Qu'est qu'ils vont penser (What will they think?)
Quand je me changerai (When I change myself)
Je m'en bats les couilles (I don't give a damn.)
Pendant la nuit (During the night)
Tous les chats sont gris (All cats are gray; meaning that in the dark, differences are not noticeable)
Comme un lion je me débrouille (Like a lion, I manage; meaning handling things with strength and determination)
Qu'est qu'ils vont penser (What are they going to think?)
Quand j'irai danser (When I go dancing)
Je m'en bats les couilles (I don't give a damn.)
Pendant la journée (During the day)
Esprit verouillé (Mind is locked up)
La nuit je déverrouille (At night, I unlock it.)
If you wanna
Feel another way
Mami

Close your eyes
And dance the Macarena
Пока (Bye)
Пока (Bye)
Uh-huh/mami
No, they don't know
Who I really am
When I'm alone
I just wanna dance
But all my bros
Wouldn't understand
How I get down with no hands
C'est-ça (3×) *ouais* (That's it, that's it, that's it, yeah.)
Elle n'arrête pas de bader (She doesn't stop looking)
Mais je m'en balek (But I don't care.)
Elle (She)
Sait pas (3×) *tout à fait* (doesn't know, doesn't know, doesn't really know for sure)
Qui je suis dans ma vie (Who I am in my life)
En parallèle (In parallel)
« Ça va
Et toi » (I'm fine and you?)
« Comme ci comme ça » (So, so)
Mais elle ne voit (But she doesn't see)
Que l'apparence (Only the appearance)
« On sort ce soir » (Are we going out tonight?)
« Il faut que je me change (I need to change)
Avant que la nuit commence » (Before the night begins.)
Haaannnh
(Backing vocal harmonies before)
When I'm coming through
Slide
When I'm in the room
Rise
You know what to do
To survive (yeah)
I got all the moves
After five
Don't act so surprised
I know you wanna try
For he who knows not vice
Doesn't know what's wrong from right

(Ethereal backing vocals in bridge)
In the day
Do what they say
But that's just a disguise
And in the night
On the dark side
I live my private life
When morning breaks
I'm too afraid
To show you what I'm like
'Cause after dark
I fall apart
So I won't turn off the light
When I'm coming through
Slide
When I'm in the room
Rise
You know what to do
To survive (yeah)
I got all the moves
After five
Don't act so surprised
I know you wanna try
'Cause if don't know vice
You don't know what's wrong from right
Qu'est qu'ils vont penser
Quand je me changerai
Je m'en bats les couilles
Pendant la nuit
Tous les chats sont gris
Comme un lion je me débrouille
Qu'est qu'ils vont penser
Quand j'irai danser
Je m'en bats les couilles
Pendant la journée
Esprit verouillé

Dominique's work illustrates what researchers call **novel concept combination**. This term refers to the way multilingual individuals bring together ideas, images and meanings from their different languages to create something original. In everyday life, this might appear when a child invents playful expressions, mixes languages while storytelling or blends cultural references from several backgrounds at once.

Multilingualism does more than expand vocabulary. It strengthens mental flexibility, creativity and perspective-taking. Children who grow up with multiple languages often engage in creative play, invent expressions and connect ideas across cultures. Moving between languages fosters pattern recognition, divergent thinking and empathy, enriching learning and communication (Kharkhurin, 2015).

Sensitivity to a variety of sounds

Children who grow up with more than one language develop more flexible and intricate sound systems. Early exposure to multiple phonetic frameworks, including rhythm, intonation and pronunciation, promotes heightened auditory sensitivity that extends beyond language into domains such as music and voice recognition (Fecher & Johnson, 2019). Research shows that multilingual infants are better at detecting subtle phonetic contrasts across languages, which sharpens their acoustic perception and supports later pronunciation accuracy and additional language learning (Werker & Tees, 1984).

Although all infants are born with the capacity to perceive the full range of sounds across languages, by around 6 months differences begin to appear. Multilingual infants continue to distinguish a wide variety of speech sounds (Petitto *et al.*, 2012), whereas their monolingual peers start to lose this sensitivity. This ongoing flexibility helps multilingual infants detect subtle phonetic contrasts, sharpening their overall acoustic perception and supporting later pronunciation accuracy and additional language learning (Kuhl, 2004). Research also shows that multilingual babies demonstrate stronger pitch discrimination in music, and multilingual children outperform monolinguals in recognizing voices across both familiar and unfamiliar languages, suggesting an advantage in processing speaker-specific cues that are important for social communication.

I have observed these sensitivities in my own children, Léandre and Dominique. For example, in high school, Dominique was deeply into rap. If you listened to him without seeing him, you might have assumed he was an African American rapper. He even recorded his voicemail in an African American accent. The same was true of his rapping in French, where he captured the style and rhythm of the rapper Grand Malada very convincingly. Both children can also imitate accents with remarkable precision, often passing temporarily as native speakers in Russian, Italian or German, only revealing the truth when grammatical errors surface. Their ability to move fluidly across accents brings to mind New York City's newly elected mayor, Zohran Mamdani, who can speak with either a Ugandan English accent or a standard American one, reflecting his own multilingual exposure. Similarly, my children tend to learn new languages quickly, especially in mastering pronunciation and accent. These observations align with research showing that multilingualism fine-tunes the auditory system for perceiving and reproducing a wide range of linguistic and social cues (Kremin *et al.*, 2021).

In short, growing up multilingual enhances sound perception not only for language development but also for music, voice recognition and social interaction, highlighting the broad auditory benefits of early multilingual exposure (Krizman *et al.*, 2012).

Adaptive language strategies

Multilingual children often show greater **metacognitive awareness** (the ability to think about and regulate their own thinking) and enhanced problem-solving skills when faced with language-related tasks, especially unfamiliar vocabulary. In a study (Barbosa *et al.*, 2017) where seven- to ten-year-old bilingual and monolingual children retold a wordless cartoon narrative, bilingual participants used a wider range of **lexical** (vocabulary) strategies when they could not produce the exact target word. Rather than omitting the concept, they more often used category-related terms (e.g. 'animal' for 'panther') or relied on **circumlocution** (using other words to explain something when one does not know or cannot remember the exact word; for example, saying 'the thing you use to cut paper' instead of 'scissors'), coining creative, functional descriptions of what an object does or looks like instead of naming it. These compensatory strategies let them convey the story clearly despite having a smaller vocabulary in each individual language, and more closely resembled the strategies used by adult second-language learners than the word-omission pattern typical of younger, less-developed speakers. The authors note this as preliminary evidence that a smaller per-language vocabulary does not necessarily limit bilingual children's ability to communicate effectively in a narrative context, though they caution that further research is needed to confirm how well the pattern generalizes beyond this specific task and population.

The third space in meaning-making

Exposure to multiple languages and cultures provides multilinguals with a significantly broader set of reference points for interpreting and engaging with the world. Because each language carries its own conceptual categories, metaphors and cultural scripts, multilinguals learn to navigate shifting frames as a matter of daily practice. This means that the multilingual mind is not simply multiple monolingual systems placed side by side but a dynamic, integrated system in which languages interact to create new cognitive possibilities (Pavlenko, 2014). Over time, this interaction becomes automatic, enabling multilinguals to develop lateral associations that are less readily available within a single cultural-linguistic worldview.

A clear example of this expanded interpretive space comes from Léandre in his early twenties. While dining in China, he spontaneously compared 豆腐卤 (braised tofu) to foie gras. The connection was not about taste but about the distinct cultural worlds evoked through Chinese and French. 豆腐卤 signaled domestic comfort and everyday simplicity, whereas foie gras carried connotations of refinement and special occasions. By drawing on both systems, he created an analogy that exists in neither culture alone but in the **third space**, a hybrid cognitive zone where multilinguals blend cultural resources to generate new meanings (Bhabha, 1994).

Another example occurred at the Confucius Temple market in Nanjing, where Léandre noticed preserved red peppers in clay pots and immediately associated them with relics he had seen in Pompeii, Italy, and discussed with his father in French. This connection was not simply the product of travel memory; it emerged from the transcultural associations woven into his linguistic repertoire. A visual cue in a Chinese context activated a historical schema encoded in French, illustrating how multilingual memory often operates independently of the language of the immediate environment.

These moments reveal how multilinguals regularly inhabit this third space, a mental territory where cultural frameworks interact fluidly and meaning arises through the interplay of languages rather than within a single linguistic frame. A monolingual traveler might notice similarities between Nanjing and Pompeii or between foie gras and 豆腐卤, but their interpretations would remain anchored in one linguistic and cultural system. Multilinguals, by contrast, layer multiple frameworks at once, expanding the range of possible meanings and cultivating cognitive flexibility that reaches beyond the limits of a single language.

Unique discourse and pragmatic styles

Exposure to multiple languages early on cultivates a distinct **discourse style** (the way language is used for specific social and communicative purposes) in multilingual individuals. This style emerges as children navigate between languages, blending linguistic and cultural elements to create fluid, adaptive modes of expression. Language blending and language play across languages are two major strategies multilingual children use to achieve communicative goals across languages, an ability not typically accessible to monolingual children (Wang, 2022a).

Dynamic language mixing for social and pragmatic goals

One hallmark of multilingual discourse is the creative use of language mixing to achieve different communicative objectives. This type of mixing is often not caused by linguistic deficiency, as is sometimes assumed, but is rather a deliberate strategy to enhance communication (Grosjean, 2010). As multilingual children mature, their language mixing becomes increasingly strategic. One distinctive function of cross-linguistic mixing is its ability to soften criticism, as shown in Box 2.2. This effect is often more difficult to achieve when speaking in only one language because switching to a different language can mitigate the force of a negative utterance (Auer, 1998) and create an emotional distance between the speaker, the listener and the critical content (Pavlenko, 2005).

Box 2.2 Example of creative language blending

Dominique (18;5;21)[1] received a gift card on Christmas Eve from his mother (me.) He did not really like it – in fact, he hated it! Instead of expressing, in Chinese, his dissatisfaction to me and his desire to get a better gift, he mixed English in making his comments: '让我打开这个礼物 (Let me open this gift), Oh, it's GREAT! Thank you VERY much!' He blended English with a heavy Chinese accent (even though I do not have a heavy Chinese accent) and he placed the stress on the words *great* and *very*. He rolled his eyes with a smirk while he was saying *great* and *very*.

In this example, Dominique achieved multiple purposes in a single act of creative language blending. By inserting English with a heavy Chinese accent and a playful tone, he distanced himself from directly blaming his mother, conveyed dissatisfaction with the gift, poked gentle fun at his mother by exaggerating an accent she did not have and indirectly signaled his wish for a better present. This example demonstrates how multilingual children can combine strategic mixing, intonation and body language to communicate complex emotions in a humorous yet socially acceptable way (Wang, 2022b).

Language play for achieving intended communication purposes

Multilingual children display remarkable linguistic dexterity through language play, creatively manipulating different levels of language with humor, wordplay and structural blending. This practice not only strengthens their social bonds but also hones their metalinguistic awareness, i.e. the ability to think about and manipulate language itself.

This creative engagement is evident across various linguistic domains.

- **Phonological play:** Multilingual children often exploit the sound systems of their languages through mimicry, exaggerating intonations and playing with tonal features. In tonal languages like Mandarin, for instance, a child might joke by saying *tāng* (汤, soup) instead of *táng* (糖, candy), teasing a sibling by pretending to offer 'soup' instead of 'candy'. This type of acoustic manipulation is a documented feature of ludic language play (Heller, 1988).
- **Lexical creativity:** Multilinguals commonly coin hybrid words by blending languages. Léandre's invention of the term *fromage criminel* (French *fromage*, cheese + English *criminal*), humorously implying that the cheese is 'criminal' because it is so fatty, is a clear example (Wang, 2008). This creation of **nonce forms** (words or expressions created spontaneously for a single occasion, often invented to meet a momentary communicative need) is a hallmark of creative vocabulary use in multilingual settings (Poplack *et al.*, 1988).
- **Semantic and grammatical play:** Multilinguals demonstrate a sophisticated understanding of language structure by playing with words that sound alike or deliberately misapplying grammatical rules. For example, Léandre and Dominique enjoyed confusing *shí liù* (十六, sixteen) and *shí liu* (石榴, pomegranate), leading to the humorous request for 'sixteen tea.' Similarly, Léandre once joked, 'I have one *pǐ* dog' (一匹狗), deliberately using the classifier *pǐ* (normally reserved for horses) instead of the correct *zhī* (只). This intentional violation of grammatical norms to create humor demonstrates a high level of **metalinguistic awareness**, the ability to look at language objectively rather than just using it (Bialystok, 2001).
- **Morphosyntactic innovation:** Multilinguals also engage in creative experimentation with grammar by fusing languages at the word level. For example, Léandre used the English suffix *-ing* with Chinese, jokingly saying '大便-ing' (pooping). By applying the English progressive marker to a Chinese verb, he created a hybrid form solely

for humor. This deliberate manipulation of grammatical rules is a classic example of ludic language play, where the speaker treats language as a playground rather than just a tool for information (Broner & Tarone, 2001).

- **Pragmatic layering:** Multilingual children sometimes engage in **stylization**, a form of **double voicing** where a speaker temporarily adopts a persona or voice that is clearly distinct from their 'normal' self to achieve a specific social effect. While monolinguals might shift their pitch or accent to 'do a voice', multilinguals can achieve this by switching languages entirely. For example, when his mother reminded him about homework in Chinese, Dominique replied in English, 'Yes, teacher,' playfully shifting from his role as a son to a performative role of a student. This switch allowed him to layer his compliance with irony, signaling that he understood the instruction but viewed the 'nagging' as formal and school-like. This ability to manipulate language to project different identities is a sophisticated communicative strategy (Rampton, 1995).

These discourse patterns transcend language boundaries. Through cross-linguistic mixing and play, multilingual children engage in humor, resolve conflicts and bridge cultural contexts. This flexible use of language makes their communication richer, more engaging and more creative than that of their monolingual peers, ultimately strengthening their ability to achieve intended communication purposes effectively (Wang, 2022b).

Language brokering

Language brokering refers to the practice of children interpreting and translating between languages for others, commonly observed in immigrant or multilingual families. This role often emerges in early childhood, as children naturally mediate communication between family members and broader society, especially when the adults have limited proficiency in the dominant community language.

Although much of the literature focuses on children translating for parents in interactions with the mainstream culture, language brokering also takes place within the family itself. It can occur between parents who do not share a common native language, as well as brokering for outsiders who do not know the family language. These less discussed but equally significant instances highlight the versatility and adaptability of multilingual children. Even when the communication stakes are lower, children play a crucial role in sustaining family cohesion across linguistic divides.

For example, at just 1 year and 4 months old, Léandre demonstrated an early form of language brokering by translating Mandarin words into French for his father. He translated 面包 (bread) as *pain* and 手 (hand) as *main*, showing an emerging ability to bridge languages and map meaning across them, well before reaching full fluency. Though a small moment, it illustrates how language brokering can begin intuitively and early in multilingual households.

Similarly, at 2 years and 2 months, Léandre engaged in an early instance of language brokering with his English babysitter, a high school student who often played with him. He explained, 'In Chinese, we call this 卡车 (truck), and in French we call this *camion*.'

This playful interaction shows how even very young children can begin to mediate across languages, offering others access to words and concepts from their multilingual repertoire.

These early brokering is more than a practical tool for communication; it lays the groundwork for lifelong skills in linguistic dexterity, cognitive flexibility and cross-cultural awareness. Children who act as brokers develop heightened metalinguistic awareness and learn to adjust their language according to context and audience, skills that are both cognitively demanding and socially rich (Orellana, 2009a).

Indeed, research shows that language brokering goes beyond translation, involving complex cognitive, cultural and interpersonal processes. Young brokers interpret meaning, shift registers and navigate cultural expectations, acting as active cultural agents rather than passive language users (Orellana, 2009b).

Theory of mind

The **Theory of Mind** (ToM) means understanding that other people have their own thoughts, feelings, beliefs and perspectives, which may be different from your child's own. The Theory of Mind is essential for making friends, taking turns, solving conflicts and having meaningful conversations. Without it, children may struggle to connect with others, because they cannot easily imagine what someone else might be thinking or feeling (Astington & Baird, 2005).

Multilingual children often show an advantage in developing ToM. One reason is that they constantly adjust the way they speak depending on who they are talking to. For example, they may use one language with grandparents, another with friends and a different tone or style with teachers. This daily practice makes them more aware that other people have different needs, preferences and perspectives (Kovács, 2009).

This heightened awareness of others' perspectives also extends beyond language choice to how meaning itself is interpreted. A key feature is a stronger understanding of **referential intent**, the ability to infer meaning beyond words. Multilingual children more readily read cues such as gaze, gesture and tone, likely because they regularly navigate multiple languages and cultural contexts (Yow & Markman, 2011). This sensitivity supports perspective-taking, empathy and more thoughtful social interaction across the lifespan.

Better self-regulating and flexible thinking

Children who grow up speaking more than one language often develop stronger skills in flexible thinking and self-regulation. Because they are used to switching between languages and adjusting how they speak depending on the situation, they learn to pay closer attention to their own speech and even revise their sentences midway. This kind of monitoring is linked to stronger mental control and **executive function** (Carlson & Meltzoff, 2008) (a set of mental skills that help plan, focus attention, remember instructions and manage multiple tasks effectively).

These benefits extend beyond language. Multilingual children often outperform their monolingual peers on tasks that involve identifying patterns or solving puzzles, such as finding simple shapes hidden within complex designs (Bialystok & Martin, 2004). They also perform better on activities that require mental flexibility and focused attention, like imagining how objects would look if rotated or moved (Costa *et al.*, 2008).

Even in mathematics, multilingual children may stand out. Studies suggest that they are more likely to approach problems creatively, often generating multiple strategies rather than relying on a single method (Adesope *et al.*, 2010). This ability to view challenges from different angles demonstrates how multilingualism fosters not only linguistic agility but also broader cognitive strengths that support learning across many domains.

Stronger academic performance

When we add together the many advantages of growing up multilingual, including stronger executive control, greater flexibility in thinking, heightened sensitivity to social cues and richer problem-solving skills, the benefits naturally extend into their academic performance. Research shows that multilingual children often demonstrate stronger overall academic performance than their monolingual peers (Rutgers *et al.*, 2024).

Similar results have also been found in Swiss multilingual primary schools, where children were taught in language pairs such as German–Italian or German–Rhaeto-Romansch. These students outperformed their monolingual classmates in listening and reading comprehension, particularly on complex questions requiring inference and interpretation (Hollenweger & Moretti, 2012). Interestingly, the multilingual children excelled precisely because they had developed such strong analytical skills: They were so used to analyzing language and meaning that their brains did a better job of handling tricky, complicated questions. Their experience gave them a more nuanced and careful approach to reading.

I can also confirm from personal experience that I witnessed my two sons Léandre and Dominique's academic performance from pre-kindergarten to graduate school. They consistently demonstrated the advantages discussed above. Multilingualism did not hinder any part of their progress. On the contrary, it added benefits to their problem-solving abilities and beyond.

Even students who enter school as second language learners, though they have historically faced challenges on large-scale assessments because of limited early exposure to the school language, have recently significantly narrowed the achievement gap with their monolingual peers. Analyzing National Assessment of Educational Progress (NAEP) data from 2003 to 2015 in the United States, one study found that multilingual students' reading and math scores improved two to three times faster than monolingual students' scores, in both grades 4 and 8 (Kieffer & Thompson, 2018). This progress held even after accounting for cohort changes in racial, ethnic, socioeconomic, and regional composition, though it is often obscured in analyses that focus only on students currently classified as English learners rather than the broader multilingual student population.

This demonstrates a broad-based academic advantage rooted in the cognitive and strategic strengths multilingual learners develop across subjects and contexts.

Taken together, the findings from multiple contexts challenge the misconception that learning more than one language might hold children back academically. Instead, multilingualism emerges as a powerful asset that strengthens learning across domains, culminating in higher achievement and deeper understanding (Adesope *et al.*, 2010).

A Few Important Caveats

Although the benefits of multilingualism discussed above are compelling, it is important to recognize that these advantages are not guaranteed or experienced in the same way by every child. Just as no two children are alike, the trajectory of multilingual development varies widely. Factors such as frequency of use, quality of input and the balance between or among languages all shape outcomes (De Houwer, 2009). Some children may develop strong phonological awareness or social sensitivity, while others may have uneven skills if exposure is inconsistent. As the cognitive psychologist Ellen Bialystok (2001) has pointed out, variation is natural, and not every multilingual child will follow the same developmental path.

Multilingualism can also bring its own set of complexities, particularly in how the brain manages multiple languages. When speaking one language, the others do not simply 'turn off'. They remain active in the background, which can occasionally slow word retrieval or lead to those frustrating 'tip-of-the-tongue' moments (Kroll & Bialystok, 2013). Vocabulary in each individual language may be smaller compared with monolingual peers, but the total vocabulary across languages is often comparable to or larger than monolingual norms (Core *et al.*, 2013; Pearson *et al.*, 1993). Language mixing or mid-sentence switches are not signs of confusion or deficiency; instead, they reflect the multilingual brain's ability to juggle multiple linguistic systems at once (Grosjean, 2010).

Beyond processing differences, multilinguals may also face practical and social challenges. In school or workplace settings, there may be pressure to prioritize one language over another, which can impact self-expression or cultural identity. Navigating multiple cultural frameworks, code-switching across contexts, or experiencing discrimination based on accent or language background may create emotional or social strain (De Houwer, 2020). However, research also shows that these challenges often build resilience, adaptability and empathy (Yeager & Dweck, 2012).

Despite these caveats, the long-term rewards far outweigh the early hurdles. I have witnessed this with my own children as they navigated languages and cultures with an adaptability unique to multilingualism. One vivid observation stands out: Watching Dominique switch fluidly between languages while chatting with a multilingual cab driver (English, German and a few other languages), his curiosity and confidence shining through. Such moments reveal the true gift of multilingualism: it is not merely about language mastery but about cultivating flexible minds, creative spirits and deeper human connections.

Pause and Reflect

Imagine the Gift

After reading about the many benefits of multilingualism, how do you feel?
Does it make you excited to raise a multilingual child?
What excites or inspires you most about giving your child the gift of your heritage language?

Picture the Moments

- How do you imagine your child greeting a grandparent in the family language?
- How might this make you and your family feel?

Think About the Future

How do you picture your child benefiting from multilingualism as she grows up; for example, shifting between cultures, building friendships or connecting across communities?

Anchor Your Motivation

What does it mean to you to pass on this gift?
Write down your personal reason.

____

____

____

____

____

Tip:

Return to this page whenever the journey feels challenging.
Your reflections will remind you why these matters and keep your motivation strong.

Family Language Planning

Now that we have explored the many benefits of multilingualism, I hope you can see from the examples how deeply valuable this gift can be. However, understanding the benefits is only the beginning. The real art begins with planning. This stage is not just about setting rules or routines; it is about creating an environment where languages, relationships and identities can grow together. It is here that the art of raising a multilingual child truly takes shape.

Research (King & Fogle, 2006) and our family experience suggest that making a family language plan before your child is born is one of the critical steps you can take. Think of it like planning a road trip: you may not know every bump or detour ahead of time, but having a map helps you stay on course and makes the journey smoother. A clear plan gives you direction, helps you anticipate challenges and keeps you motivated when the road feels long.

Successful multilingual upbringing does not happen by chance. It grows from intentional choices about how, when and where different languages are used in your family's daily life. These choices look different for every household, depending on your family's background, goals and circumstances (King *et al.*, 2008). We will explore below key areas that can significantly shape your child's heritage-language development and make your journey not only more effective but also more enjoyable.

Clarifying your motivations

Before you begin your multilingual parenting journey, it is important to reflect on *why* you want to pass on your heritage language or languages. Clarifying your motivation gives you a clear sense of direction. It serves as your anchor when challenges arise and helps you focus your time and energy on what matters most for your family. For example, if your motivation is to help your child communicate with grandparents, you might prioritize daily or weekly conversations with them in the heritage language. If your motivation is to strengthen cultural identity, you may choose to celebrate holidays, cook traditional foods or read stories that carry family traditions. If your motivation is to prepare your child for future academic or career opportunities, you might commit to supporting literacy in both the community language and your heritage language.

It is also possible that you want all these benefits for your child. Many families do. In that case, your family language plan can weave these motivations together. You might decide to set aside time for both heritage language conversations with relatives and cultural traditions at home, while also supporting your child's formal literacy in school and community settings. Wanting multiple outcomes is not only realistic but also enriching because it reflects the many roles that language can play in your child's life.

Clarifying your motivation is like setting a compass before a journey. It may not prevent every obstacle, but it ensures that you know where you are heading and allows you to keep your efforts focused in the right direction.

Research on **family language policy** (the beliefs, decisions and practices that guide how languages are used at home, shaping when, where and by whom children learn and use each language) shows that parental beliefs and motivations strongly shape children's opportunities to develop multilingual skills (King *et al.*, 2008). Parents who are clear about their goals are more likely to create consistent routines, provide meaningful input and persist even when difficulties arise. In other words, knowing why you are committed to multilingualism helps you translate that intention into everyday actions that support your child's development.

Pause and Reflect

Clarifying Your Motivations

Write Down Your Motivations
What are your top reasons for wanting to raise your child with more than one language?

1.
2.
3.

Think About Why These Matter
How will these goals shape the way you interact with your child each day?

____

____

____

Parent as Researcher in Action

Choose One Motivation to Explore
Example: I want my child to communicate with grandparents.

My focus is on: ____

Turn It into a Question
Example: What does research say about how children learn to use a heritage language with grandparents?

My question: ____

Look for Evidence
Use a book, article, or reliable website. You can also check the references at the end of this chapter.

What I found: ____

____

____

Compare and Reflect
Did the evidence confirm or challenge your expectations?

My reflection: ____

____

____

Draft a Small Action Plan
Write down one concrete step you can take based on your motivation and what you learned.

Example: We will make Sunday afternoon a regular video call time with grandparents in Spanish.

My plan: ____

____

____

Setting goals

Once you've thought through why you want to raise your child with your heritage language(s), it helps to consider what 'success' might look like for your family. Your goals do not have to be elaborate, but having a sense of direction can guide your choices and make daily decisions feel more intentional.

As discussed in the previous section, motivations for raising children with heritage languages vary widely. For some, it is about being able to chat comfortably with grandparents. For others, it might include reading and writing in a heritage language to support school or future work. Some families focus mostly on speaking and listening, whereas others aim for a more balanced mix of skills. There is no single right answer; what matters is that your goals make sense for your family's values, situation and hopes.

That said, it's useful to keep your expectations realistic. Sometimes, our hopes are bigger than what our time or resources allow. Expecting too much can lead to frustration. Starting with manageable goals, ones you can build on, tends to be more sustainable and encouraging.

Goals can also shift over time. What you prioritize now might look different a few years down the road, depending on your child's interests or your family's changing circumstances. Maybe you start by focusing on conversation at home, then later introduce reading and writing as school or travel opportunities come up.

Having clear, flexible goals can take some pressure off. It helps keep the focus on progress instead of perfection and makes it easier to notice and celebrate the small wins, like your child using a new word or asking a question in the heritage language. Most of all, it's about working with what you've got and adjusting as you go. Language development takes time, and every family's path is different. With a bit of planning and a lot of patience, your child can grow their skills while staying connected to the people and cultures that matter to you.

Pause and Reflection

Define What Success Means for Your Family (Please note that you and your spouse may have different definitions)

When you picture your child using your heritage language(s), what do you hope to see?

- Talking with grandparents?
- Reading and writing?
- Using the language for school or work?
- Feeling proud of their cultural identity?

Write your vision here:

____

____

____

____

Identify Your Starting Goals
What feels realistic for your family right now? Think about your time, energy and resources.

My immediate goals:

____

____

____

____

Think About Longer-Term Goals
What would you like your child to be able to do in a few years? These may grow or shift as your child develops.

My longer-term goals:

____

____

____

____

Balance Hope with Realism
Are your goals manageable with your family's current situation? If not, how could you adjust them to feel more achievable?

Reflection:

____

____

____

____

Celebrate Small Wins
List three examples of small milestones you will celebrate along the way.

1.
2.
3.

> Your goals do not need to be perfect or fixed. They can shift as your child grows and as life changes. What matters most is that your goals reflect your family's values and keep your child connected to the languages and cultures that matter to you.

Evaluating your heritage language proficiency

Since you and your spouse are likely the primary or only speakers of the heritage language in your household, you serve as your child's main language models and sources of input. The proficiency levels of you and your spouse will significantly shape your child's language development. For this reason, it is essential to honestly assess your ability to model and sustain the home language(s). If you are only comfortable speaking the language but lack reading or writing skills, recognize that your child's exposure will be limited unless you supplement their learning with tutors, language apps, media or other resources.

A few years ago, an English-speaking couple approached me for advice. Neither had any background in Russian or Chinese, yet they were determined to raise their child in both languages, believing it would offer future advantages. While I admired their ambition, I cautioned them that without prior knowledge and consistent reinforcement through tutors, immersion programs or structured education, their plan would face significant challenges. Occasional passive exposure would not be enough for their child to achieve proficiency.

Equally important is evaluating how well each partner understands the other spouse's heritage language, since this directly affects the family's communication dynamics and cohesion. For example, in my own family, my husband does not speak Chinese and has little motivation to learn it, whereas I studied French in college and can follow most conversations. When my husband and children converse in French, I can usually keep up and shift to Chinese if necessary. However, when I speak Chinese with my children, my husband feels excluded, sometimes appearing disengaged or distracted by looking at his phone. This type of imbalance can influence family wellbeing, as one parent may feel left out of the conversation, potentially creating frustration or emotional distance (Wang, 2013, 2016).

For couples, it is crucial to openly discuss these situations and set up communication protocols. Ideally, each spouse would try to learn at least the basics of the other's heritage language to foster shared understanding. If that is not possible, then the parent using the language should consciously relay the gist of the conversation for the other partner. This practice strengthens inclusivity and reduces the risk of one parent feeling isolated, while also modeling for the children that both languages are valued in the family. Research on family language policy confirms that such cooperative strategies play a key role in sustaining multilingual development and maintaining family harmony (Schwartz & Verschik, 2013).

Pause and Reflect

Evaluating Heritage Language Proficiency

Willingness to Learn Each Other's Heritage Language

Rate from 1 (not at all willing) to 5 (very willing)

- My spouse is willing to learn my heritage language.
  ☐ 1 ☐ 2 ☐ 3 ☐ 4 ☐ 5
- I am willing to learn my spouse's heritage language.
  ☐ 1 ☐ 2 ☐ 3 ☐ 4 ☐ 5

Comment:
Write your thoughts here.

Self-Evaluation of Proficiency
Rate your skills from 1 (very limited) to 5 (very strong)

My heritage language

- Speaking: ☐ 1 ☐ 2 ☐ 3 ☐ 4 ☐ 5
- Listening/understanding: ☐ 1 ☐ 2 ☐ 3 ☐ 4 ☐ 5
- Reading: ☐ 1 ☐ 2 ☐ 3 ☐ 4 ☐ 5
- Writing: ☐ 1 ☐ 2 ☐ 3 ☐ 4 ☐ 5

My Spouse's heritage language

- Speaking: ☐ 1 ☐ 2 ☐ 3 ☐ 4 ☐ 5
- Listening/understanding: ☐ 1 ☐ 2 ☐ 3 ☐ 4 ☐ 5
- Reading: ☐ 1 ☐ 2 ☐ 3 ☐ 4 ☐ 5
- Writing: ☐ 1 ☐ 2 ☐ 3 ☐ 4 ☐ 5

Reflect on how likely these situations may occur in your future family interactions. Rate each item from 1 (very unlikely) to 5 (very likely).

One parent may feel left out of conversations in the heritage language.
☐ 1 ☐ 2 ☐ 3 ☐ 4 ☐ 5

One parent may become less engaged when the other parent speaks his/her heritage language.
☐ 1 ☐ 2 ☐ 3 ☐ 4 ☐ 5

We will try to summarize or translate so everyone feels included.
☐ 1 ☐ 2 ☐ 3 ☐ 4 ☐ 5

Comment:
Write your reflections here. ______________________________

Parent as Researcher in Action

Identify a Question
Example: If one parent does not understand the heritage language, how can we keep family conversations inclusive?

Write your question here

Gather Evidence

- What does research say?
- What do other families do?

Write notes here ____

Compare With Your Own Reflection

- Did the evidence confirm or challenge your assumptions?

Write here ____

Draft a Family Plan
Example: We will try to summarize key points in English after speaking Arabic so everyone stays connected.

Write your plan here ____

Assessing your personality

Parental personality traits are often overlooked in the literature on multilingual childrearing. Yet the way you naturally think, respond and adapt plays a major role in how you guide language use with your child and, ultimately, in the success of your efforts.

This is not about judging what is right or wrong, or what is suitable or not suitable, but about developing self-awareness. For instance, if you notice that you are easily influenced by others, whether by your child's preferences or by societal pressures, you may need to remind yourself not to compromise on your language goals simply for convenience. This does not mean you should never adapt. Instead, it means being mindful of why you are making a change so that your choices remain intentional.

Imagine, for example, that your child begins to favor the mainstream language and resists using your heritage language. You may feel tempted to give in to avoid conflict. Or if people around you question your approach, you might second-guess yourself. In these moments, it helps to pause and ask: Is this shift necessary for my family's wellbeing, or am I responding to outside pressure? By being aware of your personality traits, you can better identify which approaches will work best for your family and which pitfalls you may need to avoid.

Pause and Reflection

Thinking Ahead: How Do You Usually Handle Challenges?
Rate yourself on each statement from 1 (strongly disagree) to 5 (strongly agree).

I tend to stick firmly to plans once I set them.
□ 1 □ 2 □ 3 □ 4 □ 5

I adapt quickly when things do not go as planned.
□ 1 □ 2 □ 3 □ 4 □ 5

My approach to handling challenges will help me stay consistent with my language goals.
□ 1 □ 2 □ 3 □ 4 □ 5

Comment:
Write your reflections or examples here.

____

____

____

Rate Your Confidence in Following Through (1 = not confident, 5 = very confident):
1 □ 2 □ 3 □ 4 □ 5 □

Considering Outside Influence
Rate each statement from 1 (strongly disagree) to 5 (strongly agree).

I usually stay confident in my decisions, even when others express strong opinions.
□ 1 □ 2 □ 3 □ 4 □ 5

I tend to second-guess my choices when others challenge my ideas.
□ 1 □ 2 □ 3 □ 4 □ 5

I can balance listening to others' advice with staying true to my own language goals.
□ 1 □ 2 □ 3 □ 4 □ 5

Reflection:
Write your thoughts or examples here.

____

____

Imagining Future Conflict
Picture your child, a few years from now, preferring to answer you in the majority language.

How do you imagine yourself responding?
Rate how ready you feel to handle each option (1 = not ready and 5 = very ready).

I would gently insist on using the heritage language.
□ 1 □ 2 □ 3 □ 4 □ 5

I might switch to the majority language to avoid conflict.
□ 1 □ 2 □ 3 □ 4 □ 5

I would try a creative compromise (for example, playful reminders, songs or routines).
□ 1 □ 2 □ 3 □ 4 □ 5

I am not sure yet how I would respond.
□ 1 □ 2 □ 3 □ 4 □ 5

Comments and Reflection:
Write your thoughts or plans here: ______________________________________

____

____

Parent as Researcher in Action

Identify a Personality Trait
Which personality trait of yours might help or hinder your ability to raise a multilingual child?
(Example: 'I avoid conflict, so I may give in too easily' or 'I am persistent, which may help me stick to our plan.')

Your Trait:

Rate how much you think this trait will impact language goals (1 = very little, 5 = very strongly):
1 □ 2 □ 3 □ 4 □ 5 □

Explore the Research
Choose one question to investigate. For example:

- Does persistence in speaking a heritage language at home make a difference in long-term outcomes?
- How do flexible parents adapt their strategies when children resist?

My research question:

Where I looked for answers (books, websites, articles):

Draft a Response

Imagine someone (a friend, relative or even a future teacher) says, 'Why bother teaching your child two languages? It will only confuse them.'

Given your reflection and research, how would you respond?

My Draft Response:

____

____

Rate how prepared you feel to respond to criticism (1 = not prepared, 5 = very prepared):

1 ☐ 2 ☐ 3 ☐ 4 ☐ 5 ☐

Based on my rating, my plan is to respond to criticism by:

____

____

Examining your support and commitment

Raising multilingual children successfully also requires a variety of resources and supports, as well as unwavering parental commitment.

Extended family networks and heritage language communities play especially vital roles. They create a **language ecology** (Haugen, 1972) (a context where language learning unfolds organically within everyday social and cultural interactions). When children regularly engage with grandparents, relatives and other heritage language speakers, they receive rich, authentic input that transcends vocabulary and grammar. These interactions expose them to idiomatic expressions, embedded cultural knowledge and the emotional resonance that gives language its meaning (De Houwer, 2021; King *et al.*, 2008).

Another essential source of support comes from heritage language schools. These programs offer structured instruction that complements home use and plays a support role in language maintenance. Through literacy development, grammar lessons and peer interactions, children come to view their heritage language as valuable not just at home but also in wider social and academic contexts. Research shows that such formal instruction significantly boosts language retention among second-generation immigrant children, helping to close the gap between passive understanding and active use (Guardado, 2018).

Media resources also offer meaningful reinforcement. Curated selections of books, music, films and digital content in the heritage language provide consistent and engaging exposure. These materials not only build comprehension but also create positive emotional associations with the language, a factor shown to have a lasting impact on language learning motivation and success (Curdt-Christiansen, 2016).

Among all the abovementioned resources, parental engagement remains the linchpin. Decades of research in early language development underscore that it is the frequency and quality of caregiver interaction that most powerfully shapes language outcomes (De Houwer, 2009; Hart & Risley, 1995). It is in daily life – storytime at bedtime, conversations in the car or laughter during meals – where language takes root and meaning flourishes. These ordinary moments are deceptively powerful, embedding not only linguistic input but also emotional connection, shared attention and cultural understanding.

Our own experience brings this to life. During our children's critical multilingual development years, we made intentional choices to center language in our family routines, even when that meant sacrifices elsewhere. My husband and I integrated our children into most of what we did, professional, social and personal (Wang, 2008), a kind of **concerted cultivation** (Lareau, 2003) (a parenting practice that deliberately fosters children's development through active structuring of their environments and experiences). Of course, this came at a cost: For example, my husband's doctoral completion timeline stretched over 11 years as we balanced parenting with academic life. But research (De Houwer, 2009) affirms that such dedication pays dividends, fostering not only linguistic growth but also secure attachment and cognitive development (Bruner, 1983).

In fact, the time invested in nurturing multilingualism has broader implications for a child's overall growth. Daily interactions that facilitate language development also serve as channels for transmitting values and shaping identity. Studies on family discourse highlight how routine conversations convey cultural beliefs, worldviews and interpersonal conventions (Blum-Kulka, 1997). Activities such as shared reading or playful exchanges in the heritage language served as **emotional scaffolding** (Wood *et al.*, 1976) (supportive interactions through which caregivers help children manage emotions and build confidence, creating a secure environment that promotes learning and development). Emerging neuroscience supports such parental interaction. Research shows that emotionally rich face-to-face communication activates the neural systems responsible for both language acquisition and emotional regulation (Kuhl, 2004). When parents commit to maintaining such interactions, they provide a 'triple reward': Linguistic competence, cultural continuity and deepened family relationships (Baker, 2011). Children raised in this way gain enduring connections to their heritage, to those who raised them and to their own evolving identities.

In sum, identifying support and committing time early shapes what follows. Though the effort can be significant, when family, community, school and media align, the rewards extend beyond language proficiency to lasting connections with heritage, family and self.

Pause and Reflect

Your Support and Commitment

Family Language Support Rating

Use the scale below to rate the level of support available in each area.

(1 = very weak, 2 = limited, 3 = moderate, 4 = strong, 5 = very strong)

Area of support	Your rating (1–5)	Notes/examples
Extended family support	□1 □2 □3 □4 □5	e.g. grandparents or relatives speaking the heritage language regularly
Community/heritage groups	□1 □2 □3 □4 □5	e.g. cultural associations, friends, local meetups
Heritage language schools	□1 □2 □3 □4 □5	e.g. weekend programs, after-school classes
Media resources	□1 □2 □3 □4 □5	e.g. books, music, TV, apps
Daily routines at home	□1 □2 □3 □4 □5	e.g. family meals, bedtime stories
Parental time commitment	□1 □2 □3 □4 □5	e.g. willingness to adjust schedules, prioritize language moments

Comment and Reflection:____________________________________

Parent as Researcher in Action 1: Reflection Scenarios

Rate how ready or confident you feel in handling each situation (1 = not ready, 2 = somewhat ready, 3 = moderately ready, 4 = ready, 5 = very ready)

Scenario 1: Staying Connected with Distant Family

If your parents or in-laws live far away and only visit once or twice a year, how might you keep your child connected to them through your heritage language (e.g. video calls, letters, shared stories)?

□ 1 □ 2 □ 3 □ 4 □ 5

Reflections: ____________________________________

____

Scenario 2: Finding Energy After Long Days

Picture a busy weekday evening when you and your spouse are both tired from work. Will you still make time to use the heritage language during dinner or bedtime?

□ 1 □ 2 □ 3 □ 4 □ 5

Reflections: ____________________________________

____

Scenario 3: Seeking Alternatives to Heritage Schools

Suppose there are no heritage language schools nearby. What other resources (apps, books, online tutors, community groups) could you turn to?

□ 1 □ 2 □ 3 □ 4 □ 5

Reflections: ____

____

Scenario 4: Handling Resistance
Imagine your child begins resisting the heritage language once they enter preschool. How would you handle this without giving up on your goals?

☐ 1 ☐ 2 ☐ 3 ☐ 4 ☐ 5

Reflections: ____

____

Parent as Researcher in Action 2: Action Steps

1. Which area did you rate the strongest? What helps make this possible?

   ____

2. Which area did you rate the weakest? Why do you think this is?

   ____

3. What one action could you take in the next month to strengthen this weaker area?

   ____

4. Choose one scenario above and reflect. How would you respond? What strategies could you use to stay consistent with your goals?

   ____

5. What question about support or commitment do you want to research further? (For example, do heritage language schools really make a long-term difference? How much exposure does a child need each week to make steady progress?)

   ____

   ____

Deciding on a family language plan

Having reflected on the areas discussed above, you are now ready to create a family language plan, often called a family language policy in the research literature.

Why language planning matters in multilingual success

Consider two families with the same goal: raising multilingual children, yet their outcomes couldn't be more different.

The Costa family developed and followed a clear language plan. The father spoke only Portuguese at home, the mother consistently used English, and the children learned German through school and social interactions. This intentional and structured exposure to all three languages ensured a steady and balanced linguistic environment. As a result, their children became confident users of Portuguese, English and German, equipped to thrive across multiple cultural and linguistic settings.

In contrast, the Chao family took a more spontaneous approach. The mother alternated between Chinese and English, while the father, a native Korean speaker, shifted to using only English once the children entered school. With inconsistent exposure and reinforcement, English quickly became dominant. Today, the Chao children speak only English, have limited understanding of Chinese and no knowledge of Korean, leading to a significant disconnection from both heritage languages and the cultures they represent.

What separates these two families is not intent but planning. A well-defined **family language policy** can make all the difference. Family language policy refers to the explicit and implicit planning around language acquisition and use within the home, distinct from broader societal language policies (Spolsky, 2012). It consists of three key components: Language practices (how languages are used at home), language ideologies (beliefs about languages and their value) and language management (deliberate strategies to shape language use) (Spolsky, 2004). Without intentional planning, the dominant community language inevitably seeps into and overtakes the home.

The message is clear: Intentional planning matters. While no plan can predict every turn in a child's linguistic journey, families that develop and stick to a thoughtful strategy are far more likely to nurture multilingualism. In a world where majority languages almost always prevail, preserving heritage languages and cultural identity requires conscious, consistent effort.

Optimizing timing and exposure

Even though we previously discussed that even older children and adults can develop multiple languages, the timing of language exposure plays a critical role in determining how well a child acquires and maintains multiple languages. Research has shown that certain aspects of language, such as **phonology** (sound), are best acquired during the early stages of development, beginning in utero and peaking within the first year as infants undergo 'perceptual narrowing' (Singh, 2024). **Syntax** (grammar) is most efficiently learned during a window of high plasticity that, while starting early, remains robust until approximately age 17 before declining (Hartshorne *et al.*, 2018). In contrast, **vocabulary and semantic development** (word and meaning) are lifelong processes that continue to expand throughout adulthood (Bloom, 2000).

Moreover, you may also want to consider whether you are introducing your heritage languages simultaneously or sequentially. **Simultaneous multilingualism,** where children are exposed to multiple languages from birth (or early on), generally results in more balanced proficiency in each language, though never exactly equal in proficiency. In contrast, **sequential multilingualism**, where a second heritage language is introduced later can still lead to high levels of proficiency, though it may take longer to achieve fluency in the second heritage language.

Therefore, earlier exposure to multiple languages increases the chances of achieving high proficiency, but older children can still become proficient with structured language input and exposure.

Determine the family communication style

If I had to highlight one of the most important aspects of family language planning, it would be the choice of family communication style. This foundational decision plays a key role in supporting a child's multilingual development. That's why it's essential to thoughtfully consider – and ideally decide on – your family's communication strategy before your child is born.

Multilingual families adopt different communication strategies to support their children's language development. Table 2.2 lists the major family communication styles, and their pros and cons.

One of the most widely used strategies by multilingual families is the **one parent–one language (OPOL)** method (Koelewijn *et al.*, 2025), where each parent consistently speaks a different language to the child. The strength of this strategy is that it helps children associate each language with a specific parent, fostering clear boundaries and aiding the differentiation of grammatical structures.

Research supports OPOL as an effective foundation for multilingual development, particularly when applied with consistency and enriched with meaningful input. Studies have shown that children in OPOL families often switch fluidly between languages when parents consistently use their designated language (De Houwer, 2007; Koelewijn *et al.*, 2025). Structured exposure of this kind is most successful when the heritage language is actively reinforced beyond daily conversation, such as through extended family, community groups or media.

My own children illustrate how the OPOL approach can work in practice. From birth, my husband and I each spoke our designated languages, French and Chinese, with them. This consistent pattern laid a strong foundation in both languages. Over time, structured exposure combined with intentional daily routines helped them communicate with confidence across languages and contexts. Once these habits were established, they proved remarkably enduring.

One moment in Léandre's adulthood stands out as an example of how deeply OPOL patterns can take root. When he was in his mid-twenties, we were checking out of a hotel in Belgium with his English-speaking girlfriend. To be polite, I asked Léandre a question in English, breaking the Chinese-only rule. He smiled and said that it felt strange because he had to look at his girlfriend while answering me in English, as he had never associated English with me. This small incident revealed how naturally and consistently OPOL had shaped his linguistic instincts, even years later.

Table 2.2 Family language policy approaches

Family language policy (FLP) approach	Description	Strengths/challenges
One parent–one language (OPOL)	Each parent consistently speaks a different language with the child. For example, one parent always speaks French while the other always speaks English. Research shows this approach supports balanced exposure but requires consistency at home (De Houwer, 2007).	Strength: Provides clear boundaries between languages. Challenge: Difficult to maintain if one parent is less proficient or not present as often.
Time and place	Families allocate specific times (e.g. weekends) or settings (e.g. meals, car rides) for the heritage language. This offers flexibility and works well when strict OPOL is not realistic (Barron-Hauwaert, 2004).	Strength: Flexible and adaptable to family routines. Challenge: Risk of inconsistency if not reinforced regularly.
Minority language at home	The heritage or minority language is spoken at home; the majority/community language is learned in school or society. This strategy ensures strong input in the heritage language (Spolsky, 2012).	Strength: Ensures steady exposure to heritage language. Challenge: Children may resist using it once they are immersed in the community language.
Mixed or flexible policy	Parents switch languages depending on the context, conversation or participant. Though less structured, it reflects natural multilingual practices in many households (Lanza, 2007).	Strength: Mirrors real-life multilingual use. Challenge: May confuse caregivers or weaken heritage language if the majority language dominates.
Heritage language only with extended family	Children are encouraged or required to use the heritage language specifically with grandparents or relatives, reinforcing intergenerational bonds and cultural continuity (King & Fogle, 2006).	Strength: Builds strong emotional and cultural ties. Challenge: Exposure is limited if extended family is not nearby or available.
Literacy focused FLP	Parents prioritize reading, writing and storytelling in the heritage language, often through books, homework or heritage schools, ensuring deeper literacy skills (Curdt-Christiansen, 2009).	Strength: Builds long-term literacy and academic skills. Challenge: Requires strong parental commitment and resources (e.g. access to books or schools).
Community-supported FLP	Families integrate community resources, such as heritage language schools, religious institutions and cultural associations, to supplement home practices and reinforce language use (Schwartz, 2010).	Strength: Expands children's exposure beyond the home. Challenge: Availability varies depending on where families live.

Although OPOL can be an effective strategy, it works best when reinforced by complementary practices such as the following.

- **Ensuring consistent and rich exposure:** Daily, meaningful interaction gives depth to language use and supports sustained proficiency.
- **Creating opportunities for use beyond the home:** Heritage language community groups, media and contact with extended family expand the range of authentic contexts for use.
- **Fostering positive attitudes:** When both parents value and respect each language, children are more likely to internalize them as integral to their identity.

It is also important to recognize OPOL's limitations. The method tends to be most effective in early childhood, when linguistic habits are still forming at home. As children grow and their worlds expand through school, peers and media, a single parent's input may not fully capture the richness of their social and academic experiences. OPOL can also feel demanding, especially when one parent is the sole source of a heritage language and lacks additional support for academic or cultural references.

Social situations can present another challenge. Families often feel pressure to switch to the majority language to include others, which may unintentionally weaken consistency, particularly during the early years. In my own family, we chose to stay committed to our languages even in mixed settings. When necessary, we offered brief translations or explained what we were saying, but we maintained our pattern of French and Chinese. Families in similar situations may find it useful to agree on strategies such as alternating explanations, code-switching purposefully or setting expectations with relatives to preserve balance while keeping communication inclusive.

In summary, OPOL offers a research-supported path to multilingualism (De Houwer, 2007), thriving through consistency, reinforcement and flexibility over time. In our family, once woven into daily life, it shaped our children's linguistic habits and identities into adulthood, as Léandre's example shows.

Decide on a common language to use when all family members are together

When raising multilingual children, one of the most challenging decisions is determining which language or languages to use when the entire family is together, particularly when the parents' heritage languages differ. Families who follow the OPOL approach often establish a routine where children speak one language with each parent. However, complications arise when parents do not understand each other's languages, making group conversations difficult, especially as the children grow older and discussions become more complex (De Houwer, 2007; Döpke, 1992).

In my own family, we maintain OPOL: I speak Chinese with our children; my husband speaks French. I can follow the French conversations, but my husband does not understand Chinese. As a result, when all four of us are together, I often sacrifice speaking Chinese with my children to keep the conversation inclusive. Though this promotes family cohesion, it reduces my children's exposure to Chinese in group settings. I also often feel that I miss the chance to fully tell my side of the story and sometimes must jump into the conversation, even at the risk of breaking the flow of French between my husband and the children.

Some families use the community's dominant language for group discussions (Döpke, 1992), reserving heritage languages for one-on-one interactions. Others encourage passive multilingualism, where a non-speaking parent follows without actively speaking (Lanza, 2007). Families may also set specific times or contexts for each language. Because each approach involves trade-offs (see Box 2.3 for a summary of the pros and cons), families benefit from discussing which language to use when everyone is present, as this choice influences family cohesion, heritage language exposure and the overall success of the family language plan (King *et al.*, 2008).

Box 2.3 Possible ways for family-wide communication

Maintaining OPOL in Family Conversation
In this approach, one parent continues using the heritage language with the children, while the other uses a different language. Even in group settings, the OPOL pattern is maintained.
Pros: Helps children associate each language with a specific parent, strengthening consistency and supporting language boundaries.
Cons: If parents do not understand each other's language, family conversations may feel limited. Although nonverbal cues and shared context can sometimes bridge the gap, one parent may feel excluded or disconnected. When choosing this practice, parents need to be aware of the potential imbalance and make deliberate efforts to manage it so that all family members feel included (Wang, 2016).

Flexible OPOL with Translation
Parents continue speaking their respective languages, but the children (or the multilingual parent) provide brief translations for key points (Piller, 2002).
Pros: Maintains heritage language exposure.
Cons: Can feel unnatural and disrupt conversation flow.

Dominant Community Language as a Lingua Franca
The multilingual families default to the majority language (e.g. English, Spanish or another widely spoken language) when everyone is together (Baker, 2006).
Pros: Ensures full participation and minimizes exclusion.
Cons: Reduces heritage language input in group settings.

Encourage Passive Multilingualism
The non-understanding parent learns to comprehend (but not necessarily speak) the other language over time (Barron-Hauwaert, 2004).
Pros: Gradually reduces language barriers without demanding fluency.
Cons: Requires long-term effort and may not work for all families.

Structured Language Time
Designate certain family activities (e.g. meals, game nights) for one language, rotating between/among them (Spolsky, 2004).
Pros: Balances exposure and inclusivity.
Cons: Requires discipline and may feel artificial.

As children grow older, group conversations often shift toward more complex topics, such as emotions, values or personal struggles, which can be difficult to navigate if one parent is excluded. Language exclusion may create tension or feelings of isolation, and many families find that adolescents naturally gravitate toward the community language for convenience, even when heritage languages are actively supported.

Weighing linguistic goals alongside family harmony (Spolsky, 2012), and revisiting these decisions as children's needs change help families adapt over time.

Pause and Reflect

Choosing a Common Family Language

As you think about how your family will communicate when everyone is together, take a moment to reflect.

- When you picture family meals, trips or holidays, which language(s) do you imagine being used?
  ☐ Heritage Language A
  ☐ Heritage Language B
  ☐ Community language
  ☐ A mix of languages
- How important are the following you? (1 = not important 2 = slightly important 3 = moderately important 4 = important 5 = very important)

- Everyone participates fully in the conversation.
  Rate importance: ☐1 ☐2 ☐3 ☐4 ☐5
- Your child hears and practices the heritage language in group settings.
  Rate importance: ☐1 ☐2 ☐3 ☐4 ☐5

Reflection

____

____

Imagine your child as a teenager. Which matters more to you in group conversations?

☐ Inclusion of all family members.
☐ Strong heritage language practice.
☐ A balance between both.

Write your thoughts about what you hope your family's language use will look like when you are all together.

Parent as Researcher in Action

Explore Other Families' Solutions
Look up a story (online, in a book or among people you know) of how another multilingual family decided on a common language for group conversations.

- What approach did they use (OPOL, community language, flexible mix, etc.)?
- What worked well for them?

- What challenges did they face?
  Notes: ______________________________

Create a 'What If' Scenario
Imagine a family gathering when your child is 5 years old. Grandparents, parents and children are all present. Write down which language(s) you would realistically expect to be used and how you might keep everyone included.
Scenario: ______________________________

Small Experiment
If possible, do this before the baby arrives. If you and your partner already have opportunities to be in multilingual situations (e.g. with relatives or friends), try different strategies:

- Stick to your heritage languages.
- Switch to the community language.
- Try flexible OPOL with translation.
  Afterward, talk together. Which approach felt natural? Which was harder to sustain?

Ongoing Check-In
Plan to revisit this decision as your child grows. Write down a reminder question to ask yourselves every year, such as 'How well is our family language choice working for both inclusion and heritage language maintenance?'

Resolving conflicts in multilingual families

In multilingual families, especially those that are intercultural, interracial or interfaith, language planning is rarely just a practical matter. It reflects deeply held values, cultural identities and emotional connections. One parent may view language as a vital link to heritage and grandparents, while the other may fear that prioritizing a minority language could hinder integration, academic progress or social relationships. If such differences remain unspoken, they can create family tension.

Consider a couple in which one parent is committed to the OPOL method but the other prefers a more flexible approach or favors using only the dominant community language for convenience. On the surface, this seems like a disagreement about method. However, but at its core, it often stems from differing hopes and priorities. One parent may associate the heritage language with family continuity and identity, whereas the other emphasizes academic success, social mobility or everyday ease. If these perspectives are not reconciled, they can affect both the parental relationship and the children's exposure to and attitude toward each language (Luykx, 2005).

For this reason, it is essential for you to discuss family communication styles early (ideally before the child is born) and to revisit these conversations as the family evolves. Family language policies are dynamic and shift over time as children grow and circumstances change (Schwartz, 2010). What matters most is not eliminating differences but managing them through open dialogue, empathy and mutual respect.

Language planning within families is a living, relational process (Curdt-Christiansen, 2009). It is not about winning arguments but about co-creating a multilingual environment where the children feel secure and understood and the parents feel heard. Conflicts are natural and often inevitable; what matters is how they are navigated. With empathy, flexibility and open communication, families can turn tension into opportunities for growth, sustaining both multilingual development and family cohesion.

Pause and Reflect

1. What Languages Mean to Both of You

Before your baby is born, take time to explore what your languages represent to each of you.

Discuss together:

- What does each of our heritage languages mean to us personally?
- What memories, emotions or hopes do we associate with them?
- What values do we share? Where might we differ?

Notes:

____

____

____

____

2. Our Shared Goals

Clarify the long-term goals you want to set as parents.

List two or three goals you both agree on:

1. __________
2. __________
3. __________

3. Staying Flexible Together

Your plans may evolve once your baby arrives.

Reflect together:

- What feels realistic for us right now?

  ____

- What might need adjustment once routines or living situations change?

  ____

4. Including Extended Family

Relatives may have strong hopes or expectations about language use.

Discuss:

- How can we involve them in a positive and supportive way?

  ____

- What boundaries or expectations do we want to clarify early on?

  ____

____

5. Seeking Support

Think ahead about where you might look for guidance if needed.

Possible sources of support:

(e.g. pediatricians, early childhood educators, multilingual specialists)

____

____

____

Parent as Researcher in Action Worksheets

Activity 1: Family Language Journal

Use a shared notebook or digital journal to record prenatal reflections.

This month's reflections:

- Our hopes for our child's future languages: ______________________
- Our concerns or questions: ______________________
- Possible areas of tension we should pay attention to: ______________________

Next review date: ______________________

Activity 2: Value Mapping

Draw a simple Venn diagram with two circles labeled:

- Heritage and identity
- Academic and social goals

Then discuss what each circle means to both of you.

Shared Vision:

____

____

____

Activity 3: Storytelling Interviews

Talk with grandparents or relatives about what the heritage language means to them.

Reflect together:

- What did we learn from their stories or memories?

  ____

- How do these insights influence our hopes for our future child?

  ____

Activity 4: Imagine Your Future Child's View

Imagine how your child might eventually experience language in everyday contexts.

Discuss:

- How might our child feel using different languages at home, preschool and in social settings?

  ____

- What can we do now to prepare a warm, supportive environment for those future experiences?

  ____

Activity 5: Quarterly Language Check-In

Revisit your plans every few weeks.

This quarter:

- What feels clear and aligned between us?

  ____

- What questions or uncertainties have come up?

  ____

- Are our expectations matching our evolving goals as future parents?

  ____

Next check-in date: ______________________

What's In a Name?

There is another matter that has been rarely discussed in family language planning: How to name your child, especially what names to give a child across languages and cultures. A name stays with a person for life, shaping both how she sees herself and how others perceive her. In multilingual families, naming carries even greater significance because it becomes a powerful expression of cultural, linguistic and personal identity (Alford, 1988; Edwards, 2009).

Names are more than simple labels. They carry deep cultural meaning, often signaling heritage, values and a sense of belonging. However, across languages and cultures, the same name may be interpreted differently, sometimes leading to confusion or unintended assumptions. For instance, Andrea is typically male in Italy but female in the United States, Noa is a popular girl's name in Israel but is often assumed to be male elsewhere; Ali is a common Arabic male name but in English-speaking contexts, it is also often used as a nickname for female names such as Alison, Alice or Alexandra; and Sasha is a boy's name in Russia but is often associated with girls in the United States.

In addition, some names are perfectly acceptable in one culture but carry laughable or even embarrassing meanings in another. For example, the name Mona, common in English, can sound like a vulgar term in certain Arabic dialects, particularly in the Gulf region, leading to unintended or awkward connotations. In Spanish, '*mona*' means 'monkey' or 'cute,' which can also provoke amusement among native speakers. These variations highlight how names travel unevenly across cultures and how children may be perceived differently depending on the linguistic and cultural context (Ainiala & Östman, 2017).

Using our family as an example, we gave each of our children three names to reflect their multilingual backgrounds and to rhyme closely with their official names: In French, Léandre and Dominique (official names); in Chinese, Lǐ Áng (理昂, rationality and dignity) and Nī Kě (呢可, affectionate); in English, Leander and Dominic. Despite our intentions, their French names ended up being the ones most used in daily life, since these were the names listed on their official documents. Looking back, we have a few regrets about these choices. Although we were drawn to their elegance and cultural resonance, we did not anticipate how the names would be received in the

United States, where both are more commonly viewed as feminine. Dominique, in particular, faced awkward experiences, such as being placed on the girls' soccer team list or being mistaken for a woman, based solely on assumptions tied to his name. Though these moments may seem minor, they can be frustrating and may subtly influence a child's self-image and social experiences over time (Sue & Telles, 2007).

As you embark on a multilingual and multicultural parenting journey, naming is an area that deserves careful thought. A name rich in tradition in one culture may be unfamiliar or misread in another. Being aware of these differences can help avoid misunderstandings and support a child's comfort and confidence in diverse settings.

Ultimately, naming is a vital part of language and identity planning. It is not only about how a name sounds or what it means, but also about how it lives with the child across cultures and communities. A thoughtful choice can affirm a child's multilingual identity and provide a strong, rooted sense of self wherever they go.

Pause and Reflect

Create a 'Naming Journey' Journal
Start a shared notebook or digital document with your partner. In it, record potential names and why you like them. Include the names' origins and meanings in different languages, and any family members or cultural figures who share the name. This helps you document your process and identify themes that are important to your family.

Conduct a 'Sound Test'
Practice saying each potential name aloud, but with a twist. Say the name with your last name, with a sibling's name, and with common phrases like 'Hello, (Name)!' or 'Time for dinner, (Name)!' Try this in each of your family's languages. This simple exercise can reveal how a name feels to say and hear in everyday conversation and if any awkward sounds or phrases emerge. For example, before we had our first child and knew the gender, we prepared two names in French: Léandre for a boy and Sophie for a girl. My husband imagined, for instance, that '*Sophie, ça suffit!*' ('Sophie, that's enough!') had a playful rhyme.

Build a Family Name Map
Draw or print a world map and mark the geographic origins of the names in your family tree. This helps visualize your family's diverse linguistic and cultural heritage and can be a powerful way to find names that honor your roots. It's a great way to see how names have traveled through your family's history.

Parent As Researcher in Action

The Name Perception Audit
Choose a few top contenders for names and ask trusted friends and family members from different language backgrounds to share their first impressions. Ask them to

write the name down and guess its gender, origin and how they would pronounce it. The results can reveal potential misunderstandings or surprises you might not have anticipated.

Create an 'Unintended Meanings' Checklist
Research each potential name for unintended meanings or humorous connotations in all the languages you and your family interact with. A simple online search can often reveal surprising slang or colloquial uses. For example, search '(name) slang', '(name) meaning in Spanish', or '(name) funny.'

Gather Multilingual Naming Stories
Actively seek out and talk to other parents raising children in multilingual homes. Ask them about their own naming experiences. What names did they choose and why? What were some unexpected challenges or happy surprises they encountered? Hearing firsthand accounts can provide invaluable insight and help you anticipate potential social and cultural nuances of your own choice.

Prenatal Language Stimulation

Once you've decided on your family's language approach and considered the factors that will support your child's multilingual development, you don't have to wait until birth to begin. In fact, language development can start even before a child is born.

By around 18–20 weeks of gestation, the fetus begins to detect low-frequency sounds, such as the mother's heartbeat, digestion, and muffled environmental noise. As the auditory system develops further, consistent responses to external sounds emerge around 22–24 weeks, reflecting increasing sensitivity to auditory input. By the third trimester (approximately 28–30 weeks onward), fetuses can perceive speech patterns and show differential responses to voices, with particular sensitivity to the mother's voice. Toward the end of pregnancy, fetuses demonstrate the ability to encode and retain auditory experiences, including speech and music, forming early memory traces that influence postnatal preferences. Newborns, for example, show a preference for their mother's voice and the prosodic patterns of the language(s) they were exposed to prenatally (DeCasper & Fifer, 1980; Movalled *et al.*, 2023).

Fetuses can tune their ears to the language they are going to acquire even before they are born. A study shows that a month before their birth, fetuses carried by American mothers-to-be can distinguish between someone speaking to them in English and Japanese (Minai *et al.*, 2017). Prenatal sensitivity to the rhythmic properties of language may indeed provide children with one of the very first building blocks in acquiring language. In fact, the language a fetus is exposed to affects not only the specific sounds she makes (**phones**, the actual sounds without linguistic meaning) but also the rhythmic and melodic qualities in its later babbling, including aspects like stress, intonation and rhythm (Mampe *et al.*, 2009).

This early exposure offers an opportunity to engage with your child by talking, reading aloud or singing in your heritage language(s) during pregnancy. These simple daily interactions not only soothe your baby but also promote early familiarity with the sounds and patterns of the language(s) she will encounter after birth. In a very real sense, your voice becomes your child's first language teacher, long before her first words are spoken.

Prenatal language stimulation also serves as a powerful tool for parents. It helps establish a consistent habit of speaking the heritage language, especially when it differs from the dominant language in the surrounding environment. For example, when I was pregnant with my first child, Léandre, we had already decided that I would speak exclusively in Chinese while my husband would speak French. Since Chinese wasn't the community's majority language, I began speaking to Léandre every day during pregnancy. This practice made the transition to speaking Chinese with him after birth feel natural. By the time he was born, I felt confident using the language, which helped support our multilingual goals from Day 1.

Starting early not only gives your child a head start, but it also prepares you as a parent to create a consistent, responsive and meaningful multilingual environment from the very beginning. Small steps taken during pregnancy can have lasting effects, both in language learning and in strengthening the parent–child bond.

Pause and Reflect

Use this activity sheet to begin practicing your heritage languages.

1. Daily Language Routines

Choose one daily moment to speak, read or sing in your heritage language (e.g. morning poem, bedtime lullaby, narrating your day).

2. End of Week Reflection

- How did it feel to use your heritage language(s) consistently this week?
- How do you imagine your baby beginning to distinguish your voices and language(s)?

Notes:

____

____

____

Parent as Researcher in Action

Use the following log to track your baby's earliest exposure to language during pregnancy.

1. Log Your Language Use

Record each interaction.

Date: ____________________

Activity (reading, singing, talking): ____________________

Baby's response (kicks, movement, stillness): ____________________

(Repeat as needed)

2. Review Your Notes Every Few Weeks

Reflect as a team:

- Are we providing regular exposure to both languages?
- Does the baby seem more responsive at certain times or to certain activities?
- Is speaking our heritage languages becoming more natural?

Summary:

____

____

____

3. Looking Ahead

How will this prenatal practice help us feel more confident and prepared once the baby arrives?

Our thoughts:

____

____

Before You Leave This Chapter

As you come to the end of this chapter, take a moment to imagine the possibilities ahead. You are preparing to begin an extraordinary journey: Raising a child who will grow up hearing, feeling and expressing herself through more than one language. Even before birth, your baby is already tuning into the rhythm of your voice; one day, she will move with ease between words that open doors to different worlds.

This is more than a practical parenting choice. It is a gift of identity, belonging and connection that will stay with your child for a lifetime. Challenges will arise, but you are not stepping into this unprepared. The reflection and planning you are doing now will become a steady guide as your child grows.

Before turning the page, complete the chart below. You have already considered many of these ideas throughout the chapter; writing them down will help you clarify your intentions and mark your first concrete step in bringing your multilingual vision to life.

Once you finish, place the chart somewhere you will see it often, whether in your journal, on your desk or on the refrigerator. Let it be a gentle reminder of the hopes you hold for your child's multilingual journey.

When your baby arrives, these reflections will help you turn intention into daily practice, guiding you as you begin living the multilingual story you have imagined.

Multilingual Childrearing Planning Checklist

Areas to consider	Summary (your thoughts in a few words or sentences)	Notes/next steps
What is your motivation to raise multilingual children?		
What are your multilingual childrearing goals?		
What is your heritage language proficiency?		
What are your personality traits that will shape your approach?		
What support do you have in your heritage language(s)? How much time can you commit to your child?		
What is your family language plan? What is the family communicative style?		
Do you and your partner agree on the family language plan? If not, how will you resolve differences?		
What family values do you want reflected in your language choices?		
What name(s) have you chosen for your child? Have you researched the meanings in different cultures?		
How will you celebrate milestones and progress in your child's multilingual journey?		

Note

(1) This is a conventional way to describe a research participant's age: 18 years, 5 months, 21 days.

References

Adesope, O.O., Lavin, T., Thompson, T. and Ungerleider, C. (2010) A systematic review and meta-analysis of the cognitive correlates of bilingualism. *Review of Educational Research* 80 (2), 207–245. https://doi.org/10.3102/0034654310368803

Ainiala, T. and Östman, J.O. (eds) (2017) *Socio-onomastics: The Pragmatics of Names*. John Benjamins. https://doi.org/10.1075/pbns.275

Alford, R.D. (1988) *Naming and Identity: A Cross-Cultural Study of Personal Naming Practices*. HRAF Press.

Alladi, S., Bak, T.H., Duggirala, V., Surampudi, B., Shailaja, M., Shukla, A.K., Chaudhuri, J.R. and Kaul, S. (2013) Bilingualism delays age at onset of dementia, independent of education and immigration status. *Neurology* 81 (22), 1938–1944. https://doi.org/10.1212/01.wnl.0000436620.33155.a4

Astington, J.W. and Baird, J.A. (eds) (2005) *Why Language Matters for Theory of Mind*. Oxford University Press.

Auer, P. (ed.) (1998) *Code-Switching in Conversation: Language, Interaction and Identity*. Routledge.

Baker, C. (2011) *Foundations of Bilingual Education and Bilingualism* (5th edn). Bristol: Multilingual Matters.

Barbosa, P., Nicoladis, E. and Keith, M. (2017) Bilingual children's lexical strategies in a narrative task. *Journal of Child Language* 44 (4), 829–849. https://doi.org/10.1017/S030500091600026X

Barron-Hauwaert, S. (2004) *Language Strategies for Bilingual Families: The One-Parent–One-Language Approach* (1st edn). Multilingual Matters.

Bhabha, H.K. (1994) *The Location of Culture*. Routledge.

Bialystok, E. (2001) *Bilingualism in Development: Language, Literacy, and Cognition*. Cambridge University Press. https://doi.org/10.1017/CBO9780511605963

Bialystok, E. and Martin, M.M. (2004) Attention and inhibition in bilingual children: Evidence from the dimensional change card sort task. *Developmental Science* 7 (3), 325–339. https://doi.org/10.1111/j.1467-7687.2004.00351.x

Bialystok, E., Craik, F.I.M and Luk, G. (2012) Bilingualism: Consequences for mind and brain. *Trends in Cognitive Sciences* 16 (4), 240–250. https://doi.org/10.1016/j.tics.2012.03.001

Bloom, P. (2000) *How Children Learn the Meanings of Words*. MIT Press.

Blum-Kulka, S. (1997) *Dinner Talk: Cultural Patterns of Sociability and Socialization in Family Discourse*. Routledge.

Broner, M. and Tarone, E. (2001) Is it fun? Language play in a fifth-grade Spanish immersion classroom. *The Modern Language Journal* 85 (3), 363–379. https://doi.org/10.1111/0026-7902.00114

Bruner, J. (1983) *Child's Talk: Learning to Use Language*. Norton.

Byers-Heinlein, K. and Lew-Williams, C. (2013) Bilingualism in the early years: What the science says. *Learning Landscapes* 7 (1), 95–112. https://doi.org/10.36510/learnland.v7i1.632

Carlson, S.M. and Meltzoff, A.N. (2008) Bilingual experience and executive functioning in young children. *Developmental Science* 11 (2), 282–298. https://doi.org/10.1111/j.1467-7687.2008.00675.x

Core, C., Hoff, E., Rumiche, R. and Señor, M. (2013) Total and conceptual vocabulary in Spanish–English bilinguals from 22 to 30 months: Implications for assessment. *Journal of Speech, Language, and Hearing Research* 56 (5), 1637–1649. https://doi.org/10.1044/1092-4388(2013/11-0044)

Costa, A., Hernández, M. and Sebastián-Gallés, N. (2008) Bilingualism aids conflict resolution: Evidence from the ANT task. *Cognition* 106 (1), 59–86. https://doi.org/10.1016/j.cognition.2006.12.013

Cummins, J. (2001) Bilingual children's mother tongue: Why is it important for education? *Sprogforum* 7 (19), 15–20.

Curdt-Christiansen, X.L. (2009) Visible and invisible language planning: Ideological factors in the family language policy of Chinese immigrant families in Quebec. *Language Policy* 8 (4), 351–375. https://doi.org/10.1007/s10993-009-9146-7

Curdt-Christiansen, X.L. (2016) Conflicting language ideologies and contradictory language practices in Singaporean multilingual families. *Journal of Multilingual and Multicultural Development* 37 (7), 694–709. https://doi.org/10.1080/01434632.2015.1127926

De Houwer, A. (1999) Environmental factors in early bilingual development: The role of parental beliefs and attitudes. In G. Extra and L. Verhoeven (eds) *Bilingualism and Migration* (pp 75–95). De Gruyter.

De Houwer, A. (2007) Parental language input patterns and children's bilingual use. *Applied Psycholinguistics* 28 (3), 411–424. https://doi.org/10.1017/S0142716407070221

De Houwer, A. (2009) *Bilingual First Language Acquisition*. Multilingual Matters.

De Houwer, A. (2020) Harmonious bilingualism: Well-being for families in bilingual settings. A.C. Schalley and S.A. Eisenchlas (eds) *Handbook of Home Language Maintenance and Development* (pp. 63–83). https://doi.org/10.1515/9781501510175-004

De Houwer, A., Bornstein, M.H. and Putnick, D.L. (2014) A bilingual–monolingual comparison of young children's vocabulary size: Evidence from comprehension and production. *Applied Psycholinguistics* 35 (6), 1189–1211. https://doi.org/10.1017/S0142716412000744

De Houwer, A. (2021) *Bilingual Development in Childhood*. Cambridge University Press. https://doi.org/10.1017/9781108866002.

DeCasper, A.J. and Fifer, W.P. (1980) Of human bonding: Newborns prefer their mothers' voices. *Science* 208 (4448), 1174–1176. https://doi.org/10.1126/science.7375928

Döpke, S. (1992) *One Parent, One Language: An Interactional Approach*. John Benjamins. https://doi.org/10.1075/sibil.3

Edwards, J. (2009) *Language and Identity: An Introduction*. Cambridge University Press.

Fecher, N. and Johnson, E.K. (2019) Bilingual infants excel at foreign-language talker recognition. *Developmental Science* 22 (4), e12778. https://doi.org/10.1111/desc.12778

García, O. and Li, W. (2014) *Translanguaging: Language, Bilingualism and Education*. Palgrave Macmillan. https://doi.org/10.1057/9781137385765

Grosjean, F. (2010) *Bilingual: Life and Reality*. Harvard University Press.

Guardado, M. (2018) *Discourse, Ideology and Heritage Language Socialization: Micro and Macro Perspectives*. Mouton de Gruyter. https://doi.org/10.1515/9781614513841

Hart, B. and Risley, T. (1995) *Meaningful Differences in the Everyday Experience of Young American Children*. Paul H. Brookes.

Hartshorne, J.K., Tenenbaum, J.B. and Pinker, S. (2018) A critical period for second language acquisition: Evidence from 2/3 million English speakers. *Cognition* 177, 263–277. https://doi.org/10.1016/j.cognition.2018.04.007

Haugen, E. (1972) *The Ecology of Language*. Stanford University Press.

Heller, M. (1988) Introduction: The role of language in the construction of social identity. In M. Heller (ed.) *Code-Switching: Anthropological and Sociolinguistic Perspectives* (pp. 1–13). Mouton de Gruyter. https://doi.org/10.1515/9783110849615.1

Hoff, E. (2006) How social contexts support and shape language development. *Developmental Review* 26 (1), 55–88. https://doi.org/10.1016/j.dr.2005.11.002

Hollenweger, J. and Moretti, M. (2012) Multilingual education and academic outcomes in Switzerland. *European Journal of Psychology of Education* 27 (3), 307–324.

Ivanova, I. and Costa, A. (2008) Does bilingualism hamper lexical access in speech production? *Acta Psychologica* 127 (2), 277–288. https://doi.org/10.1016/j.actpsy.2007.06.003

Kharkhurin, A.V. (2015) Multilingual creative cognition: Theory, research and practice. In R. Jones (ed.) *The Routledge Handbook of Language and Creativity* (pp. 452–467). Routledge.

Kieffer, M.J. and Thompson, K.D. (2018) Hidden progress of multilingual students on NAEP. *Educational Researcher* 47 (6), 391–398. https://doi.org/10.3102/0013189X18777740

King, K.A. and Fogle, L. (2006) Bilingual parenting as good parenting: Parents' perspectives on family language policy for additive bilingualism. *International Journal of Bilingual Education and Bilingualism* 9 (6), 695–712. https://doi.org/10.2167/beb362.0

King, K.A., Fogle, L. and Logan-Terry, A. (2008) Family language policy. *Language and Linguistics Compass* 2 (5), 907–922. https://doi.org/10.1111/j.1749-818X.2008.00076.x

Koelewijn, A., Hoevenaars, E. and Verhagen, J. (2025) How do parents think about multilingual upbringing? Comparing OPOL parents and parents who mix languages. *Journal of Multilingual and Multicultural Development* 46 (3), 230–248. https://doi.org/10.1080/01434632.2023.2202633

Kovács, Á.M. (2009) Early bilingualism enhances mechanisms of false-belief reasoning. *Developmental Science* 12 (1), 48–54. https://doi.org/10.1111/j.1467-7687.2008.00742.x

Kramsch, C. (2009) *The Multilingual Subject*. Oxford University Press.

Kramsch, C. (2011) The symbolic dimensions of the intercultural. *Language Teaching* 44 (3), 354–367. https://doi.org/10.1017/S0261444810000431

Krashen, S.D. (2012) *Second Language Acquisition: Theory, Applications, and Some Conjectures*. Cambridge University Press.

Kremin, L.V., Netelenbos, N., Ibáñez, A.M. and Krizman, J. (2021) Bilingualism and voice recognition: Evidence for an advantage in speaker processing. *Cognition* 214, 104751.

Krizman, J., Marian, V., Shook, A., Skoe, E. and Kraus, N. (2012) Subcortical encoding of sound is enhanced in bilinguals and relates to executive function advantages. *Proceedings of the National Academy of Sciences* 109 (27), 11075–11080. https://doi.org/10.1073/pnas.1201575109.

Kroll, J.F. and Bialystok, E. (2013) Understanding the consequences of bilingualism for language processing and cognition. *Journal of Cognitive Psychology* 25 (5), 497–514. https://doi.org/10.1080/20445911.2013.799170

Kuhl, P.K. (2004) Early language acquisition: Cracking the speech code. *Nature Reviews Neuroscience* 5 (11), 831–843. https://doi.org/10.1038/nrn1533

Lanza, E. (2007) Multilingualism in the family. In P. Auer and Li, W. (eds) *Handbook of Multilingualism and Multilingual Communication* (pp. 45–67). Mouton de Gruyter. https://doi.org/10.1515/9783110198553.1.45

Lareau, A. (2003) *Unequal Childhoods: Class, Race, and Family Life*. University of California Press.

Luk, G., de Sa, E. and Bialystok, E. (2011) Is there a relation between onset age of bilingualism and enhancement of cognitive control? *Bilingualism: Language and Cognition* 14 (4), 588–595. https://doi.org/10.1017/S1366728911000010

Luykx, A. (2005) Children as socializing agents: Family language policy in situations of language shift. In J. Cohen, K.T. McAlister, K. Rolstad and J. MacSwan (eds) *Proceedings of the 4th International Symposium on Bilingualism* (pp. 1407–1414). Cascadilla Press.

Mampe, B., Friederici, A.D., Christophe, A. and Wermke, K. (2009) Newborns' cry melody is shaped by their native language. *Current Biology* 19 (23), 1939–1940. https://doi.org/10.1016/j.cub.2009.09.064

Minai, U., Gustafson, K., Fiorentino, R., Jongman, A. and Sereno, J. (2017) Fetal rhythm-based language discrimination: A biomagnetometry study. *NeuroReport* 28 (10), 561–564. https://doi.org/10.1097/WNR.0000000000000794

Movalled, K., Sani, A., Nikniaz, L. and Ghojazadeh, M. (2023) The impact of sound stimulations during pregnancy on fetal learning: A systematic review. *BMC Pediatrics* 23 (1), 18. https://doi.org/10.1186/s12887-023-03990-7

Orellana, M.F. (2009a) The work of language brokering: A discourse-analytic approach to the study of children's translations. *Linguistics and Education* 20 (4), 309–324.

Orellana, M.F. (2009b) *Translating Childhoods: Immigrant Youth, Language, and Culture*. Rutgers University Press.

Paradis, J., Genesee, F. and Crago, M.B. (2021) *Dual Language Development & Disorders: A Handbook on Bilingualism and Second Language Learning* (3rd edn). Brookes Publishing.

Paradowski, M.B. (2013) *Myths about Bilingualism*. Institute of English Studies, University of Warsaw.

Pavlenko, A. (2005) *Emotions and Multilingualism*. Cambridge University Press.

Pavlenko, A. (2014) *The Bilingual Mind: And What It Tells Us About Language and Thought*. Cambridge University Press.

Pearson, B.Z., Fernández, S.C. and Oller, D.K. (1993) Lexical development in bilingual infants and toddlers: Comparison to monolingual norms. *Language Learning* 43 (1), 93–120. https://doi.org/10.1111/j.1467-1770.1993.tb00174.x

Petitto, L.A., Berens, M.S., Kovelman, I., Dubins, M.H., Jasinska, K. and Shalinsky, M. (2012) The 'perceptual wedge hypothesis': How early bilingual experience provides advantages in neural processing for speech perception. *Brain and Language* 121 (2), 130–140. https://doi.org/10.1016/j.bandl.2011.05.003

Piller, I. (2002) *Bilingual Couples Talk: The Discursive Construction of Hybridity*. John Benjamins. https://doi.org/10.1075/sibil.25

Poplack, S., Sankoff, D. and Miller, C. (1988) The social correlates and linguistic processes of lexical borrowing and assimilation. *Linguistics* 26 (1), 47–104. https://doi.org/10.1515/ling.1988.26.1.47

Rampton, B. (1995) *Crossing: Language and Ethnicity Among Adolescents*. Longman.

Rutgers, D., Evans, M., Fisher, L., Forbes, K., Gayton, A. and Liu, Y. (2024) Multilingualism, multilingual identity and academic attainment: Evidence from secondary schools in England. *Journal of Language, Identity & Education* 23 (2), 210–227. https://doi.org/10.1080/15348458.2021.1986397

Saiz, A. and Zoido, E. (2005) Listening to what the world says: Bilingualism and earnings in the United States. *Review of Economics and Statistics* 87 (3), 523–538. https://doi.org/10.1162/0034653054638256

Schwartz, M. (2010) Family language policy: Core issues of an emerging field. *Applied Linguistics Review* 1 (1), 171–192. https://doi.org/10.1515/9783110222654.171

Schwartz, M. and Verschik, A. (2013) *Successful Family Language Policy: Parents, Children and Educators in Interaction*. Dordrecht: Springer. https://doi.org/10.1007/978-94-007-7753-8

Singh, L. (2024) Generalizability and representation in studies of infant perceptual narrowing: Considerations for future research. *Infant Behavior and Development* 77, 101998. https://doi.org/10.1016/j.infbeh.2024.101998.

Spolsky, B. (2004) *Language Policy*. Cambridge University Press. https://doi.org/10.1017/CBO9780511615245

Spolsky, B. (2012) Family language policy – the critical domain. *Journal of Multilingual and Multicultural Development* 33 (1), 3–11. https://doi.org/10.1080/01434632.2011.638072

Sue, C.A. and Telles, E.E. (2007) Assimilation and gender in naming. *American Journal of Sociology* 112 (5), 1383–1415. https://doi.org/10.1086/511801

Tsimpli, I.M., Peristeri, E. and Andreou, M. (2016) Narrative production in monolingual and bilingual children with specific language impairment. *Applied Psycholinguistics* 37 (1), 195–216. https://doi.org/10.1017/S0142716415000478

University of Cambridge (2021) Students who self-identify as multilingual perform better at GCSE. University of Cambridge Research News, 11 November. https://www.cam.ac.uk/news/students-who-self-identify-as-multilingual-perform-better-at-gcse

Wang, X.-L. (2008) *Growing up with Three Languages: Birth to Eleven*. Multilingual Matters.

Wang, X.-L. (2013) Multilingualism and family welfare. In T.K. Bhatia and W.C. Ritchie (eds) *The Handbook of Bilingualism and Multilingualism* (2nd edn) (pp. 542–562). Wiley-Blackwell. https://doi.org/10.1002/9781118332382.ch22

Wang, X.-L. (2016) *Maintaining Three Languages: The Teenage Years*. Multilingual Matters.

Wang, X.-L. (2022a) Multilingualism and language play. In A. Stavans and U. Jessner (eds) *The Cambridge Handbook of Childhood Multilingualism* (pp. 235–254). Cambridge University Press. https://doi.org/10.1017/9781108669771.013

Wang, X.-L. (2022b) Phrasing it differently: Understanding multilingual children's social and communicative competence through language mixing. [Conference session]. 10th European Conference on Language Learning, London, UK.

Werker, J.F. and Byers-Heinlein, K. (2008) Bilingualism in infancy: First steps in perception and comprehension. *Trends in Cognitive Sciences* 12 (4), 144–151. https://doi.org/10.1016/j.tics.2008.01.008

Werker, J.F. and Tees, R.C. (1984) Cross-language speech perception: Evidence for peceptual reorganization during the first year of life. *Infant Behavior and Development* 7 (1), 49–63. https://doi.org/10.1016/S0163-6383(84)80022-3

Wood, D., Bruner, J.S. and Ross, G. (1976) The role of tutoring in problem solving. *Journal of Child Psychology and Psychiatry* 17 (2), 89–100. https://doi.org/10.1111/j.1469-7610.1976.tb00381.x

Yeager, D.S. and Dweck, C.S. (2012) Mindsets that promote resilience: When students believe that personal characteristics can be developed. *Educational Psychologist* 47 (4), 302–314. https://doi.org/10.1080/00461520.2012.722805

Yow, W.Q. and Markman, E.M. (2011) Young bilingual children's heightened sensitivity to referential cues. *Journal of Cognition and Development* 12 (1), 12–31. https://doi.org/10.1080/15248372.2011.539524

3 The Multilingual Formative Years (Birth to Age 5): Building the Foundation

You are holding your newborn. Your gaze meets his for the first time. Months of anticipation have boiled down to this joyful moment as you welcome him into the world, greeting him in the heritage language you chose. What began before birth now continues as you enter the journey of multilingual childrearing.

The first five years offer an extraordinary window for learning multiple languages. His mind is like fertile soil, ready to absorb the sounds and rhythms around him. Every song you hum, every story you tell and every conversation you share plants seeds that will shape his growth. The languages he hears guide not only his communication but also his sense of belonging in the world.

By his fifth birthday, you may marvel at the child he has become. He might describe his day in one language, sing in another and ask a question in a third. In his voice, you hear both his growing mind and the depth of his feelings.

This chapter invites you into these first five years, a time rich with possibility for raising a multilingual child. Through intentional strategies, you can help him grow up confident, curious and rooted in the languages that shape his life. It also encourages you to observe his progress as a parent-researcher and let your strategies evolve with him.

Biological Windows for Early Language Acquisition

Although humans can learn languages at any age, early childhood is the most favorable period for **language acquisition** (the unconscious process of absorbing language through interaction and exposure). This is why it is often described as a **sensitive**, **critical** or **optimal period**. During these years, the brain is especially flexible and responsive to language input, allowing children to absorb one or more languages naturally through everyday interaction. Even before babies speak, their brains are preparing for language. Newborns show activation in the same brain regions involved in adult language processing (Perani *et al.*, 2011) and can distinguish the sounds of all the world's languages (Werker & Tees, 2005). Infants are highly sensitive to subtle **phonetic** (sound) differences, but this ability declines between 6 and 12 months (Kuhl *et al.*, 2003), a process known as **perceptual narrowing** (Kuhl, 2004).

Because of this sensitivity, the timing of exposure is crucial. Early and consistent input supports nativelike phonology, and delays of even a few years can lead to lasting differences in pronunciation. Even in cases of exceptional learners who appear native to the casual listener, detailed phonetic analysis often reveals subtle deviations from native norms (Abrahamsson & Hyltenstam, 2009).

This is especially relevant for heritage languages, which often receive less support from the surrounding environment. Some researchers suggest that the brain's peak readiness for language acquisition is most robust in early childhood, with a gradual shift in learning mechanisms occurring between ages 7 and 10 (Johnson & Newport, 1989). After **puberty** (when the body develops the ability to reproduce), achieving native-like fluency becomes significantly more challenging, particularly regarding pronunciation and complex grammatical structures (Abrahamsson & Hyltenstam, 2009).

Furthermore, the age of first exposure shapes the neural architecture. Children who begin learning after age 7 often utilize different neural pathways from those exposed from birth (Kim *et al.*, 1997). In contrast, heritage speakers who are exposed to their home language from infancy often maintain nativelike neural processing patterns in areas like phonology and basic syntax, even if their formal proficiency is lower than that of a monolingual peer (Montrul, 2016). This suggests that early exposure hardwires certain linguistic foundations that are difficult for later learners to replicate.

However, this sensitive period does not end all at once. Instead, it unfolds in stages linked to different aspects of language. Sensitivity to sound patterns is strongest from late pregnancy to the first year. Grammar learning peaks around age four, and understanding word meanings continues to expand into adolescence (Kuhl, 2010). This layered timeline helps explain why adults may retain an accent though they still build strong vocabulary and literacy skills.

Early exposure to multiple languages also supports broader brain development. Research shows that multilingual children often have more gray matter and stronger neural connections in areas related to memory, attention and cognitive flexibility (Mechelli *et al.*, 2004). These differences can lead to advantages such as better focus, greater adaptability, and more efficient problem-solving (Bialystok, 2011). Even at seven months, multilingual infants show early signs of stronger attention control.

To give your child the best start on his multilingual journey, the approaches in the 'Try These Strategies' box can help him build a strong foundation for years to come.

Try These Strategies

Expose Your Child to the Heritage Language Early

Early exposure, even before birth, supports phonological and cognitive development. Infants recognize rhythm and sound patterns long before they produce words.

Birth to Age 2
Example: During diapering or feeding:
'Let's put on your soft socks. One… two.'
Tip: Use short, melodic phrases and repetition.

Ages 3 to 5
Example: During pretend play:
'You're cooking soup? What should we put in next?'
Tip: Storytelling and role-play build vocabulary and narrative skills.

Establish Consistent Heritage Language Use

Research shows that children develop stronger heritage language skills when their parents are consistent in their language use (De Houwer, 2009).

Birth to Age 2
Example: Speak exclusively to your baby in your heritage language, even if he responds with sounds or gestures.
Tip: Use the same phrases during daily routines to build predictability.

Ages 3 to 5
Child: 'I want a snack.' (in the mainstream language, English)
You: '*¿Tienes hambre? Vamos a ver qué tenemos.*' (in your heritage language, Spanish)
Tip: Continue to speak your heritage language even when your child answers in the dominant community language.

Increase Quantity and Quality of Input

Children need enough exposure to learn a language well. A general guide is at least 20–25% of waking hours or about 2.5–3 hours per day, woven naturally into routines (Hoff *et al.*, 2012).

Daily examples:

- Morning routine, 20–30 minutes
- Storytime, 20–30 minutes
- Playtime, 30–40 minutes
- Mealtime talk, 30–40 minutes
- Bedtime routine, 20–30 minutes

High-quality input matters just as much as quantity.

Birth to Age 2
'This is your red shirt. One arm… now the other.'
Tip: Use gestures and objects to support understanding.

Ages 3 to 5
'What do you think the squirrel is looking for?'
Tip: Ask open-ended questions and extend responses.

Nurture Language Through Responsive Talk

Children learn language most effectively when adults respond promptly and meaningfully to their sounds and words. These interactions support vocabulary, grammar, turn-taking and early storytelling skills (Bruce *et al.*, 2022).

Birth to Age 2

Baby coos. You respond:
'Oh, you're talking to me? Tell me more.'

Baby says 'ba' while holding a ball. You expand:
'Yes, your ball. A big red ball.'
Tip: Treat every sound as communication and expand with simple, rich language.

Ages 3 to 5
Child: 'I drawed a monster.'
You: 'You drew a monster? What color is it?'

Child: 'Water.'
You: 'You want cold water? Here it is. So refreshing.'

Tip: Build on what your child says by extending the idea into a full, natural sentence without correcting the form.

Foster Joint Attention

Joint attention refers to the shared focus of a caregiver and child on the same object, event or activity. Shared focus helps children attach meaning to words.

Birth to Age 2
Baby looks at a toy. You say:
'You see the bear? He's waving.'
Tip: Follow your baby's gaze and label objects of interest.

Ages 3 to 5
Child: 'Look at that bug.'
You: 'Yes, an ant! Where do you think it's going?'
Tip: Build language around what interests your child.

Use Child-Directed Speech

Child-directed speech, known as **motherese** or **baby talk,** is a specialized speech style characterized by a higher pitch, exaggerated intonation, slower tempo, repetition and simplified vocabulary. Child-directed speech supports vocabulary and early comprehension (Weisleder & Fernald, 2013).

Birth to Age 2
'Shoe time. One shoe, two shoes.'
Tip: Slow, expressive speech helps infants process sound patterns.

Ages 3 to 5
'Let's cut the tomatoes. They are juicy.'
Tip: Use child-directed speech if culturally appropriate; what matters most is responsive communication.

Learn Through Play

Pretend and symbolic play naturally expand vocabulary and narrative skills (Quinn *et al.*, 2018).

Birth to Age 2
'Where's mama? Peekaboo. There she is.'
Tip: Use simple, predictable games.

Ages 3 to 5
'Do you want milk or bread? Put it in the basket.'
Tip: Follow your child's lead and enrich play with descriptive language.

Essential Language Development Tasks from Birth to Age 5

To become competent language users, children must develop skills across several core domains of language. These foundational components include the following:

- **Phonology** refers to the sound system of a language, including **phonemes**, the smallest sounds that change meaning (such as /b/ and /p/ in *bat* and *pat*).
- **Lexicon** (or vocabulary) is the mental dictionary a child continuously builds. It includes the sound, meaning and correct use of every word they know.
- **Semantics** involves understanding word meanings and how they relate to one another.
- **Morphology** concerns how words are built from smaller meaningful parts, such as markers for plural (*books*), tense (*walked*) or possession (*Tom's book*). Languages differ in how they create these forms. For example, Turkish expresses meaning through multiple endings, as in *evlerinizden* ('from your houses', where *ev*=house, *-ler*=plural, *-iniz*=your, *-den*=from). Chinese, in contrast, relies more on word order and helper words, as in 我去了学校 ('I went to school'), where 了 signals a completed action and the sequence of words carries much of the grammatical meaning.
- **Syntax** refers to how words combine to form phrases and sentences.

- **Pragmatics** is the ability to use language appropriately in social contexts, such as greetings, taking turns or adjusting speech for different listeners.
- **Emergent literacy** includes the early skills that prepare children for later reading and writing. These skills grow long before formal instruction and include vocabulary development, interest in stories, recognition of print and symbols, and active engagement with books, pictures and digital media. During this stage, children begin understanding that print carries meaning, that stories have structure, and that written and spoken language are connected.

As these domains develop, children also begin to show **metalinguistic awareness** (the ability to think about and reflect on language itself). For example, a child may notice that two words rhyme or that a single word can have more than one meaning.

Variations Among Children Learning One or More Than One Language

Now that we have identified the major language tasks of the first five years, we can look more closely at how these areas typically unfold in children learning one language and how they may vary in children learning more than one during this period.

Phonology

Birth to age 2

General developmental pattern: Infants begin life able to hear many speech sound differences and gradually tune in to the sound contrasts, rhythm and intonation patterns of their environmental language. By the end of the first year, they become more efficient at recognizing sounds used in their language and less sensitive to those not needed.

Multilingual variation: Infants exposed to more than one language tend to maintain sensitivity to a wider range of sounds for a longer period. They track different rhythmic or tonal patterns depending on the languages they hear, which helps them begin forming separate sound systems before recognizable words appear.

Ages 3 to 5

General developmental pattern: Children refine their articulation, master more complex sounds and use the rhythm and intonation patterns characteristic of their language.

Multilingual variation: Children may master some sounds earlier in one language than another, depending on how often they hear them. For example, a child may produce the English *r* before the Spanish trilled *rr*, or take longer with English blends like *sp* if these do not appear in their other language. These differences are typical and resolve with regular exposure.

Lexicon

Birth to age 2

General developmental pattern: Infants and toddlers learn their first words from people and routines in their environment, building vocabulary steadily through repetition and interaction.
Multilingual variation: Vocabulary grows across languages based on context, need and **interlocutor** (the person a child is speaking or interacting with in a conversation). When all words are counted across languages, the **conceptual vocabulary** (total size) of a multilingual child is typically similar to or larger than that of monolingual peers. However, the vocabulary measured in each separate language may be smaller than that of a monolingual counterpart.

Ages 3 to 5

General developmental pattern: Vocabulary grows rapidly. Children learn new words through play, books and conversations.
Multilingual variation: Children build word knowledge in both shared and language-specific ways. For example, a child may know *hamer* in Dutch but not yet know *hammer* in English; with exposure, he learns that both words refer to the same object.

Semantics

Birth to age 2

General developmental pattern: Children start linking words to people, actions and objects and begin forming basic categories, such as grouping words like *dog*, *cat* and *rabbit* as animals.
Multilingual variation: Children learning more than one language learn that the same object can have different labels. They may temporarily treat words across languages as equivalent until they learn how each language divides meaning.

Ages 3 to 5

General developmental pattern: Children expand their understanding of word relationships, including similarities, differences and simple abstract meanings.
Multilingual variation: Children notice that one language may use broader categories while another is more specific. For example, English uses *cousin*, whereas French distinguishes *cousin* and *cousine*.

Morphology

Birth to age 2

General developmental pattern: Toddlers begin to understand basic grammatical markers, such as plural or tense, although their early forms are often simplified.

Multilingual variation: Children learning more than one language must absorb how each language builds or marks meaning. They may rely on simpler forms at first while their systems are still emerging. Occasional mixing of the rules is common and temporary.

Ages 3 to 5

General developmental pattern: Children begin using plural, tense and possession markers more consistently and understand how small word parts change meaning.
Multilingual variation: Children gradually apply the correct markers in each language. They learn when to use endings, when to use helper words and when word order matters. They keep these patterns separate with continued exposure.

Syntax

Birth to age 2

General developmental pattern: Children begin combining words into short phrases using the basic word order of their language.
Multilingual variation: Young multilingual children may sometimes use the word order of one language when speaking another while both systems are still developing.

Ages 3 to 5

General developmental pattern: Children expand their sentences, use more complex structures and follow the grammatical patterns of their language.
Multilingual variation: Children learn to select and switch between grammatical rules across languages depending on context, keeping structures largely distinct as their systems mature. Occasional code-mixing is a normal part of multilingual communication.

Pragmatics

Birth to age 2

General developmental pattern: Children learn early social routines such as pointing, greeting, taking turns and making simple requests.
Multilingual variation: Young multilingual children rapidly begin mastering the social rules of their languages, learning who speaks which language to whom and adjusting their vocalizations, gestures or early words accordingly.

Ages 3 to 5

General developmental pattern: Children learn how to participate in conversations, adjust their tone and use polite forms.
Multilingual variation: Children learn to use their different languages for specific social functions, adjusting what they say, how they say it and to whom, while recognizing differences in politeness and directness across languages.

Emergent literacy

Birth to age 2

General developmental pattern: Children enjoy being read to, explore books and begin noticing that print carries meaning.
Multilingual variation: Children may see books or print in different languages and begin recognizing different script shapes or symbol types across their environments.

Ages 3 to 5

General developmental pattern: Children start connecting letters or symbols with sounds or meanings and begin recognizing familiar words.
Multilingual variation: Multilingual children follow similar paths but show cross-linguistic transfer. Skills in one language can support another (e.g. Spanish rhyming can support English phonological awareness) but differences in writing systems may require adjustment, such as learning to read Arabic from right to left after reading English left to right.

Metalinguistic awareness

Birth to age 2

General developmental pattern: Children begin noticing that people use different sounds or words, even if they cannot yet describe these differences.
Multilingual variation: Children exposed to more than one language become aware earlier that different languages exist and may separate them according to the speaker or context.

Ages 3 to 5

General developmental pattern: Children begin to notice rhymes, sound similarities and simple grammatical patterns.
Multilingual variation: Multilingual children often show strong metalinguistic awareness. They compare their languages, notice structural differences and develop flexible thinking that supports later reading and problem-solving.

The following intentional strategies can help support your child's multilingual development, especially his heritage language development.

Try These Strategies

Phonology

Birth to 2
Example: During daily routines, highlight and exaggerate key sound features in each language to draw attention to their distinct phonological patterns. For example, in Mandarin, emphasize tones such as mā (妈-mother, first tone, high

level) and mǎ (马-horse, third tone, dipping) with clear tonal contours, and in English, stress patterns such as MOMmy, with strong emphasis on the first syllable.
Tip: Use facial expressions and hand or body movements, such as clapping, to highlight differences in rhythm and tone.

Ages 3 to 5
Example: Play a 'sound match' game. Ask, 'Which words start the same?' using French words such as *soleil* (sun), *savon* (soap) and *sourire* (smile).
Tip: Focus on listening first, production follows naturally.

Lexicon

Birth to 2
Example: During bathtime, use simple words and repetition in the heritage language: 'Here's the warm water. Splash, splash! Let's wash your hands... one, two!'

Tip: Use short, rhythmic phrases paired with physical actions or gestures to anchor words in memory (Hostetter, 2011). Support word learning with gestures, including **deictic** (pointing) and **iconic** (showing actions or shapes); for example, point while naming objects or act out words, and invite your child to move with you.

Ages 3 to 5
Example: Read picture books together and extend the story into conversation. After reading a gardening book, ask, 'What do we need to plant a flower?'

Tip: Use books as springboards for conversation, pretend play and personal connections. This reinforces vocabulary through active use and supports **incidental learning**, as children acquire new words through repeated exposure in meaningful contexts rather than direct instruction (Nagy & Anderson, 1984).

Sample interaction (incidental learning):
Child: 'Seeds!'
You: 'Yes, seeds. What else?'
Child: 'Water.'
You: 'Right, water helps it grow. And what do we put the seeds in?'
Child: 'Dirt.'
You: 'Yes, soil. Can you help me scoop the soil into the pot? Let's pretend we're planting sunflowers.'
(You and your child then act out the planting process together, reinforcing words such as *seeds*, *soil*, *water* and *grow*.)

Semantics

Birth to 2
Example: During mealtime, hold up each item as you name it: 'Banana... apple... orange. Yummy fruits!' Then add, '*These are all fruits. Fruits are sweet and we can eat them.*'

Tip: Grouping objects by category helps your child build a **semantic network** (a mental web of related words and concepts). For example, learning that *banana*, *apple* and *orange* are all 'fruits' links them together in memory, so when your child thinks of one fruit, it becomes easier to recall others in the same category (Gelman & Markman, 1986).

Ages 3 to 5
Example: Sort toy animals together. Ask in your heritage language, 'Which ones live on a farm? Which ones live in the jungle?' Your partner asks the same questions in their heritage language.
Tip: When you and your partner reinforce categories in both languages, even if the terms differ, you help strengthen your child's cross-linguistic semantic mapping (Peterson & McCable, 1994).

Morphology

Birth to 2
Example: Naturally model plural or verb forms in the heritage language during daily routines, e.g. emphasizing plural markers or verb endings while naming objects or actions.
Tip: Avoid drilling. Repeated exposure to correct forms in meaningful contexts is sufficient at this stage.

Ages 3 to 5
Example: Play 'one or many?', focusing on its specific morphological patterns. For example, in French, contrast *un chat* and *des chats* while pointing to one cat or several cats.
Tip: Emphasize meaning first. Morphological accuracy develops gradually with continued exposure and use.

Syntax

Birth to 2
Example: During bath time, one parent (speaking Korean) says, '물이 뜨거워요' ('Water hot is'; 'The water is hot'); the other (speaking English) says, 'The water is warm.'
Tip: Keep sentences short, consistent, and tied to the immediate activity. This builds awareness of parallel forms without overwhelming the child.

Ages 3 to 5
Example: On a walk, one parent (speaking Turkish) says, '*Çocuk top oynuyor*' ('The child is playing ball'); the other (speaking English) says, 'The child is playing with the ball.'
Tip: Keep each parent's language consistent during the activity so your child hears a complete model of the grammar in one language at a time. This helps strengthen the boundaries between languages.

Pragmatics

Birth to 2
Example: Observe how your child adjusts language use. A toddler may gesture more with a Mandarin-speaking grandparent and use words with an English-speaking caregiver.
Tip: Respond warmly to all attempts; social awareness grows through interaction.

Ages 3 to 5
Example: Role-play greetings, for example, practice the polite form in Korean: '안녕하세요' (*annyeonghaseyo*), meaning 'Hello.'
Tip: Model context-appropriate language rather than correcting.

Emergent Literacy

Birth to 2
Example: Point to pictures and print during shared reading. Trace the direction of the text with your finger.
Tip: Emphasize enjoyment, not decoding.

Ages 3 to 5
Example: Read and re-read stories in your heritage language, drawing attention to how the text looks and works, such as letter shapes, characters or reading direction.
Tip: Encourage scribbling and pretend writing in the heritage script, as these early attempts count as emergent literacy.

Monitoring Your Child's Multilingual Development: Parent As Researcher in Action

We have explored the key language milestones children build in the first five years to become confident communicators and to form a strong base for later academic success. Because your child is exposed to more than one language, and the heritage language is often learned in more limited contexts, you may wonder whether his development is keeping pace with that of monolingual children. In most cases, there is no cause for concern as long as your child is developing typically, growing in a nurturing environment, having his needs met and being regularly spoken to in one or more languages. Although some multilingual children show minor differences across languages early on, most reach milestones similar to their monolingual peers, even when exposure varies (Byers-Heinlein *et al.*, 2013).

It is also important to remember that multilingualism does not cause language-related disabilities. Conditions such as developmental language disorder occur in monolingual and multilingual children at similar rates. A multilingual child with such a condition would experience similar challenges even with only one language (Paradis *et al.*, 2011).

The following steps can help you monitor language development across different languages using the parent as researcher approach. This process offers reassurance and highlights areas where support may be needed.

Step 1: Understanding general language development milestones and possible multilingual variations

In the previous sections, you were introduced to broad patterns of language development and multilingual variation from birth to age five. Table 3.1 builds on this overview by presenting age-specific developmental milestones for typically developing children, highlighting possible multilingual variations and offering practical ways to observe your child's progress, along with areas that may warrant closer attention or additional support.

One note of caution: The milestones listed in Table 3.1 are intended as flexible reference points, not rigid rules. As long as your child reaches these milestones in at least one language, there is usually no cause for concern.

Another note of attention: Although language milestones tend to follow a universal developmental trajectory, their expression is profoundly influenced by the structural and orthographic features of specific language systems. Cross-linguistic variations shape how these milestones unfold, influencing phonological, lexical-semantic, morphosyntactic and pragmatic development in unique ways. The following two areas illustrate how such differences can serve as useful reminders for observing your child's early multilingual growth.

The influence of orthography

In alphabetic languages (e.g. English, Spanish), early reading grows out of this letter-sound matching. In **transparent systems** like Italian or Finnish, where letters consistently map to sounds, many children around age 5 can sound out new words they have not memorized, such as Italian p-a-s-t-a → 'pasta' or Finnish k-i-s-s-a → '*kissa*' ('cat'). In **opaque systems** like English, the mapping is less consistent. A 5-year-old may read *cat* or *sun* easily but stumble on high-frequency words like *said* or *one*, where the letters do not make the expected sounds. Because print–sound links are more predictable in transparent systems, children learning them often show earlier success in phonemic awareness activities such as blending (/m/+/a/='ma') and segmenting ('pasta'→/p/ /a/ /s/ /t/ /a/).

Challenges in semitic systems

Semitic alphabetic systems such as Arabic and Hebrew use consonant-based scripts but present distinct challenges because of their non-linear morphological structure and **abjad orthography**, where short vowels are typically omitted in writing. In Arabic, for instance, the **root structure** (e.g. K-T-B, related to writing) is combined with vowel patterns to create words like *kitāb* ('book') or *kātib* ('writer'). Early readers must rely heavily on **morphological awareness** to interpret texts. Diacritics used in early learning

Table 3.1 Language and emergent literacy milestones, variations and when to pay attention

Age range	General developmental milestone	Possible multilingual variation	How to observe/assess your child	When to pay attention
Birth to 6 months	Infants can distinguish different speech sounds and begin to recognize familiar voices. They often respond to their name and show interest in speechlike sounds.	Multilingual infants may remain sensitive to a wider range of speech sounds for longer than their monolingual peers, recognizing phonemes from each language (Kuhl, 2004; Werker & Byers-Heinlein, 2008).	Try calling your baby's name from different directions. Use each parent's language when you do this and watch to see if your baby responds or shows recognition.	The baby does not respond to familiar voices, sudden loud sounds or her own name by the end of this period.
6 to 12 months	Infants can understand simple words like *bye-bye* and *no*, and begin producing first words. Babbling reflects the sounds and rhythms of the home language.	Babbling may vary with the language being spoken to them at the time. Early words may come from different languages, depending on context and frequency of use (Vihman, 2014).	Use routine phrases in each parent's language and watch how your baby responds. Listen for early word attempts in either language.	The baby is not babbling with consonant–vowel combinations or showing interest in speech; no response to common phrases in any language.
1 to 2 years	Vocabulary grows to about 50 words; children begin combining two or more words meaningfully.	The language with less exposure may have a smaller vocabulary, although the total vocabulary across all languages often matches that of monolingual peers (Pearson *et al.*, 1993).	Keep a combined word list from all languages; note when your child starts putting two words together in any language.	Fewer than about 50 total words across all languages by age 2 or no two-word combinations; vocabulary growth stalls for several months.
2 to 3 years	Children can use pronouns, speak in short sentences and understand more complex language.	Some grammatical structures may develop later in one language if not equally reinforced. Code-switching (language mixing) is common and part of normal development (Genesee *et al.*, 2004).	Listen for sentences of 3+ words and for correct pronoun use in each language; give simple instructions and observe comprehension in both.	No short sentences (three or more words) in at least one language; difficulty understanding simple instructions in both languages.
3 to 4 years	Children can hold basic conversations, ask questions and use past tense. They understand simple stories and multistep instructions.	May master certain tenses or vocabulary earlier in one language depending on exposure. Narrative style may vary by language and cultural norms (Minami & McCabe, 1991).	Ask your child to retell a short story in the language you used; check if they can follow two- to three-step instructions.	Struggles to follow two-step directions or cannot retell a simple story; very limited discussion of past or future events.
4 to 5 years	Children can sustain longer conversations, use future tense and understand complex storylines. They show interest in letters, sounds and early writing.	Emergent literacy-related skills (letter–sound awareness, storytelling structure) may transfer positively between languages, but orthographic differences can also cause interference (Ziegler & Goswami, 2005).	Read a story and ask your child to predict what happens next; watch for recognition of letters, sounds or characters in the language you use.	Cannot hold a short conversation or use basic past/future tenses; shows no interest in letters/sounds despite repeated exposure.

Table 3.2 Multilingual development tracking chart

Child's Name: ________________ **Day/Month/Year:** ________________

Age range	General developmental pattern in Language 1	General developmental pattern in Language 2	General developmental pattern in Language 3	Notes	Concerns
Birth–6 months					
6 to 12 months					
1 to 2 years					
2 to 3 years					
3 to 4 years					
4 to 5 years					

texts (e.g. 'حِمار' [*ḥimār*, 'donkey']) are gradually phased out, requiring children to infer meaning and pronunciation from context, developing strong semantic parsing and inference skills. Similarly, in Hebrew, children must distinguish between morphologically similar roots such as ש.מ.ר (*sh.m.r*, to guard) and ס.פ.ר (*s.f.r*, to count) using on subtle context cues.

Table 3.2 offers a multilingual tracking chart that you can use to record your observations across languages. Keeping this ongoing record will help you notice emerging patterns and changes over time, giving you a clearer picture of your child's overall progress. If any concerns arise, the chart will also provide language professionals with meaningful, real-life context to support a more accurate and individualized assessment of your child's language development.

Step 2: Conducting deeper observation

Alongside general developmental milestones, I will focus on two targeted measures that offer insight into early language development, **mean length of utterance** (MLU) and **non-word repetition** (NWR). I will also briefly outline several additional measures.

Mean length of utterance

Before we dive in, here is a quick heads-up. If this section feels technical, do not worry. Read what you can. By the end, you will see an easier way to measure MLU, but it helps to first understand the basic idea.

MLU is a simple way to look at a young child's language productivity. A higher MLU usually reflects more advanced early language skills. Although researchers debate some details, MLU is still a useful measure of expressive language development (Owens, 2014).

MLU is calculated by dividing the number of morphemes by the number of utterances (MLU=morphemes÷utterances). An **utterance** is a complete thought with a natural pause. For example, 'I want juice.' is one utterance and 'More please.' is another.

A **morpheme** is the smallest meaningful unit in a language.

In *eats*, there are two morphemes: *eat* and *-s*. Here is an example morpheme count:

The (1) little (1) boy (1) eat (1) -s (1) two (1) un- (1) wash (1) -ed (1) apple (1) -s (1) each (1) day (1)=13 morphemes. Below is a quick demo.

To estimate your child's MLU, record a short speech sample of about 50–100 utterances using your phone to provide a more accurate estimate of your child's language development. The sample does not need to be collected all at once. After recording, transcribe the sample verbatim, count the number of morphemes in each utterance and then calculate the average. For example,

- *I like play-ing with my truck-s* = 8 morphemes
- *The big truck is my favorite* = 6 morphemes
- *Grandpa brought it* = 3 morphemes

Total morphemes: 17
Total utterances: 3
MLU $= 17 \div 3 \approx 5.7$

Table 3.3 provides step-by-step guidance for collecting, transcribing and analyzing your child's speech samples so you can calculate her MLU in each language.

Table 3.3 How to collect, transcribe and compute MLU

Step	What to do	Tips
Collect a sample of utterances	Record your child speaking naturally in different settings using a phone or recorder. Aim for about 100 utterances (50 is okay for very young children).	Include playtime, mealtime, conversations with family – capture lots of everyday moments.
Transcribe utterances verbatim	Write down exactly what your child says, word for word, including pauses or repeated words. To make this process easier and more accurate, you can use an AI-powered transcription tool to capture the speech sample verbatim.	Use simple writing or apps that help with transcription. Accuracy is important.
Count morphemes or words in languages like Chinese	Count all meaningful parts of speech in each utterance: morphemes for languages like English and Turkish; words for languages like Chinese.	Remember, some words have parts like prefixes or suffixes – count each meaningful piece separately.
Exclude mixed-language utterances	If your child mixes languages in one sentence, set those aside when calculating MLU for each language.	Mixed sentences show multilingual skills but don't count for MLU in a single language.
Calculate MLU	Divide the total number of morphemes (or words) by the number of utterances for each language separately.	This gives you the average utterance length, a helpful measure of language growth.
Monitor progress	Repeat this process regularly to track your child's language development over time, using Table 3.1 as a reference.	Language skills develop at different rates in each language – that's normal!
Consult professionals if concerned	If you notice big differences or delays in your child's language skills, ask a pediatrician or speech therapist for advice.	Early support helps your child thrive in all their languages.

If you prefer a quicker method, you can use an AI-based tool (e.g. ChatGPT or Google Gemini) to calculate MLU automatically. Record a natural speech sample (ideally 50–100 utterances), ask the AI to transcribe it and then have it calculate the MLU.

Table 3.4 lists the average MLU for monolingual children at different ages. You can use it to gain a basic understanding of each of your child's languages. These measures are best used with children between 18 and 36 months, as you may be able to collect better speech samples in this age range (Miller, 1981).

It is important to note that MLU varies across languages because of structural differences. For example, in languages like English, Spanish or Turkish, we count each meaningful part of a word. Here is an illustration with the meaning 'She is eating cookies.'

- English: 'She's eating cookies' = 6 morphemes *(she + is + eat + -ing + cookie + -s)*
- Spanish: '*Está comiendo galletas*' = 5 morphemes *(está + com + -iendo + galleta + -s)*
- Turkish: '*O kurabiye yiyor*' = 4 morphemes *(O + kurabiye + yi + -yor)*

However, in a language like Mandarin Chinese, words are not changed with endings like '-ing' or '-s,' so it's harder to count morphemes. Instead, words or syllables are counted. For example: '她在吃饼干' (她 (1) 在 (1) 吃 (1) 饼干 (1) 'She is eating cookies') = 4 words

If your child is growing up with more than one language, avoid directly comparing the MLU across languages. Each language constructs meaning in its own way, so the

Table 3.4 MLU and corresponding age (based on Miller and Chapman (1981))

Age (months)	MLU
18	1.31
21	1.62
24	1.92
30	2.54
33	2.85
36	3.16
39	3.47
42	3.78
45	4.09
48	4.40
51	4.71
54	5.02
57	5.32
60	5.63

most important thing is that your child is making progress in each language according to its unique structure. To illustrate this, Table 3.5 presents different language types and shows how MLU is calculated using the same meaning ('I am playing with my friends').

MLU provides only a general estimate of your child's language productivity. It is common for a child's MLU to be higher in one language (typically the one they are most frequently exposed to) than in another. As long as your child's MLU in at least one language falls within the expected developmental range, there is usually no cause for concern.

However, if you do have worries (which many parents intuitively sense,) it is advisable to consult a professional, such as your child's pediatrician or a

Table 3.5 MLU calculation in different language types

Writing system	Language example	Sample sentence	MLU unit	MLU	Morpheme-by-morpheme breakdown
Fusional	English	I'm playing with my friends.	Morphemes	8	I (1) + am (1) + play (1) + -ing (1) + with (1) + my (1) + friend (1) + -s (1)
Isolating	Chinese	我跟朋友玩。	Words	4	我 (I) (1) + 跟 (with) (1) + 朋友 (friend) (1) + 玩 (play) (1)
Fusional/ agglutinative	Hindi	मै अपने दोस्तों के साथ खेल रहा हूँ	Morphemes	9	मै (I) (1) + अपने (my) (1) + दोस्त (friend) (1) + -ों (plural) (1) + के (oblique marker) (1) + साथ (with) (1) + खेल (play) (1) + रहा (progressive participle) (1) + हूँ (auxiliary "am") (1)
Semitic	Arabic	ألعب مع أصدقائي.	Morphemes	6	أ- (I) (1) + لعب (play) (1) + -ُ (indicative) (1) + مع (with) (1) + أصدقاء (friends) (1) + -ي (my, genitive) (1)
Agglutinative	Japanese	友達と遊んでいます。	Morphemes	5	友達 (friend) (1) + と (with) (1) + 遊 (play root) (1) + んで (gerund/ te-form) (1) + います (progressive + polite present) (1)
Agglutinative	Turkish	Arkadaşlarımla *oynuyorum.*	Morphemes	7	*Arkadaş* (friend) (1) + *-lar* (plural) (1) + *-ım* (my) (1) + *-la* (with) (1) + *oyna* (play) (1) + *-yor* (progressive) (1) + *-um* (first person) (1)
Agglutinative[1]	Korean	친구들과 놀고 있어요.	Morphemes	7	친구 (friend) (1) + 들 (plural) (1) + 과 (with) (1) + 놀 (play) (1) + 고 (connective, used in progressive construction) (1) + 있 (progressive) (1) + 어요 (polite ending) (1)
Isolating/ agglutinative	Hawaiian	*Ke pā'ani nei au me ko'u mau hoa.*	Words	8	*Ke* (progressive marker) (1) + *pā'ani* (play) (1) + *nei* (aspect) (1) + *au* (I) (1) + *me* (with) (1) + *ko'u* (my) (1) + *mau* (plural) (1) + *hoa* (friend) (1)
Polysynthetic	Inuktitut	*Piqatikkalu pinnguaqtunga*	Morphemes	5	piqati (friend) (1) + -kka (my, plural possessed) (1) + -lu (with) (1) + pinnguaq (play) (1) + -tunga (I, present indicative) (1)

speech-language pathologist. If any language-related issues are present, early intervention can make a meaningful difference in your child's development.

Non-word repetition

Another widely used method in child language assessment is the NWR task. In this task, children are asked to repeat invented, nonsense words such as 'woogalamic' or 'noitauf' (Archibald, 2008). Because the words are novel, children cannot rely on memory or prior vocabulary knowledge. Instead, they must use their phonological processing skills, which include the ability to hear, hold and reproduce sequences of sounds (Gathercole & Baddeley, 1990). NWR performance is considered a reliable indicator of phonological working memory and has been shown to predict vocabulary growth and, to a lesser extent, grammatical development, sometimes more accurately than traditional language tests (Melby-Lervåg & Lervåg, 2012). One advantage of NWR is that it minimizes the influence of a child's existing knowledge of words or grammar, which makes it a useful way to measure their underlying language learning capacity (Chiat & Roy, 2007).

Research also shows that children's performance on NWR tasks is shaped by their linguistic environment. For example, children learning languages with longer average word lengths, such as Spanish, Portuguese or Greek, often perform better on longer non-words than children acquiring English (Dispaldro *et al.*, 2013). This suggests that exposure to the sound structures of a particular language helps children practice handling longer or more complex sequences. Across languages, NWR tasks consistently provide insight into a child's phonological awareness and capacity for learning new words (Gathercole, 2006). These tasks are especially informative around age 3, when children's ability to immediately repeat unfamiliar sound patterns begins to strongly correlate with later vocabulary and morphosyntactic skills. Table 3.6 provides some examples of NWR activities.

Some of you may wonder whether asking your child to repeat made-up 'non-words' (through what is called an NWR task) could confuse her or slow language development. You can rest assured that this concern is unfounded. NWR tasks are designed to check how well a child can remember and process sounds in her mind (called **phonological working memory**), rather than to test vocabulary. They are used successfully with both monolingual and multilingual children, as long as the task is adjusted to match the child's language background.

Researchers have looked at many studies on this topic in what is called a **meta-analysis** (a way of combining results from multiple studies to get a clear overall picture). These studies confirm that NWR can help identify possible language difficulties in children. In some cases, researchers use **quasi-language-independent stimuli**, which means that the made-up words are designed to avoid favoring one language over another (Grimm, 2022). For example, the sounds might be chosen so they could exist in many different languages, making the test fair for children who speak more than one language.

In short, when NWR is used in a supportive and intentional way, it is safe and can give valuable insight into your child's language skills. It is not a risk to their language development.

Table 3.6 Examples of NWR activities

Language	Non-word example	Activity	Skill focus
English	*flompie, zoodle*	'Silly Sandwich Words': Invent a nonsense word, have your child repeat it, then find rhyming words together.	Rhyming and sound manipulation
Mandarin Chinese	*māgōu* (马沟), *tìfēi* (替飞)	'Funny Two-Syllable Friends': -Create two-syllable nonsense words, such as māgōu (妈沟) and tífěi (提匪), repeat them with tone variations, and see how tones change meaning or remove meaning.	Tone recognition and syllable segmentation
Spanish	*picaluna, tronipe*	'*Palabras Locas*': Make a pretend word, ask your child to guess what it could mean and clap each syllable together.	Syllable awareness and phoneme blending
Arabic	*mafroon, faarin*	'كلمة غريبة' ('Strange Word'): Invent a nonsense root and create different pretend words using that root; compare it with real roots.	Root–pattern recognition
French	*broustique, zanoufle*	'*Mots Rigolos*':Invent a silly word, ask imaginative questions about it and play with French endings like *-ette* or *-on*.	Morphological endings and sound play
Japanese	もりこぴ, たぬぺん	'へんなことば' ('Weird Words'): Make hiragana-based nonsense words; repeat them slowly, then faster; change one mora to make a 'new' word.	Mora awareness and sequencing
Hindi	लोपकिा, झुनाली	'मज़ेदार शब्द' ('Fun Words'): Create a made-up word, ask what it could be and break it into syllables while clapping.	Syllable segmentation and vowel–consonant patterns
Hebrew	קוניל, גפלור	'מילים מצחיקות' ('Funny Words'): Invent a nonsense word using Hebrew root patterns, then create new pretend words from that root.	Root–pattern recognition and consonant–vowel structure

Table 3.7 Other measures of multilingual development

Measure	Age range	What it tracks	How to observe (example)
Vocabulary inventory	Birth to 2 years	The total number of words understood or spoken across all languages (Fenson et al., 2007).	Use a checklist to mark every word your child says in both languages (e.g. '*mesa*' and 'table').
Receptive language	Birth to 2 years	The ability to understand concepts and instructions before the child is able to speak them.	Give a simple command like 'Touch your nose' to see if they understand the word without you pointing.
Pragmatics	3 to 5 years	How language is used socially, such as turn-taking and adjusting speech for the listener (Montrul, 2016).	Observe if your child uses simpler words when talking to a younger baby or a pet.
Narrative skills	3 to 5 years	The ability to organize thoughts into a logical story with a beginning, middle and end.	Ask your child to retell a movie plot or describe their day at the park in sequence.
Metalinguistic awareness	3 to 5 years	The ability to think about language as a system and recognize different languages.	Notice if your child 'corrects' a translation or asks, 'How do we say this in Grandpa's language?'

Besides MLU and NWR, there are several other ways to check the deep level of your child's multilingual development; see Table 3.7 for a summary and examples.

Together, these measures offer a complementary approach to understanding your child's multilingual development.

Step 3: Making reflection a habit

Reflective journaling lies at the heart of mindful parenting. A simple journal records what your child did, whereas a reflective one captures what it meant (Duncan *et al.*, 2009). Writing down your thoughts or recording them when time is short turns daily moments into lasting insights. Reflection transforms brief notes into understanding, helping you see patterns, celebrate growth and gently adjust your strategies.

In my own journey of raising multilingual children, journals became quiet companions that revealed what videos could not. Although recordings preserved laughter and newly spoken words, my journals held the invisible qualities of wonder, frustration, pride and awe. Re-reading them years later felt like rediscovering the rhythm of our shared story, the small miracles that built fluency, confidence and connection.

Both parents' voices can enrich this process. My husband's notes often captured details I had missed, such as small exchanges or gestures tied to the languages. Together, our reflections created a fuller picture that deepened over time.

You do not need long entries. A few lines are enough. What matters is doing it regularity.

Here is a simple reflective journal format:

Date: (day/month/year). Noting the day, month and year is important when observing young children's language development. From birth to age 5, language growth is often rapid and uneven, and meaningful changes can occur within days. Research shows that early language development tends to progress in spurts rather than in a steady, linear manner, making precise dates essential for tracking real developmental change (Brown, 1973).

Event: Reading a picture book in French before bed.

Observation: Child named animals easily but paused on *écureuil* (squirrel). Used gesture instead.

Reflection/progress: Vocabulary is strong overall; hesitation may signal a less familiar word rather than a lack of understanding. Gesture use shows communicative competence.

Next step: Reintroduce *écureuil* during play tomorrow and model it naturally in context.

Regular reflections preserve meaningful moments and guide future choices. One day, when your child is grown, revisiting them together may reveal not only how language was learned but also how attention, patience and love shaped that journey.

Step 4: Putting it all together: Keeping a multilingual development log

Finally, keeping a multilingual development log provides a clear place to record your child's progress. It gathers your observations on milestones, MLU, NWR and reflections, helping you track growth, notice changes over time and adjust your support as needed. Below is a template of the multilingual development log that you can use and adapt to your own needs.

Multilingual Development Log

Date (Day/Month/Year):____________

1. Language Development Journal

Date: ___________________________

Observation (milestone, new word, sentence or code-switching moment):

____

____

Context (where/with whom it happened):

____

____

Your reflections:

____

____

Strategies used (e.g. bedtime story, song, playdate):

____

____

Next steps/ideas:

____

____

2. Monthly Language Snapshot

Date: ____

Languages used in snapshot: ___________________________

Recorded activity (short video, audio, written notes):

____

Examples of new words/phrases:

____

____

Language Progress Tracker

Language	Changes observed	Vocabulary inventory	Receptive language	MLU	NWR	Pragmatics	Narrative skills	Metalinguistic awareness	Notes/ reflections
Language A									
Language B									
Language C									

3. Video Diary Clip Log

Date of clip: ______________________________

Activity recorded: __________________________

Language(s) used: __________________________

Notable features (pronunciation, grammar, confidence):

____

____

Comparison with earlier clips:

____

____

4. Strategy Tracker

Date Strategy tried How often used Child's reaction Impact observed Next steps

5. Play-Based Language Observation

Date: ____

Type of play (solo play, sibling play, peer play): _____________________

Language(s) used in play: ___________________________________

Examples of role-play or creative language use:

____

____

Your thoughts:

____

____

____

6. Family Reflection Notes (for Both Parents)

Date: ______________________________

Participants: __________________________

Highlights/successes:

____

____

Challenges/questions:

____

____

Agreed actions for next month:

____

____

Your Reflections:

____

____

____

Major Takeaways of Chapter 3 (Birth to Age 5)

The first five years of your child's life offer a remarkable window of opportunity for nurturing multilingual development, especially in his heritage language. By using intentional strategies, the heart of the art of raising multilingual children, you lay a strong foundation for his future success in all his languages. Here is a recap of some key practices to keep in mind as you support your child's multilingual development.

- Start early and embed the heritage language in everyday life through stories, songs, traditions and conversations that create emotional connections.
- Be consistent in speaking the heritage language, even if your child replies in another language, and provide opportunities for him to hear it in authentic social and cultural contexts, such as with extended family or in heritage language communities.
- Offer a variety of activities where you use richer words and more complex sentences to expand vocabulary and sentence skills.
- Use intentional strategies to address language-specific features such as classifiers, tone distinctions or unique grammatical patterns.
- Support learning through play so that heritage language practice feels enjoyable rather than forced.
- Document and reflect on your approaches like a 'parent-researcher' so you can adapt to your child's needs over time.

The first five years of your child's life are a time of wonder when language takes root and begins to shape who he will become. In the quiet rhythm of daily life, telling stories, singing or talking while preparing a meal, you are giving him more than words. You are offering love, connection and the assurance that he belongs in more than one world. These early moments, rich with warmth and meaning, form the roots of his communication and confidence.

Parents who regularly use the heritage language at home and involve their children in related activities, such as storytelling, songs and cultural events, foster stronger vocabulary, literacy development and family bonds (Luo & Wiseman, 2000). What matters most is the shared, lived experience of speaking and doing together.

As the seasons pass, the foundation you have built will continue to grow in new directions. In the next stage, middle childhood (ages 6 to 12), your child's world will expand through school, friendships and discovery. With your steady presence and continued care, he will carry his languages forward with confidence and joy.

Notes

(1) Japanese, Korean and Turkish are all listed as agglutinative languages because they share a core linguistic structure, yet they are distinct languages listed separately to demonstrate a key principle of language typology.

References

Abrahamsson, N. and Hyltenstam, K. (2009) Age of onset and nativelikeness in a second language: Listener perception versus linguistic scrutiny. *Language Learning* 59 (2), 249–306. https://doi.org/10.1111/j.1467-9922.2009.00507.x

Archibald, L.M.D. (2008) The promise of nonword repetition as a clinical tool. *Canadian Journal of Speech-Language Pathology and Audiology* 32 (1), 21–28.

Bialystok, E. (2011) Reshaping the mind: The benefits of bilingualism. *Canadian Journal of Experimental Psychology* 65 (4), 229–235. https://doi.org/10.1037/a0025406

Brown, R. (1973) *A First Language: The Early Stages.* Harvard University Press.

Bruce, M., McFayden, T.C., Ollendick, T.H. and Bell, M.A. (2022). Expressive language in infancy and toddlerhood: The roles of child temperament and maternal parenting behaviors. *Developmental Psychobiology* 64 (6), e22287. https://doi.org/10.1002/dev.22287.

Byers-Heinlein, K., Fennell, C.T. and Werker, J.F. (2013) The development of associative word learning in monolingual and bilingual infants. *Bilingualism: Language and Cognition* 16 (1), 198–205. https://doi.org/10.1017/S1366728912000417

Chiat, S. and Roy, P. (2007) The preschool repetition test: An evaluation of performance in typically developing and clinically referred children. *Journal of Speech, Language, and Hearing Research* 50 (2), 429–443. https://doi.org/10.1044/1092-4388(2007/030)

De Houwer, A. (2009) *An Introduction to Bilingual Development.* Multilingual Matters.

Dispaldro, M., Leonard, L.B. and Deevy, P. (2013) Real-word and nonword repetition in Italian-speaking children with specific language impairment: A study of diagnostic accuracy. *Journal of Speech, Language, and Hearing Research* 56 (1), 323–336. https://doi.org/10.1044/1092-4388(2012/11-0304)

Duncan, L.G., Coatsworth, J.D. and Greenberg, M.T. (2009) A model of mindful parenting: Implications for parent–child relationships and prevention research. *Clinical Child and Family Psychology Review* 12 (3), 255–270. https://doi.org/10.1007/s10567-009-0046-3

Fenson, L., Marchman, V.A., Thal, D.J., Dale, P.S., Reznick, J.S. and Bates, E. (2007) *MacArthur–Bates Communicative Development Inventories: User's Guide and Technical Manual* (2nd edn). Paul H. Brookes.

Gathercole, S.E. (2006) Nonword repetition and word learning: The nature of the relationship. *Applied Psycholinguistics* 27 (4), 513–543. https://doi.org/10.1017/S0142716406060383

Gathercole, S.E. and Baddeley, A.D. (1990) Phonological memory deficits in language-disordered children: Is there a causal connection? *Journal of Memory and Language* 29 (3), 336–360. https://doi.org/10.1016/0749-596X(90)90004-J

Gelman, S.A. and Markman, E.M. (1986) Categories and induction in young children. *Cognition* 23 (3), 183–209. https://doi.org/10.1016/0010-0277(86)90034-x

Genesee, F., Paradis, J. and Crago, M.B. (2004) *Dual Language Development and Disorders: A Handbook on Bilingualism and Second Language Learning.* Paul H. Brookes Publishing.

Grimm, A. (2022) The use of the LITMUS quasi-universal nonword repetition task to identify DLD in monolingual and early second language learners aged 8 to 10. *Languages* 7 (3), 218. https://doi.org/10.3390/languages7030218

Hoff, E., Core, C., Place, S., Rumiche, R., Señor, M. and Parra, M. (2012) Dual language exposure and early bilingual development. *Journal of Child Language* 39 (1), 1–27. https://doi.org/10.1017/S0305000910000759

Hostetter, A.B. (2011) When do gestures communicate? A meta-analysis. *Psychological Bulletin* 137 (2), 297–315. https://doi.org/10.1037/a0022128

Johnson, J.S. and Newport, E.L. (1989) Critical period effects in second language learning: The influence of maturational state on the acquisition of English as a second language. *Cognitive Psychology* 21 (1), 60–99. https://doi.org/10.1016/0010-0285(89)90003-0

Kim, K.H., Relkin, N.R., Lee, K.M. and Hirsch, J. (1997) Distinct cortical areas associated with native and second languages. *Nature* 388 (6638), 171–174. https://doi.org/10.1038/40623

Kuhl, P.K. (2004) Early language acquisition: Cracking the speech code. *Nature Reviews Neuroscience* 5 (11), 831–843.

Kuhl, P.K. (2010) Brain mechanisms in early language acquisition. *Neuron* 67 (5), 713–727. https://doi.org/10.1016/j.neuron.2010.08.038

Kuhl, P.K., Tsao, F.-M. and Liu, H.-M. (2003) Foreign-language experience in infancy: Effects of short-term exposure and social interaction on phonetic learning. *Proceedings of the National Academy of Sciences of the United States of America* 100 (15), 9096–9101. https://doi.org/10.1073/pnas.1532872100

Luo, S.H. and Wiseman, R.L. (2000) Ethnic language maintenance among Chinese immigrant children in the United States. *International Journal of Intercultural Relations* 24 (3), 307–324. https://doi.org/10.1016/S0147-1767(00)00003-1

Mechelli, A., Crinion, J.T., Noppeney, U., O'Doherty, J., Ashburner, J., Frackowiak, R.S. and Price, C.J. (2004) Structural plasticity in the bilingual brain. *Nature* 431 (7010), 757. https://doi.org/10.1038/431757a

Melby-Lervåg, M. and Lervåg, A. (2012) Oral language skills moderate nonword repetition skills in children with dyslexia: A meta-analysis of the role of nonword repetition skills in dyslexia. *Scientific Studies of Reading* 16 (1), 1–34. https://doi.org/10.1080/10888438.2010.537715

Miller, J.F. (1981) *Assessing Language Production in Children: Experimental Procedures.* University Park Press.

Miller, J.F. and Chapman, R.S. (1981) The relation between age and mean length of utterance in morphemes. *Journal of Speech and Hearing Research* 24 (2), 154–161. https://doi.org/10.1044/jshr.2402.154

Minami, M. and McCabe, A. (1991) Haiku as a discourse regulation device: A stanza analysis of Japanese children's personal narratives. *Language in Society* 20 (4), 577–599. https://doi.org/10.1017/S0047404500016730

Montrul, S. (2016) *The Acquisition of Heritage Languages.* Cambridge University Press.

Nagy, W.E. and Anderson, R.C. (1984) How many words are there in printed school English? *Reading Research Quarterly* 19 (3), 304–330. https://doi.org/10.2307/747823

Owens, R.E. (2014) *Language Development: An Introduction* (8th edn). Pearson.

Paradis, J., Genesee, F. and Crago, M.B. (2011) *Dual Language Development and Disorders: A Handbook on Bilingualism and Second Language Learning* (2nd edn). Paul H. Brookes Publishing.

Pearson, B.Z., Fernández, S.C. and Oller, D.K. (1993) Lexical development in bilingual infants and toddlers: Comparison to monolingual norms. *Language Learning* 43 (1), 93–120.

Perani, D., Saccuman, M.C., Scifo, P., Anwander, A., Spada, D., Baldoli, C., Poloniato, A., Lohmann, G. and Friederici, A.D. (2011) Neural language networks at birth. *Proceedings of the National Academy of Sciences* 108 (38), 16056–16061. https://doi.org/10.1073/pnas.1102991108

Peterson, C. and McCabe, A. (1994) *Developmental Psycholinguistics: Three Ways of Looking at a Child's Narrative.* Plenum Press.

Quinn, S., Donnelly, S. and Kidd, E. (2018) The relationship between symbolic play and language acquisition: A meta-analytic review. *Developmental Review* 49, 121–135. https://doi.org/10.1016/j.dr.2018.05.005

Vihman, M.M. (2014) Early phonological development: Babbling. In P. Brooks and V. Kempe (eds) *Encyclopedia of Language Development* (pp. 21–25). Sage Publications.

Weisleder, A. and Fernald, A. (2013) Talking to children matters: Early language experience strengthens processing and builds vocabulary. *Psychological Science* 24 (11), 2143–2152. https://doi.org/10.1177/0956797613488145

Werker, J.F. and Byers-Heinlein, K. (2008) Bilingualism in infancy: First steps in learning two languages. *Trends in Cognitive Sciences* 12 (4), 144–151.

Werker, J.F. and Tees, R.C. (2005) Speech perception as a window for understanding plasticity and commitment in language systems of the brain. *Developmental Psychobiology* 46 (3), 233–251. https://doi.org/10.1002/dev.20060

Ziegler, J.C. and Goswami, U. (2005) Reading acquisition, developmental dyslexia and skilled reading across languages: A psycholinguistic grain size theory. *Psychological Bulletin* 131 (1), 3–29. https://doi.org/10.1037/0033-2909.131.1.3

4 The Multilingual Testing Years (Ages 6 to 12): Sustaining a Shifting Linguistic Landscape

Your child has now stepped into middle childhood, a time of blossoming independence, curiosity and rapid growth. The little one who once relied on you for just about everything is now becoming an increasingly independent individual, full of opinions, questions and imagination. If the previous five years were about acquiring and learning language, this stage is about using language to explore new ideas, understand school subjects and make sense of the world.

This is also a pivotal moment for your child's heritage language development. During middle childhood, formal schooling typically takes place in the community's dominant language, and your child begins spending more time with peers outside the home. As a result, her daily linguistic environment gradually shifts, and the dominant community language often takes center stage. If you have been able to sustain communication in your heritage language at home despite this outside influence, that is something to truly celebrate. But it is worth keeping in mind that this balance can be fragile. Without consistent support, the influence of school and society can quickly tip the scales, making the home language less visible, less practiced and harder to maintain.

This shift is not merely speculation; research supports it. For example, one study found that many Turkish-speaking children growing up in other countries began early childhood with Turkish skills that were similar to those of their monolingual peers in Turkey. However, after starting school and spending increasing time in a dominant-language environment, they fell behind in areas such as grammar, vocabulary and pronunciation. These gaps tend to persist into later childhood and beyond, especially in the absence of sustained support, making full catch-up unlikely (Karayayla & Scmid, 2019).

In fact, it is not uncommon for children during middle childhood to gradually lose their home language(s), using only the community's dominant language both inside and outside the home. It is also during this period that many families abandon their multilingual childrearing aspirations, often because of the mounting challenges and frustrations. This underscores how heritage language development outside of heritage-speaking communities is vulnerable to attrition or even loss if intentional maintenance strategies are not in place.

I still vividly remember how this shift felt during my own children's middle childhood years, as I described in *Growing up with Three Languages: Birth to Eleven*:

> *The joy and excitement we once felt with every small step of their home-language achievement were gradually replaced by frustration. Worst of all, many home-language activities the boys used to enjoy slowly became chores or a struggle* (Wang, 2008: 153).

Recognizing that middle childhood is a critical period for sustaining a child's heritage language amid the growing dominance of the school language, this chapter offers practical suggestions to help you meet the challenges and embrace the possibilities of this stage. It first discusses the common difficulties multilingual families often encounter, then presents age-appropriate strategies to address them. It also introduces ways to monitor your child's heritage language progress, supported by research-based linguistic developmental milestones. The overarching goal is to support your child in navigating an increasingly shifting linguistic landscape while continuing to develop both the heritage language and the mainstream community language.

Major Challenges and Opportunities During Middle Childhood

Middle childhood is the stage where children build on their existing language abilities and begin to develop a **functional balance**[1] across their languages and between the dominant school language and the home language, while also beginning the important work of developing literacy in the heritage language. The challenges that arise during this period can be significant, but with purposeful and consistent efforts, they can be addressed. What you do during these years will have a lasting influence on your child's language development, identity and connection to culture.

When one language begins to dominate

I did a sample calculation about my younger son Dominique's exposure to his surrounding languages during his early and middle childhood (see Table 4.1). As you can see, he was spending increasingly more time each week at school, along with additional time with friends and extracurricular activities, all in his community's dominant language, English. Meanwhile, his time hearing or using his home languages (French and Chinese) had dropped to just a few hours a day. No matter how committed we were with his home languages at home, the numbers told a different story.

This kind of shift is common. Once your child starts school, his exposure to the community's dominant language often skyrockets, while his heritage languages fade into the background (Unsworth, 2016). If this trend continues, your child may begin to lose his home language, sometimes without you noticing until much later.

But don't lose heart. What matters most isn't doing everything perfectly; it's doing something consistently. Simple, meaningful interactions in your heritage language can

Table 4.1 Dominique's average exposure to heritage language and the community's dominant language

	French	Chinese	English
Before Age 6	7 hours	7 hours	2 hours
Age 6	5 hours	5 hours	6 hours
Age 7	4.5 hours	4.5 hours	7 hours
Age 8	4 hours	4 hours	8 hours
Age 9	3.5 hours	3.5 hours	9 hours
Age 10	3 hours	3 hours	10 hours
Age 11	3 hours	3 hours	10 hours
Age 12	2.5 hours	2.5 hours	11 hours

Note: The hours listed are average waking hours. The dominant language, English, was increasingly associated with time spent in school, extracurricular activities, interactions with peers and media.

make all the difference. Two practices can make a difference: Keep speaking your heritage language regularly and provide your child with varied, meaningful opportunities to hear and use it in daily life. Whether you're chatting during dinner, telling a bedtime story or sharing a silly moment in the car, every word counts. Even if your child responds in the dominant community language, don't be discouraged. Keep speaking your heritage language. Your child is still listening, still learning and still feeling the emotional bond that comes with your voice and your words. These interactions, however simple, help sustain the language and nurture a sense of belonging rooted in family, culture and love.

Try These Strategies

Virtual Family Time

Set up regular video calls with relatives who speak the heritage language.

Ages 6 to 9

Example: During a video chat, guide your child to greet a grandparent using the culturally appropriate form of address and share a short update in the heritage language, such as 'Grandma, I went to the park today and played with my friends.' This supports everyday storytelling and respectful communication.

Tip: Before the call, help your child prepare three things to share or ask about, such as school, pets or a drawing. Provide some key vocabulary in advance. For example, if you want your child to talk about a school trip to the botanical garden, introduce words like 'rose', 'sunflower', 'bamboo' or 'pond'. Practicing beforehand builds confidence during the real conversation.

Ages 10 to 12

Example: Invite your child to ask a relative questions about his/her childhood or cultural traditions.

Tip: Practice related vocabulary ahead of time. You can rehearse a few conversation starters or sample questions together to help your child feel more confident before the call.

Playgroup Participation

Organize or join a small group of families who share the same heritage language.

Ages 6 to 9

Example: Organize outdoor games like 'Simon Says' or 'Duck, Duck, Goose' in the heritage language.

Tip: Focus on repetition and clear commands. Children this age learn well through movement and imitation.

Ages 10 to 12

Example: Host a game night with card games, charades or board games in the heritage language.

Tip: Encourage light conversation in the heritage language during breaks or transitions between games.

Media Exposure

Use age-appropriate media to expose your child to the heritage language in enjoyable ways.

Ages 6 to 9

Example: Watch a 20-minute cartoon in the heritage language and ask, 'Who was your favorite character?'

Tip: Use subtitles in the heritage language and pause occasionally to explain new words.

Ages 10 to 12

Example: Watch a short film or episode and discuss what the characters felt or what might happen next.

Tip: Ask open-ended questions to prompt reflection: 'Why do you think she said that?' or 'Would you have done the same?'

Language Apps and Tools

Introduce interactive tools that support heritage language use in a playful format.

Ages 6 to 9

Example: Use a vocabulary app to match images with words like 'apple', 'house' or 'happy'.

Tip: Sit with your child and repeat words aloud together to reinforce pronunciation.

Ages 10 to 12

Example: Let your child use a gamified app with voice recognition to practice full sentences like 'I am going to school.'

Tip: Encourage independent use, but ask her to teach you one new word or phrase after each session.

Everyday Tasks

Turn daily routines into rich language opportunities.

Ages 6 to 9

Example: Ask your child to help label items around the house, like 'table', 'window' or 'shoes', using sticky notes in your heritage language.

Tip: Adapt the game based on the structure of your language. For **alphabetic languages** (e.g. Spanish, French, English), try: 'Can you find five things in the kitchen that start with the letter B?' For **character-based languages** (e.g. Chinese), try: 'Can you find three items that include the character for "木" (wood) or "水" (water)?' For **abjad languages** (e.g. Arabic, Hebrew), try: 'Can you point to three things in the room that have the letter "ب" (ba) or "ש" (shin) in their names?' For **abugida languages** (e.g. Hindi or Amharic), try: 'Can you find four objects whose names begin with the syllable "का" (*ka*) or "ሀ" (*hä*)?' For **tonal languages** (e.g. Thai, Yoruba or Vietnamese), try: 'Can you name three foods and say their names in different tones to hear how the meaning changes?' For **agglutinative languages** (e.g. Turkish, Swahili or Finnish), try: 'Can you find three objects and say their names in both singular and plural?' For **polysynthetic languages** (e.g. Inuktitut or Mohawk), try: 'Can you choose one object and try to make a long word that describes it in detail?'

Ages 10 to 12

Example: Involve your child in planning meals or writing grocery lists in the heritage language.

Tip: Let her take charge of writing, reading aloud or even explaining recipes in the heritage language.

Mealtime Conversations

Use shared meals as a time to connect through language.

Ages 6 to 9

Example: 'Tell me one thing that made you laugh today.'

Tip: Don't require a full response in the heritage language. If your child answers in the dominant language, restate or expand her response in your target language.

Ages 10 to 12

Example: 'What's one thing that surprised you or made you think today?'

Tip: Invite deeper reflections and model your own answers in the heritage language to spark conversation.

Housework Talk

Make chores a playful time to speak the heritage language.

Ages 6 to 9

Example: 'Let's fold these together. Can you guess whose socks these are?'

Tip: Describe actions out loud and invite your child to name objects, give instructions or guess what's next.

Ages 10 to 12

Example: 'Can you sort these groceries and tell me where each item belongs?'

Tip: Let your child take the lead. Use this as a time to introduce new vocabulary related to household routines.

Story Swap

Invite storytelling as a playful and creative exchange.

Ages 6 to 9

Example: 'Tell me about the funniest thing that's ever happened at school.'

Tip: Don't worry about grammar. Focus on keeping the exchange lively. Use props or drawings to support the story.

Ages 10 to 12

Example: 'Tell me a story you'd write if you were the main character.'

Tip: Encourage creative storytelling with emotion, suspense or humor. You can co-create a story together by taking turns.

Car Conversations

Turn travel time into spontaneous language play.

Ages 6 to 9

Example: 'Guess what I saw on the way home? It had four legs and was wearing a raincoat!'

Tip: Try games like 'I Spy' or 'Would You Rather?' using your home language for a fun and informal way to reinforce vocabulary.

Ages 10 to 12

Example: 'If you could change something you saw today, what would it be and why?'

Tip: Use open-ended questions to spark critical thinking. Let your child ask you questions back in the heritage language.

Message Relay

Use real-time messages to encourage speaking and listening.

Ages 6 to 9

Example: 'Can you tell your sister that dinner will be ready in 10 minutes?'

Tip: Use this as a regular routine. Keep messages simple and encourage full-sentence repetition.

Ages 10 to 12

Example: 'Tell your sister we need to leave in 15 minutes and ask her if she fed the dog.'

Tip: Include multipart instructions to challenge memory and comprehension. Encourage your child to summarize or confirm the message.

Personal Reflections

Share memories and associations to build emotional ties through language.

Ages 6 to 9

Example: 'I saw a little girl drawing with sidewalk chalk today. Remember how you used to cover the driveway with rainbows and flowers?'

Tip: Use sensory language and positive emotions to draw connections and promote vocabulary.

Ages 10 to 12

Example: 'I saw someone skipping down the sidewalk today, and it reminded me of how you used to skip everywhere when you were little.'

Tip: These personal moments build emotional connection and deepen the habit of sharing in your home language.

Word of the Day Challenge

Play with one word throughout the day to build vocabulary and connection.

Ages 6 to 9

Example: 'Today's word is "happy". Can you show me a happy face or draw something that makes you feel happy?'

Tip: Use visuals, gestures or simple drawings to reinforce meaning. Repeat the word in songs, games or snack-time talk.

Ages 10 to 12

Example: 'Today's word is "generous". Can you describe someone you know who is generous or tell me about a time you were generous?'

Tip: Encourage your child to use the word in a sentence, story or journal entry. Connect the word to real-life examples or current events for deeper engagement.

Travel Immersion

If possible, travel to a country or region where the heritage language is spoken.

Ages 6 to 9

Example: During a family trip, help your child order simple items like 'juice' or 'bread' in the heritage language at a café.

Tip: Practice key phrases before each outing. Use visuals or flashcards to reinforce vocabulary.

Ages 10 to 12

Example: Encourage your child to handle small tasks such as asking for directions or buying tickets on her own in the heritage language.

Tip: Create mini challenges (e.g. 'Ask someone what time the museum opens') to build independence and motivation.

Connection to Local Heritage Community

Look for opportunities in your local area where the heritage language is used naturally.

Ages 6 to 9

Example: Join a weekend craft or storytelling group conducted in the heritage language.

Tip: Choose activities with hands-on components, like puppet shows or painting, that make the language experience fun and active.

Ages 10 to 12

Example: Enroll your child in a culture or language enrichment program where she can engage in projects or group discussions.

Tip: Look for opportunities where she can speak, present or perform in the heritage language.

When peer pressure undermines heritage language use

As children enter middle childhood, peer relationships grow in importance. Around ages 9 or 10, many become increasingly sensitive to their peers' opinions and begin adjusting their behavior to fit in. This developmental shift can significantly affect heritage language use. Your child may avoid speaking her home language in public or school settings if she fears being perceived as different or excluded from peer groups (Van Gorp & Verheyen, 2024). For example, my older son, Léandre, refused to speak French with a new classmate from Geneva, despite her repeated attempts to initiate conversation in French. They only managed to speak French together when no one else was around. His reluctance didn't reflect a lack of ability or interest but rather a desire to avoid drawing attention from English-speaking peers. This moment marked a subtle but important shift, as peer influence was beginning to shape his linguistic choices.

Such behavior is not uncommon. Research shows that children often perceive minority or heritage languages as socially marked, particularly if those languages are not supported in their peer environments (Guardado, 2002). They may worry about being teased or misunderstood, or simply standing out at a time when fitting in feels crucial to their social identity.

Try These Strategies

Boost Self-Confidence Beyond Language

Ages 6 to 9

Example: After your child accomplishes something she is proud of, scoring a goal, helping a friend or completing a puzzle, link the moment to her overall identity: 'You're such a great helper! And when you explained it in Mandarin, Grandma understood right away!'

Tip: Celebrate not only the achievement but how your child used her language to contribute, reinforcing that the heritage language is part of her strength, not separate from it.

Ages 10 to 12

Example: When your child shares a personal success, encourage her to reflect on how her language skills are part of what makes her capable. For instance, if she helped a teacher translate something for another student, acknowledge it as leadership: 'You really stepped up, and it was impressive to hear you use Spanish like that,' (Bandura, 1997).

Tip: Let your child overhear you praising her efforts in the heritage language to others. This indirect reinforcement boosts confidence without putting her on the spot.

Connect with Heritage Language Peers

Ages 6 to 9

Example: Enroll your child in weekend programs that use the heritage language through storytelling, crafts, music or cultural celebrations. Activities like making festival lanterns, preparing holiday food or learning traditional songs and dances help children build friendships and experience the language as a natural part of cultural life.

Tip: Choose programs that emphasize play and connection rather than academic rigor to keep engagement joyful.

Ages 10 to 12

Example: Encourage participation in culture or language clubs where your child can work on group projects or performances (e.g. preparing a short skit in Hebrew for a community showcase). These shared experiences make the language socially meaningful.

Tip: Invite a friend from school to attend a cultural event with your child; it bridges both peer groups and shows that the heritage language has value in both spaces.

Create Positive Emotional Associations (Schumann, 1997)

Ages 6 to 9

Example: Plan a family movie night featuring animated films in the heritage language with subtitles. Choose a familiar story so your child can follow along while reinforcing vocabulary.

Tip: Afterward, act out favorite scenes together using heritage language phrases to add playful engagement.

Ages 10 to 12

Example: Connect your child's interests, such as dance, art or music, to the heritage language. If she admires a singer like Céline Dion, watch interviews in French together and talk about what she understands.

Tip: Use tools like karaoke, heritage language Spotify playlists or film festivals to create joyful, culturally rich experiences.

Let Your Child Take the Lead

Ages 6 to 9

Example: Ask your child to read a short story in the heritage language to a younger sibling or family member. Even partial reading or using gestures is valuable.

Tip: Praise her effort: 'You read that so clearly, and your little brother loved hearing you tell the story in Amharic!'

Ages 10 to 12

Example: Invite your child to teach a few phrases from the heritage language to a friend or create a video explaining cultural greetings or traditions.

Tip: Let her choose the content and format. Teaching others builds competence and pride (Vygotsky, 1978).

Respect Your Child's Feelings; Keep the Door Open

Ages 6 to 9

Example: If your child hesitates to speak the heritage language in front of others, reassure her with phrases like, 'That's okay, we'll just use it here at home; it's our special way of talking.'

Tip: Use whispered conversations in the heritage language to keep it private, safe and fun.

Ages 10 to 12

Example: When your child expresses discomfort, validate her experience: 'It's okay to feel awkward. Just know that speaking Arabic with us is something we'll always value, even if it stays between us for now.'

Tip: Keep the home a space where the heritage language is warmly accepted but never forced.

Embrace and Celebrate Multilingual Identity and Share What Makes You Unique

Ages 6 to 9

Example: Help your child see multilingualism as part of who she is. 'Show and Tell' is a great chance to share her heritage language and culture. Support her in preparing a brief presentation about a meaningful item, such as a toy, holiday dish or family heirloom. Practice key heritage language words together. For example: 'This is *injera*. We eat it during special celebrations in Ethiopia.'

Tip: Stay involved. When you help organize events or volunteer in the classroom, your child feels proud and supported. When my children were in early elementary school, I visited during Chinese New Year to share food and customs and wrote a small booklet. Dominique proudly told his classmates, 'My mom wrote this.'

Ages 10 to 12

Example: Encourage your child to bring the heritage language into school projects. She might create a multilingual cookbook, a short video about a cultural holiday or a slideshow introducing greetings in Korean. If she enjoys cooking, she could explain the meaning behind a traditional recipe and how it connects to your family. She might also share a traditional piece of clothing or an artifact and tell its story.

Tip: If appropriate, ask the teacher whether your child can include multilingual or cultural elements in assignments. These authentic, child-led moments build confidence, spark pride and promote curiosity among her classmates. When your child sees her language welcomed at school, she is more likely to embrace it as a meaningful part of her identity.

Make the Most of Digital and Online Communities

Ages 6 to 9

Example: Find engaging YouTube channels in the heritage language that focus on crafts, animals or storytelling. Watch together and pause to ask questions or talk about what you see.

Tip: Use heritage language subtitles to boost reading and listening comprehension simultaneously.

Ages 10 to 12

Example: If your child enjoys Minecraft, Roblox or similar platforms, explore servers or forums that use the heritage language. With supervision, she can join Discord communities, follow YouTube channels or respond to family WhatsApp messages for casual practice. Heritage language comics, digital magazines and eBooks also offer fun ways to build reading skills.

Tip: Let your child create or follow content creators who use the heritage language; this can normalize and update the language's relevance in her digital life (Gee, 2003).

When the gap between heritage and school languages grows wider

As children grow older and spend more time at school and with friends, it becomes harder for parents to stay involved in every part of their daily lives. When children are young, it is easy to maintain heritage language conversations through shared routines like meals, play and bedtime stories. But once school subjects, friendships and activities take center stage, the gap between home and school languages often widens.

This raises a real challenge: How do you keep using the heritage language when much of your child's daily life now happens in the school language? I remember feeling frustrated when helping Léandre and Dominique with English homework while speaking Chinese. They could understand terms like *ecosystem* or *fractions* in English but had no idea how to say them in Chinese. I often struggled too, since academic vocabulary rarely appears in everyday home conversations.

This disconnect is common in multilingual families. The home language usually covers daily routines, whereas the school language introduces academic and abstract terms that children may never learn at home. As a result, heritage language communication can feel limited for both parents and children.

The gap also grows during ages 6 to 12, when reading and writing develop rapidly in the school language through formal instruction. Heritage language literacy usually receives far less structured attention, especially if it uses a different writing system, such as Chinese characters, Hebrew or Arabic scripts, or Devanagari. Without intentional support, heritage language literacy can lag behind, widening the divide even further.

Try These Strategies

Expand Home Language Vocabulary for Academic Topics

Ages 6 to 9

Example: Watch short educational videos in the heritage language that relate to classroom topics and pause to explain new words naturally. When your child speaks in the school language, gently recast in the heritage language. For example, in French: '*Ah, tu veux dire que tu as fait de la peinture aujourd'hui?*' ('Oh, you mean you did some painting today?')

Invite your child to share part of her day. If she switches languages because she lacks a word, supply it gently and rephrase. In Spanish, you might respond: '*Ah, plantaste semillas en la tierra. ¿Qué tipo de semillas eran?*' ('Oh, you planted seeds in the soil. What kind of seeds were they?')

Tip: The **recasting approach** (Taeschner, 1983) (gently supplying words in context and repeating them naturally) helps your child build vocabulary while keeping interactions warm, supportive and engaging.

Ages 10 to 12

Example: Choose a non-fiction topic your child is studying at school, such as fractions, ancient Egypt or ecosystems, and find heritage language books or videos on that subject. Read or watch together, noting how terms differ across languages. Create a home vocabulary list. For example: '*habitat*' in English becomes *hábitat* in Spanish or 栖息地 in Chinese. Use these words in follow-up conversations about schoolwork. Encourage your child to give short oral summaries in the heritage language. For instance, you might ask: 'Can you explain your science project in French?' This practice strengthens academic vocabulary while connecting school learning to the heritage language.

Tip: Recasting and expanding school-related content in the heritage language helps your child develop subject-specific vocabulary, deepens comprehension and shows her that the heritage language is a valuable tool for academic learning, not just for everyday conversation.

Connect School Experiences to the Heritage Language and Make School Talk Part of Home Talk

Ages 6 to 9

Example: After school, recreate a mini 'Show and Tell' using the heritage language. Ask: 'What did you bring or do at school today? Show me and tell me.'

If your child struggles with vocabulary, turn it into a guessing game: 'What do you call this thing that we used to glue paper? Hmm, was it صمغ (ṣamgh)?'

Books like *Le Petit Nicolas* or heritage language children's books about school routines can spark relatable conversations and help reinforce vocabulary.

Tip: Keep activities playful and interactive so the focus stays on communication, not correction. Games, props and stories help your child feel relaxed and willing to experiment with new words in the heritage language.

Ages 10 to 12

Example: Ask your child to role-play a school activity or teacher explanation in the heritage language: 'Pretend I'm a new student and explain the math game you played today.' Use open-ended prompts like: 'Tell me about your science experiment. What did you observe?' Respond with heritage language follow-up questions to encourage elaboration.

Tip: Role-play and open-ended prompts allow your child to practice academic vocabulary in meaningful ways. By prompting explanations and asking further questions, you show that the heritage language can be used for complex ideas, not just everyday conversation.

Use Hand Gestures to Support Communication

Ages 6 to 9

Example: When your child struggles to find a word, use gestures to support communication and model vocabulary. For example, if your child does not yet know the word *volcán* in Spanish, you can say the word while mimicking lava flowing with your hands. Encourage your child to use gestures as well when a word is missing, as iconic gestures engage motor systems in the brain and support memory (Hostetter, 2011). Combining speech with movement creates an embodied context that makes new vocabulary more accessible and memorable.

Tip: Pair words with gestures and invite your child to act out meanings with their hands or body. Mirror your child's movements as you supply the heritage language word, turning vocabulary learning into an engaging multisensory experience.

Ages 10 to 12

Example: Introduce culturally embedded gestures (**emblems**). For example, the Italian chin-flick gesture, commonly used to mean 'I don't care.'

Tip: Highlighting gestures that carry cultural meaning deepens both language learning and intercultural awareness.

Support Reading with Purposeful, Motivating Materials

Ages 6 to 9

Example: Select heritage language books that match your child's interests (e.g. fairy tales, animal stories or comics). Read aloud together, pausing to ask: 'Who is this character? What do you think will happen next?' Use familiar stories like *The Very Hungry Caterpillar* in the heritage language version. Familiar content boosts engagement and supports comprehension (Ghosn, 2002).

Tip: Make reading interactive. Encourage your child to point to pictures, act out parts of the story or predict what comes next. This keeps attention high and turns reading into a shared, playful experience rather than a lesson.

Ages 10 to 12

Example: Introduce chapter books like *Harry Potter* in the heritage language. Read together or use audiobooks to build listening and vocabulary skills.

Use **TPRS®** (Teaching Proficiency through Reading and Storytelling®) (Ray & Seely, 2004). TPRS® integrates reading, storytelling, acting and discussion to promote language acquisition through compelling and personalized narratives. Its power lies in combining literacy, creativity and cultural resonance. Stories, often humorous or rooted in cultural contexts, are developmentally appropriate and memorable, making them ideal for home language support. In a TPRS-informed home setting, you can co-construct a story with your child using familiar events or family memories. Ask simple questions in the heritage language ('Where did we go?' 'Who was there?' 'What happened next?') and build the story together. Then retell it orally or in writing. Your child can draw scenes, rewrite the story with a twist or record themselves reading it aloud. These multimodal practices enhance fluency, agency and confidence. As research (Son & Wee, 2024) shows, home-based, creative literacy fosters not only language growth but also a stronger sense of cultural identity.

Tip: Rotate around reading, listening, speaking and creating to keep your child engaged. For example, pair a chapter from the book with an audiobook segment, then have your child retell or illustrate the story. This variation strengthens different language skills while keeping the experience fresh and motivating.

Build Writing Through Personal Expression

Ages 6 to 9

Example: Encourage your child to write short notes, thank you cards or journal entries mixing drawing and text. Accept invented spelling or code-switching. Later, return to fill in heritage language vocabulary. Write a story together about a pet or trip and illustrate it. Use speech bubbles or labels in the heritage language to connect oral and written expression.

Tip: At this stage, focus on making writing enjoyable and creative. Let your child use drawings, playful spelling and mixed-language attempts as stepping stones toward confident heritage language writing.

Ages 10 to 12

Example: Invite your child to write about school life or family traditions. Provide sentence starters in the heritage language: 'Yesterday, I went to ____' or 'I celebrate _____ with my family because__________.'

Use apps with heritage language keyboards or voice-to-text features to support composition and editing. Writing for real audiences (e.g. emailing a grandparent) can boost motivation.

Tip: Connect writing to authentic purposes. Messages to relatives, blog posts or shared journals show children that heritage writing has real value beyond schoolwork, building both skill and motivation.

Introduce the Heritage Language Script Through Play

Ages 6 to 9

Example: Use tactile tools like sand trays, playdough or finger paints to practice script formation (e.g. Arabic or Chinese). Create puzzles with characters and images. Label everyday items around the house in the heritage script to support print awareness: *toothbrush, fridge, door.*

Tip: Keep script learning playful and multisensory. The more children can touch, move and manipulate letters or characters, the easier they will remember them and associate them with real-world meaning.

Ages 10 to 12

Example: Add short writing tasks using the script: Labeling a diagram, writing a grocery list or making a greeting card. Use calligraphy apps or digital tools to reinforce accuracy. Explore etymology or radicals in logographic systems. In Chinese, explain that the character for 'tree' (木) appears in 'forest' (林) and 'woods' (森), a fun way to discover meaning-building patterns.

Tip: Link script learning to patterns and logic. Show how words build from smaller parts or share roots across contexts. This makes the writing system feel less overwhelming and more meaningful for older children.

Create Digital Affinity Spaces[2]

Ages 6 to 9

Example: Introduce your child to online content in the heritage language that matches his interests, such as animated stories, craft tutorials or educational games. If he enjoys drawing, explore YouTube channels in the heritage language that teach cartooning. Watch together and ask simple questions like, 'What color did she use for the sky? Can you say that color in Arabic?'

Encourage small interactions, such as leaving a comment or sharing a drawing. These steps help your child feel part of a wider community that uses the heritage language in fun, meaningful ways.

Tip: Choose safe, age-appropriate platforms and use subtitles or transcripts in the heritage language to reinforce comprehension and script recognition.

Ages 10 to 12

Example: Support your child in joining online forums or communities, such as fan groups, game chats or Discord servers where the heritage language is used informally. If she enjoys Minecraft or anime, help her find a heritage language space to discuss builds or favorite characters. These affinity spaces encourage spontaneous, peer-driven language use.

Invite your child to create content in the heritage language, such as a fan comment, short review or labeled artwork. This builds motivation and helps her feel part of a wider cultural-linguistic community.

Tip: Focus on guiding your child to create and share content, rather than simply consume it, because this boosts literacy development and reinforces cultural identity.

Align Literacy Tasks Across Languages

Ages 6 to 9

Example: After writing a story or completing a worksheet in your child's school language, ask your child to retell it in the heritage language. Use sentence frames or drawings as support. For example, after a classroom journal entry on a zoo trip, prompt: 'Can you tell Grandma about the zoo in French?'

Tip: Turn everyday school assignments into opportunities for heritage language use. Encourage your child to share what she learned at school in the heritage language with a family member or friend. This not only strengthens vocabulary and storytelling skills but also helps your child connect academic learning with family communication.

Ages 10 to 12

Example: If your child writes a persuasive or informative paragraph in school, help her draft a heritage language version for a family newsletter, blog or class back home.

Tip: Help revise together by pointing out grammatical differences. Use tools like heritage language dictionaries or translation checkers to support accuracy and reflection.

Create a Literacy-Rich Home Environment

Ages 6 to 9

Example: Set up a cozy reading nook with heritage language books and writing tools. Use posters or alphabet charts to make the script and vocabulary visible. Read stories aloud as a bedtime routine and leave notes for your child in the heritage language.

Tip: Keep tasks light and supportive. Use pictures, prompts or short sentence starters to scaffold the retelling. This reinforces comprehension across languages without making your child feel like he is doing the assignment twice.

Ages 10 to 12

Example: Let your child see you writing in the heritage language (e.g. texts, shopping lists, social media posts). Encourage her to do the same. Incorporate digital resources: Type stories, listen to podcasts or follow YouTube science channels in the heritage language.

Tip: Treat these activities as discovery, not correction. Encourage your child to notice how ideas are expressed across languages and celebrate flexible thinking, which builds metalinguistic awareness and confidence. Praise effort rather than outcomes, and mark small milestones such as reading a sentence, writing a note or typing a short paragraph. The goal is not perfection or equal proficiency, but a joyful, consistent heritage language literacy foundation built through reading, writing, storytelling and digital tools

For further information and practical ideas on supporting your child's heritage language reading, writing and digital literacy, see Wang (2011).

When languages interfere with one another

During middle childhood, multilingual children navigate multiple linguistic systems simultaneously, which can lead to temporary cross-linguistic interference. This may appear in areas such as sounds (phonology), vocabulary (lexical and semantic), sentence structure (syntax), word formation (morphology) and the pragmatic use of language in cultural contexts. These instances of interference are developmentally typical and often diminish over time if children receive consistent support through meaningful exposure, literacy development and activities that promote metalinguistic awareness (De Houwer, 2009).

Interlanguage interference in sounds

Between ages 6 and 12, multilingual children may still experience phonological interference, especially when one language is dominant. These challenges often stem from typological differences, such as tonal contrasts, rhythm patterns or language-specific sounds.

Ages 6 to 9

At this stage, children are still consolidating their phonological representations. They may exhibit cross-linguistic influence, especially when a dominant societal language begins to shape their speech patterns in the heritage language.

In tonal languages such as Mandarin, Vietnamese and Thai, children may struggle with tone production and perception, particularly when tones do not exist in the dominant language. Mandarin's dipping third tone *mǎ* (horse), for instance, is frequently flattened or confused with the second tone *má* (hemp) among heritage speakers exposed primarily to English (Chang & Yan, 2016). **Tone merging** (loss of contrast between two or more tones) and **tonal drift** (gradual deviation from the correct tone contours over time, e.g. *lǎoshī* (teacher) may become *láoshī*) have been documented in second-generation speakers (Chang & Yan, 2016).

French-speaking children often omit required liaisons or produce them inappropriately. For example, in *les enfants arrivent*, the required liaison /z/ may be dropped. This is compounded by the mismatch between the written and spoken forms (Trancl, 1987).

Rhythm mismatches are common: English's stress-timed rhythm may be imposed on syllable-timed or tonal languages. For instance, applying English-like stress patterns to French (*photographie – photography*) or Mandarin (*wǒ yào chī fàn* – 我要吃饭 – I want to eat) may disrupt natural flow and comprehensibility (Gut, 2009).

Articulatory errors also emerge. Spanish heritage speakers may substitute the English /ɹ/ for the trilled /r/, whereas Korean–English bilinguals often collapse the aspirated and unaspirated stop distinction (e.g. /kʰ/ vs. /k/), which are phonemic in Korean but not in English (Lee & Iverson, 2012).

Children acquiring Japanese as a dominant community language, which favors a strict consonant–vowel syllable structure, may struggle with English consonant clusters and may insert vowels to break them up – a process known as **epenthesis** (Masuda & Arai, 2010). Similarly, Arabic or Tagalog dominant speakers may insert epenthetic vowels into cluster-rich words when speaking English, reshaping syllable boundaries to fit the phonotactic constraints of their native languages (Al-Abdullah & Almutairi, 2024; Tayao, 2008).

Ages 10 to 12

Older children show greater awareness of their speech and begin to self-monitor. However, interference patterns often persist, especially in tonal control, liaison and difficult phoneme production. Tone accuracy may decrease in spontaneous speech. Children may confuse similar tone contours in Mandarin or Vietnamese, especially when stressed or speaking quickly. Research suggests that metalinguistic awareness, supported by auditory feedback and visual aids, improves tone precision (Yang & Chen, 2019).

Liaison issues in French, such as overgeneralizing (*qui z'ont* for *qui ont*), may become fossilized without explicit instruction or modeling through reading and recitation (Demuth & Tremblay, 2008).

Persistent phoneme challenges also include:

- German /ç/ (often replaced with /ʃ/ or /k/).
- Arabic pharyngeals /ḥ/, /ʿ/ replaced with glottal or fricative approximations.
- Spanish trilled /r/ remaining anglicized.
- Korean aspirated stops collapsing into English /k/.

Children learning Japanese may still simplify words with multiple consonants, and Arabic-speaking children may insert unnecessary vowels to break clusters in English.

Interlanguage interference in lexical, semantic and morphosyntactic areas

In addition to sound-level interference, multilingual children in middle childhood often experience cross-linguistic influence in the lexical (word), semantic (meaning) and morphosyntactic domains (grammar), particularly in their home languages.

Ages 6 to 9

During the early school years, multilingual children are still consolidating foundational vocabulary and grammar across their languages. At this stage, language mixing is common, as children draw flexibly from their full linguistic repertoire to express themselves. For instance, a Spanish–English speaker might say, '*La* teacher *me dijo que es Lunes*' ('The teacher told me it's Monday'), inserting the English word 'teacher' into a Spanish sentence. Such mixing often reflects momentary gaps in vocabulary or a stronger association between specific concepts and the school language (Yow *et al.*, 2018).

Lexical interference also surfaces through **false cognates** or **false friends** (words that look or sound similar across languages but differ in meaning). A child may confuse French *actuellement* ('currently') with English 'actually', or she may assume the Spanish *embarazada* (pregnant) to mean the same as English 'embarrassed'. These surface-level associations are particularly common in early reading and storytelling, when children rely on visual or phonetic cues over deeper semantic knowledge.

Homophones (words that sound the same but have different meanings within or across languages) can create additional confusion. In English, for example, 'flower' and 'flour' sound alike but represent very different concepts. In Chinese, the syllable *qīng* may mean 'grayish blue' (青) or 'clear' (清).

Morphosyntactic interference can appear when children transfer grammatical rules from one language to another. For instance, a Chinese–English speaker may say, 'He go to school yesterday,' omitting the past tense marker because of Chinese's lack of verb inflection. Arabic-speaking children might omit plural or gender agreement in English, reflecting differences in morphological salience across their languages. These errors are typical at this stage and reflect the child's effort to make sense of multiple grammatical systems.

Ages 10 to 12

By ages 10 to 12, multilingual children generally have more structured exposure to academic language, particularly in the school language. However, lexical interference may persist in more subtle ways as they engage with increasingly abstract topics. For example, a Mandarin–English speaker may struggle to explain scientific concepts such as ecosystems or fractions in Mandarin after learning them only in English, leading to circumlocutions or borrowing English terms. Encouraging children to read non-fiction texts in both languages and co-create bilingual word banks can support cross-linguistic transfer.

False friends continue to pose challenges. A French–English speaker may say 'sensible' to mean 'sensitive,' based on the French *sensible*, or 'make a photo' instead of 'take a photo,' influenced by the direct translation of *faire une photo*. These errors, though seemingly minor, reveal the ongoing semantic negotiations multilingual children engage in as they navigate similar yet distinct lexical items.

In the morphosyntactic domain, interference may manifest in more complex sentence constructions. A Hebrew–English bilingual might say, 'She gave him it,' rather than 'She gave it to him,' because of differences in pronoun ordering and prepositional structures. Tense confusion, article omission and plural errors are also common in writing, especially when the heritage language lacks the corresponding grammatical features.

At both age levels, these moments of interference, whether lexical, semantic or grammatical, are best treated not as errors to correct in the moment but as opportunities for meaningful exploration. Using visual aids, real life examples, storytelling and humor, parents can gently guide children toward greater clarity and metalinguistic awareness. Over time, these efforts foster not only stronger language skills but also cognitive flexibility and a deeper appreciation of linguistic diversity.

The abovementioned cross-linguistic influences are completely normal. Consistent and meaningful exposure to the heritage language remains the most effective support.

Interference in pragmatic and cultural aspects

During middle childhood, children become increasingly attuned to social norms and peer dynamics, gradually developing **pragmatic competence** (knowing how to use language appropriately in different social contexts). In their dominant community language, this competence grows naturally through daily exposure to a wide range of interactions, including classroom discussions, peer conversations and media consumption. Through these experiences, children learn to interpret and use context-dependent expressions, sarcasm, indirect requests and appropriate levels of politeness. In contrast, children's heritage language often receives more limited and less varied input, which can hinder the development of contextually appropriate language use. As a result, children may speak the heritage language correctly in terms of vocabulary and grammar but use it in ways that are pragmatically inappropriate. For example, in Japanese, a child might use an informal form like お前何してるの？ ('What are you doing?') with an elder instead of the polite 何をしていらっしゃいますか?, unintentionally sounding rude. Similarly, in French, children may misuse *tu* instead of *vous* with teachers or unfamiliar adults, leading to perceptions of disrespect.

Similarly, children often encounter taboo or vulgar expressions in the dominant language through peers or media but may lack equivalent knowledge or cultural sensitivity when using such language in the heritage language. For example, a child might playfully say 'shut up' in English but translating it directly into Arabic ((اخرس!) would sound harsh or offensive, since the expression carries a much stronger tone in Arabic.

Without rich, context-based exposure to the heritage language in varied social settings, children can miss the subtle ways language is used to convey respect, emotion or social hierarchy. This gap highlights the importance of providing not just linguistic input but also socially and culturally grounded opportunities to use the heritage language meaningfully and appropriately.

Try These Activities

Ages 6 to 9: Notice, Play and Explore

Sound and Rhythm Games

Example: Play a sound-matching game using pictures or objects. Say two similar sounding words in the heritage language that differ in tone, stress or sound, and ask your child to point to the correct picture. You can also read short rhymes or chants and use clapping or tapping to highlight language-specific sound patterns, such as tone changes, rhythm or sound linking.

Tip: Help your child hear the differences first. Listening and playful repetition lay the foundation for accurate production later.

Word Detective Play

Example: Explore confusing words through drawings or humor. If your child mixes up Spanish *embarazada* and English *embarrassed*, draw a silly picture to show the difference and talk about when each word is used.

Tip: Treat word confusion as a puzzle to solve together. Laughter and curiosity make new meanings easier to remember.

Grammar Through Stories

Example: At bedtime, ask your child to retell something that happened that day in the heritage language. If a verb form is missing or incorrect, respond by modeling it naturally in your reply.

Tip: Keep grammar embedded in stories and meaning. Gentle modeling is more effective than direct correction.

Cultural Role-Play

Example: Use puppets or role-play with family members to act out greeting a visitor or thanking someone for a gift. Model appropriate words, tone and gestures in the heritage language.

Tip: Let your child try both roles, speaker and listener, to experience how language changes with context.

Ages 10 to 12: Reflect, Compare and Refine

Listening and Self-Monitoring

Example: Have your child record herself reading a short passage in the heritage language. Listen together and notice tone, rhythm or linking features, then try again.

Tip: Ask your child what sounded different rather than pointing it out yourself. Self-noticing builds independence.

Contrastive Language Journals

Example: Invite your child to jot down words or phrases that feel confusing across languages, such as false friends or expressions learned only in school.

Tip: Position your child as a language detective. Explaining patterns strengthens metalinguistic awareness and confidence.

Purposeful Grammar Play

Example: Ask your child to tell a short story as a reporter, detective or storyteller, focusing on past tense or sentence structure in the heritage language.

Tip: Creative roles lower pressure and encourage risk-taking with more complex forms.

Pragmatic Scenarios

Example: Role-play asking a teacher for help versus chatting with a friend, practicing appropriate register and politeness in the heritage language.

Tip: Emphasize appropriateness over perfection. Understanding *when* and *how* to speak matters more than sounding flawless.

Monitor your child's heritage language progress: Parent as researcher in action

Now that we have explored the challenges and opportunities of heritage language development in middle childhood, it is time to gather insights into your child's multilingual development as a parent-researcher.

Step 1: Understanding typical development patterns and possible multilingual variations

To support your efforts, Table 4.2 provides a developmental overview of language milestones commonly observed during middle childhood, highlights possible multilingual variations and identifies areas that may warrant closer attention or additional support.

With a general understanding of the developmental trajectories in middle childhood in the above table, you gain a foundation for observing your child's heritage language progress and identifying where to focus your support. Table 4.3 suggests ways that you can track your child's language development in different domains and actions that you need to take to support her development.

Step 2: Conducting deeper observations

Once you have a general understanding of language and literacy development, including possible multilingual variations, you can begin using more focused measures to monitor your child's multilingual growth during middle childhood. These measures allow you to observe progress in both spoken and written language across the heritage and school languages.

Table 4.2 Language development milestones and variations during middle childhood

Age range	General developmental pattern	Possible multilingual variation	How to observe/assess your child	When to pay attention
6 to 9 years	Phonological development: Children can master most phonemes, refine clusters and multisyllabic words, develop phonemic awareness (e.g. rhyming, blending).	Multilingual children may keep each language's sound system distinct. If one language has a very regular sound–letter match (a 'transparent orthography,' like Spanish, where each letter usually makes one sound), they may use those decoding skills to help read in other languages. This is called **transfer** (borrowing strategies from one language to support another).	Play rhyming or blending games in each language; listen for accurate pronunciation in clusters and longer words.	Frequent mispronunciations that interfere with understanding; difficulty in rhyming or blending despite support.
	Lexical and semantic development: Rapid vocabulary growth. Children can acquire concrete and some abstract words and begin understanding multiple-meaning words and idioms.	Building conceptual vocabulary across languages; starting linking cognates and context-specific terms.	Ask your child to explain school vocabulary in the heritage language; observe growth across languages.	Vocabulary growth stalls in all of his languages; persistent difficulty understanding simple idioms.
	Morphosyntactic development: Children can use simple and compound sentences and begin applying past tense, plurals and conjunctions consistently.	Showing structural transfer errors; mixing forms but code-switching naturally in context.	Listen for varied sentence types and tense accuracy; observe code-switching in play.	Cannot form simple sentences or struggles to use past tense in at least one language.
	Pragmatic development: Children can improve turn-taking; maintain topics and begin adapting speech for different listeners.	Adjusting politeness or formality differently across languages; responding to listener's language choice.	Observe conversations with peers vs. teachers; note politeness markers.	Trouble maintaining conversations or following conversational rules in either language.
	Reading development: Children can move from decoding to fluent reading of short texts, comprehend the main ideas and use context for meaning.	Applying decoding strategies across scripts; benefit from cross-linguistic support.	Listen to oral reading in each language; ask comprehension questions.	Struggles with decoding or refuses to read in either language.
	Writing development: Children can write simple sentences and short paragraphs, and use punctuation and transitions.	Relying on oral support in weaker language; transferring sentence structures between languages.	Review short written work in all the ambient languages; encourage journaling.	Avoids writing or cannot produce sentences with punctuation.
	Language mechanics: Children can apply capitalization, punctuation and basic grammar with support.	Spelling and punctuation may vary depending on dominant input.	Look at spelling tests or editing attempts in each language.	Frequent uncorrected errors that obscure meaning.

(Continued)

Table 4.2 *Continued*

Age range	General developmental pattern	Possible multilingual variation	How to observe/assess your child	When to pay attention
	Digital literacy: Children can learn basic typing, navigation and digital storytelling and engage with educational platforms.	Using tools in more than one language; creating simple digital stories in more than one language.	Watch how your child types captions or narrates digital work in both languages.	Cannot navigate basic digital tools or avoids the heritage language online.
10 to 12 years	Phonological development: Children can produce adult-like speech, master complex clusters and manipulate phonemes for spelling and reading.	Coordinating multiple phonological systems; managing cross-language interference more flexibly.	Ask your child to explain spelling choices or break words into sounds in both languages.	Persistent mispronunciations that affect reading/spelling or unclear speech.
	Lexical and semantic development: Children can use figurative language, metaphors, nuanced vocabulary and academic terms.	Deepening vocabulary in both languages; learning culture-specific expressions; comparing meanings across languages.	Ask your child to explain metaphors or translate expressions; discuss academic terms in both languages.	Difficulty understanding figurative language, academic words or culturally specific terms.
	Morphosyntactic development: Children can use complex sentences with subordinate clauses, and master verb tenses and irregular forms.	Using advanced code-switching strategically; showing metalinguistic awareness.	Have your child retell stories with different tenses; check for sentence complexity.	Ongoing grammatical errors or inability to form complex sentences.
	Pragmatic development: Children adapt speech to social contexts; use sarcasm, indirect language and structured storytelling.	Using culturally appropriate speech acts in each language; adjusting pragmatics to cultural norms.	Role-play speaking to a teacher vs. a peer; observe appropriateness of tone.	Difficulty adapting speech to social situations or missing pragmatic cues.
	Reading development: Children can read chapter books fluently, and analyze themes, character motivations and text structures.	Applying comprehension strategies across languages; interpreting texts in cultural context.	Discuss themes or the author's purpose in the heritage language; compare across languages.	Struggles with comprehension or avoids age-level reading.
	Writing development: Children can compose multiparagraph essays with a thesis and supporting details, and revise drafts.	Writing in both languages with audience awareness; including cultural references.	Review essays/projects in each language; note organization and cultural insight.	Cannot organize or revise writing; frequent structural weaknesses.
	Language mechanics: Children can apply grammar and punctuation effectively, and use punctuation rhetorically (semicolons, complex structures).	Demonstrating control in the dominant language; adapting rules across languages strategically.	Check editing in both languages; observe how mechanics transfer.	Persistent errors that interfere with clarity; weak editing in both languages.
	Digital literacy: C Children can conduct online research, create multimedia projects and evaluate sources.	Using tools in both languages; critically assessing sources in different contexts.	Review bilingual digital projects; ask how your child checks credibility.	Difficulty evaluating online sources or avoiding the heritage language online.

Table 4.3 Ways to track your child's heritage language development

Domain	How to check (ages 6 to 9)	How to check (ages 10 to 12)	Your observation and action (example)
Phonology (pronunciation, accent, intonation)	• Listen during play, reading aloud or singing. • Play rhyming games or simple tongue twisters. • Record and replay short conversations.	• Ask your child to read aloud from a book or news clip. • Try tongue twisters in the heritage language. • Record storytelling and review together.	**Observation:** Mispronounces French r. **Action:** Use songs, rhymes and tongue twisters. **Observation:** Flattens Mandarin tones (妈 mā vs. 马 mǎ). **Action:** Practice tongue twisters twice a week; replay recordings together.
Lexicon and semantics (vocabulary, word meanings, expressions)	• Ask your child to retell a cartoon or bedtime story. • Use picture books and pause to identify words. • Introduce playful idioms or riddles.	• Retell a movie or explain a school topic in the heritage language. • Explore idioms, metaphors and proverbs. • Compare usage of words across languages.	**Observation:** Switches to English for animal names. **Action:** Build a family word wall; play guessing games. **Observation:** Struggles with academic vocabulary in Spanish (*nutrición*). **Action:** Create subject-specific word lists and ask for oral summaries.
Morphosyntax (grammar, word forms, sentence structure)	• Listen for plurals, tenses and connectors like 'and' or 'because'. • Review notes, drawings or labels.	• Review journals, texts or short essays. • Listen for complex sentences, verb endings and word order. • Encourage debates or essays.	**Observation:** Says *yo comer* instead of *yo comí* ('I ate'). **Action:** Prompt with past-tense questions. **Observation:** Simplifies Russian case endings (*u mama*). **Action:** Use family photos, ask questions requiring case endings and model full forms.
Pragmatics (context, politeness, humor, register)	• Observe speech with adults vs. peers. • Encourage jokes, riddles or role-plays. • Ask: 'How would you say that to Grandma vs. your friend?'	• Observe how your child adapts speech to peers, elders or teachers. • Rewrite song lyrics or proverbs. • Ask: 'How would you say that differently to your cousin vs. your teacher?'	**Observation:** Uses English jokes only. **Action:** Teach simple riddles and playful expressions. **Observation:** Uses informal *tu* with French elders. **Action:** Role-play scenarios to practice *tu* vs. *vous*.

(Continued)

Table 4.3 *Continued*

Domain	How to check (ages 6 to 9)	How to check (ages 10 to 12)	Your observation and action (example)
Text and discourse (storytelling, flow organization)	• Ask your child to narrate a family outing. • Encourage journal drawings with labels. • Listen for beginning–middle–end in stories.	• Ask your child to narrate a memory or write diary/blog entries. • Check for logic, detail and transitions.	**Observation:** Leaves out linking words. **Action:** Prompt with 'What happened first? What happened next?' **Observation:** Writes list-like stories in French. **Action:** Encourage weekly journals with prompts like 'Describe your best moment this week.'
Everyday language use (code-switching, emotional vocabulary, confidence)	• Notice when switching occurs (play, emotions, school talk). • Ask reflective questions: 'What do you like about speaking our language?'	• Observe switching in school, social or online contexts. • Ask: 'What feels easy or hard about using our language?'	**Observation:** Switches to English for feelings. **Action:** Introduce emotional vocabulary during bedtime chats. **Observation:** Avoids heritage language with peers. **Action:** Encourage participation in clubs or online affinity spaces.
Digital literacy (using technology to strengthen the heritage language)	• Explore child-friendly videos, audiobooks or educational games. • Use subtitles or captions to connect spoken and written forms. • Encourage simple online contributions (e.g. leaving a 'thank you' comment with your help).	• Support participation in online communities (fan groups, coding forums, Discord). • Encourage creating digital content (blogs, short videos, reviews). • Discuss how online interactions differ across languages/cultures.	**Observation:** Enjoys heritage language cartoons but doesn't use subtitles. **Action:** Watch shows with captions and pause to read key words together. **Observation:** Reads manga forums in Japanese but rarely posts. **Action:** Encourage short weekly comments and co-create a review or caption.

For children between the ages of 6 and 9, oral language measures such as MLU, introduced in early childhood (see Chapter 3), remain useful. At this stage, you can also add a new measure called the **number of different words (NDW)**, which counts the number of unique words (types of words) your child uses in a sample. Repeated words are counted only once, so this measure focuses on variety rather than frequency, reflecting the breadth of your child's vocabulary in both speech and writing.

Spoken example: If your child says, 'I went to the park. I climbed the slide. I ran to the swing. I swing and swing,' the unique words are *I, went, to, the, park, climbed, slide, ran, swing* and *and*. The NDW is 10, even though some words are repeated.

Writing example: If your child writes, 'I like my dog. My dog is big. My dog runs fast,' the unique words are *I, like, my, dog, is, big, runs* and *fast*. The NDW is 8, even though *dog* and *my* appear several times.

At this age, literacy development also becomes increasingly important. Beyond MLU and NDW, you can observe your child's **sight word recognition** (how many words they read automatically without sounding them out) and **spelling attempts** (whether they use sound–letter correspondences, even when their spelling is not fully accurate). Together, these indicators show how oral vocabulary is beginning to transfer into reading and writing, offering a fuller picture of your child's development across languages.

For children between the ages of 10 and 12, the focus shifts toward more advanced structures in both speech and writing. Oral language at this stage can be assessed through **clausal density**, which measures how many clauses appear in a sentence and reflects your child's ability to express complex ideas. For example, a simple sentence like 'I like apples' has one clause, whereas 'I like apples because they are sweet and crunchy' contains three clauses, showing greater syntactic complexity. Another useful measure is **narrative skills**, which examine how well your child organizes ideas, connects events with cohesive devices (such as *first, then, because* and *however*) and uses more advanced vocabulary. For instance, your child might say, 'At first, I was scared to go on stage, but when I started singing, I felt proud,' demonstrating both sequencing and emotional depth.

At the literacy level, you can assess **reading comprehension** by asking your child to retell the main idea of a passage, explain why something happened or relate the story to personal experiences. For example, after reading a short fable, you might ask, 'Why do you think the fox tricked the crow?' or 'Has something like that ever happened to you?' To observe **written expression**, look for your child's ability to write multiclause sentences; use transitions such as *however, therefore or as a result*; and organize ideas into coherent paragraphs. For example, 'I didn't win the race; however, I learned that trying my best is more important than winning' shows both grammatical maturity and reflective thinking.

These measures together highlight not only increasing complexity but also how effectively your child uses language to think, express ideas and communicate across languages and modalities. Table 4.4 provides practical guidance on how to apply these measures to track your child's multilingual progress during middle childhood.

Table 4.4 How to track your child's language progress

Step	Age range	Oral measures	Literacy measures	Notes/reflections (changes/ concerns+action steps)
Step 1: Collect a sample	6 to 9	Gather 50–100 spoken sentences in natural conversation.	Ask your child to read a short text aloud and write a few sentences.	**Concern:** Child's sentences are still short and simple. **Action:** Continue weekly recordings and prompt longer responses with open-ended questions.
	10 to 12	Collect an oral story (retelling of a recent event).	Collect a short piece of writing (paragraph or journal).	**Change:** Story had more detail. **Action:** Encourage storytelling at family meals.
Step 2: Apply the measures	6 to 9	**MLU:** Count morphemes. **NDW:** Count unique words (repeated words once). **Example:** 'I climbed the slide, ran to the swing' → NDW = 7.	**Sight word recognition:** Words read instantly. **Spelling attempts:** Look for sound–letter use. Example: 'I like my dog. My dog runs fast.' → NDW = 6.	**Change:** NDW rose from 10 to 15. **Action:** Introduce new words through reading.
	10 to 12	**Clausal density:** Count clauses. **Narrative skills:** Look for connectors (*because, however*). *Example:* 'I wanted to go, but it rained, so we stayed inside.' → 3 clauses.	**Reading comprehension:** Retell, infer, connect. **Written expression:** Look for transitions and organization.	**Change:** Uses 'because' instead of 'and then.' **Action:** Give writing prompts that need explanations.
Steps 3 and 4: Reflect and encourage growth	6 to 12	**Reflect:** Is vocabulary expanding? Are sentences longer and more connected? Encourage: Model sequencing words (*first, next, finally*) and advanced connectors (*therefore*).	**Reflect:** Is reading more fluent? Is writing more organized with transitions? **Encourage:** Practice sight words, journaling and short stories.	**Change:** Heritage language weaker than English. **Action:** Schedule weekly heritage language storytime.

If you want a shortcut, record a short speech sample from your child on your phone, then use AI to transcribe it and calculate the measures described above. For writing samples, simply paste the text into an AI tool and let it complete the analysis.

For multilingual children, the goal is not monolingual equivalence but steady progress and functional proficiency within family and community contexts (Unsworth, 2016).

Step 3: Pulling it all together: Documenting and reflection

The following log is designed to help you observe your child's multilingual development, collect samples of her language use (such as stories, sentences or writing), document your observations in a structured way and reflect on your child's progress over time. By combining these steps, you can see your child's growth at a glance and identify areas where extra support may be helpful.

Multilingual Development Log

Date (Day/Month/Year): ____________

1. Language Development Journal

Date: ________________________________

Observation (milestone, new word, sentence or code-switching moment):

____

____

Context (where/with whom it happened):

____

____

Your reflections:

____

____

Strategies used (e.g. shared reading, journaling, family conversation, games or cultural activities):

____

____

Next steps/ideas

____

____

2. Monthly Language Snapshot

Date: ________________________________

Languages used in snapshot: ________________________________

Recorded activity (short video, audio or written notes):

____

Examples of new words/phrases:

____

____

Language progress tracker

Language	MIU	NDW	Sight word recognition	Spelling attempts	Clausal density	Narrative skills	Reading comprehension	Written expression
Language A								
Language B								
Language C								

3. Video Diary Clip Log

Date of clip: ______________________________

Activity recorded: ______________________________

Language(s) used: ______________________________

Notable features (pronunciation, grammar, confidence):

____

____

Comparison with earlier clips:

____

____

4. Strategy Tracker

Date	Strategy tried	How often used	Child's reaction	Impact observed	Next steps

5. Family Reflection Notes (for Both Parents)

Date: ______________________________

Participants: ______________________________

Highlights/successes:

____

____

Challenges/questions:

____

____

Agreed actions for next month:

____

____

Reflections:

____

____

Key Takeaways of Chapter 4

Middle childhood is a turning point in your child's multilingual journey. During this stage, the heritage language can begin to fade under the growing influence of school, peers and media, or it can continue to thrive with steady, joyful and intentional support at home. As you help your child navigate this changing linguistic landscape, the following principles can guide you in transforming challenges into opportunities for growth.

- **Consistency counters the pull of the dominant language:** Daily, meaningful use of the heritage language through shared routines, conversations or stories helps balance the strong influence of the school language. Even brief but regular moments of use can prevent gradual loss and keep the language alive.
- **Emotional connection strengthens commitment:** Children are more motivated to maintain their heritage language when it is tied to love, family bonds and joy. Cooking together, listening to music, celebrating holidays or sharing bedtime stories in the heritage language turns it from a task into a living part of family life.
- **Flexibility responds to a changing world:** As children grow, their interests and schedules evolve. What worked at age 6 may not work at age 10. Stay flexible and adapt your strategies to their current passions, whether it involves connecting language learning to a favorite sport, book or online game.
- **Playful engagement overcomes resistance:** When the heritage language feels like homework, children may resist it. Keeping language use fun through games, creative storytelling, humor or movies makes practice enjoyable and builds positive associations that last.
- **Modeling matters more than correcting:** Code-switching or mixing languages is a natural part of multilingual development. Instead of correcting every mistake, model the correct form through conversation. This builds confidence and allows learning to unfold naturally.
- **Celebrate progress, not perfection:** Each new word, sentence or story represents growth. Acknowledge these moments with enthusiasm. Progress, rather than perfection, nurtures your child's sense of pride and strengthens both linguistic and emotional connection.

By overcoming the challenges of middle childhood and finding the right balance between the school language and the heritage language, you create the environment for your child to thrive. With steady modeling, playful engagement and meaningful connections, the way forward opens with promise. Your child will be ready to step into adolescence with confidence, carrying the heritage language as both a strength and a source of pride.

Notes

(1) Complete equality between the school's dominant language and a child's home language is rarely possible. The school language almost always grows faster because it is used for daily instruction. Functional balance means keeping the home language active and meaningful, not matching the school

language. Supporting reading and writing in the home language, in print or digital form, helps sustain deeper growth.

(2) Digital affinity spaces are online communities where people gather around shared interests, such as games, hobbies, fandoms, or creative projects, and learn from one another through interaction and participation (Gee, 2003).

Key characteristics:

- Interest-driven: People join because they care about the topic;
- Peer learning: Newcomers learn by observing and engaging with experienced members;
- Shared purpose: Members work toward a common goal;
- Flexible participation: Users can comment, create, ask questions or simply observe;
- Multimodal communication: Text, images, video and audio enrich language use;
- Low pressure: Informal, voluntary involvement boosts motivation for language learners.

References

Al-Abdullah, S. and Almutairi, M.A. (2024) Vowel epenthesis in the pronunciation of English consonant clusters by Kuwaiti EFL learners. *Journal of Language Teaching and Research* 15 (2), 664–673. https://doi.org/10.17507/jltr.1502.35

Bandura, A. (1997) *Self-Efficacy: The Exercise of Control*. W. H. Freeman.

Chang, C.B. and Yao, Y. (2016) Toward an understanding of heritage prosody: Acoustic and perceptual properties of tone produced by heritage, native, and second language speakers of Mandarin. *Heritage Language Journal* 13 (2), 134–160. https://doi.org/10.46538/hlj.13.2.4

De Houwer, A. (2009) *An Introduction to Bilingual Development*. Multilingual Matters.

Demuth, K. and Tremblay, A. (2008) Prosodically-conditioned variability in children's production of French determiners. *Journal of Child Language* 35 (1), 99–127. https://doi.org/10.1017/S0305000907008276

Gee, J.P. (2003) *What Video Games Have to Teach Us about Learning and Literacy*. Palgrave Macmillan.

Ghosn, I.K. (2002) Four good reasons to use literature in the primary school ELT. *ELT Journal* 56 (2), 172–179. https://doi.org/10.1093/elt/56.2.172

Guardado, M. (2002) Loss and maintenance of first language skills: Case studies of Hispanic families in Vancouver. *Canadian Modern Language Review* 58 (3), 341–363. https://doi.org/10.3138/cmlr.58.3.341

Gut, U. (2009) Learner English across languages: Prosodic patterns of second-language speech. In U. Gut, R. Fuchs and A. Möhring (eds) *Learner English across Languages: Prosodic Patterns of Second Language Speech* (pp. 97–120). Mouton de Gruyter.

Hostetter, A.B. (2011) When do gestures communicate? A meta-analysis. *Psychological Bulletin* 137 (2), 297–315. https://doi.org/10.1037/a0022128

Karayayla, T. and Schmid, M.S. (2019) First-language attrition as a function of age at onset of bilingualism. *Language Learning* 69 (1), 106–142. https://doi.org/10.1111/lang.12316

Lee, S. and Iverson, G.K. (2012) Stop consonant productions of Korean–English bilingual children. *Bilingualism: Language and Cognition* 15 (2), 275–287. https://doi.org/10.1017/S1366728911000083

Masuda, H. and Arai, T. (2010) Processing of consonant clusters by Japanese native speakers: Influence of English learning backgrounds. *Acoustical Science and Technology* 31 (5), 320–327. https://doi.org/10.1250/ast.31.320

Ray, B. and Seely, C. (2004) *Fluency through TPR Storytelling: Achieving Real Language Acquisition in School* (5th edn). Command Performance Language Institute.

Schumann, J.H. (1997) *The Neurobiology of Affect in Language*. Blackwell.

Son, M. and Wee, S.J. (2024) Writing as play: Highlighting children's agency and creativity through home-based literacy. *Early Childhood Education Journal* 53 (6), 1999–2021. https://doi.org/10.1007/s10643-024-01774-x

Taeschner, T. (1983) *The Sun is Feminine: A Study on Language Acquisition in Bilingual Children*. Springer-Verlag.

Tayao, M.L.G. (2008) A lectal description of the phonological features of Philippine English. In M.L.S. Bautista and K. Bolton (eds) *Philippine English: Linguistic and Literary Perspectives* (pp. 157–174). Hong Kong University Press. https://doi.org/10.1515/9789888052639-013

Tranel, B. (1987) *The Sounds of French: An Introduction*. Cambridge University Press.

Unsworth, S. (2016) Quantity and quality of language input in bilingual language development. In E. Nicoladis and S. Montanari (eds) *Bilingualism across the Lifespan: Factors Moderating Language Proficiency* (pp. 103–121). American Psychological Association.

Van Gorp, K. and Verheyen, S. (2024) Primary school children's conflicted emotions about using their heritage languages in multilingual classroom tasks. *The Modern Language Journal* 108 (1), 101–126. https://doi.org/10.1111/modl.12893

Vygotsky, L.S. (1978) *Mind in Society: The Development of Higher Psychological Processes*. Harvard University Press.

Wang, X.-L. (2008) *Growing up with Three Languages: Birth to Eleven*. Multilingual Matters.

Wang, X. L. (2011) *Learning to Read and Write in the Multilingual Family*. Multilingual Matters.

Yang, C. and Chan, A.Y.W. (2019) Learning tonal distinctions in Mandarin among young heritage speakers. *Language Awareness* 28 (2), 169–185.

Yow, W.Q., Tan, J.S.H. and Flynn, S. (2018) Code-switching as a marker of linguistic competence in bilingual children. *Bilingualism: Language and Cognition* 21 (5), 1075–1090. https://doi.org/10.1017/S1366728917000335

5 The Multilingual Negotiation Years (Ages 13 to 19): Making Multilingualism Last

Your child is now entering the teenage years, a period known as **adolescence**[1], derived from the Latin *adolescere*, meaning 'to grow up.' This stage marks a profound transition from childhood to adulthood, bringing physical, cognitive, social and emotional changes. It can be both fascinating and challenging. As educators De Vries Guth and Pratt-Fartro (2011) noted, adolescents are 'a strange and wonderful mix of mature and childlike qualities,' able to move from seriousness to playfulness in an instant.

Although adolescence is often seen as turbulent, it is also a time filled with curiosity, idealism, a sense of justice and boundless energy. When these qualities are nurtured, they can create powerful opportunities for your teen to deepen his connection with the heritage language and bring his proficiency to new levels.

If your child has developed any level of proficiency in his heritage language with your support, that is a great accomplishment. You have given him both a strong foundation and an enduring advantage. If progress has been uneven, it is never too late to strengthen his skills. With meaningful interaction, steady practice and language introduced in manageable, engaging ways, older learners can continue to make real progress (MacWhinney, 2012). Whatever your teen's current level, it is important to recognize that adolescence brings new academic, social and emotional demands that may influence his motivation and opportunities to use the language.

During these years, the heritage language often takes on deeper meaning. It becomes a bridge for sharing personal thoughts, strengthening family bonds, navigating friendships and expressing cultural identity. As psychologist Laurence Steinberg (2014) observed, teenagers may push away from adults, yet at critical moments they need adults more than ever. Conversations in the heritage language help your teen process emotions, solve problems and feel grounded in who he is.

Your role now shifts from manager to consultant (Riera, 2003): Someone who listens, asks thoughtful questions and offers guidance when your teen is ready. Keeping the heritage language alive in these exchanges nurtures his ability to connect deeply, think clearly and carry forward a strong sense of self.

This chapter explores both the challenges and opportunities of adolescence and offers intentional strategies for sustaining your teen's heritage language during one of life's most transformative stages. It concludes with parent as researcher activities designed to help you track progress and remain an engaged partner in your child's multilingual journey.

Major Challenges and Opportunities During Adolescence

Adolescence is a time of rapid cognitive growth, expanding social connections and evolving identity. For multilingual teens, these changes often intersect with challenges such as maintaining the heritage language, navigating peer expectations and developing academic knowledge across languages. As your teen becomes more independent and reflective, he may use the heritage language less or show uneven proficiency, yet this stage also brings opportunities for renewed motivation and growth. He is learning to think about his language choices and connect them to personal and future goals. With thoughtful support, you can help him strengthen and extend his multilingual abilities. The following sections outline both the challenges and the opportunities of adolescence and offer practical ways to sustain and enrich your teen's multilingual development.

When there is a risk of language attrition

By adolescence, heritage language skills often plateau or decline if daily exposure and meaningful use diminish. Without regular and meaningful use, your teen may find it harder to recall words quickly, use grammar accurately and express himself fully in his heritage language (Schmid, 2011). Adolescents are particularly vulnerable because peer-group norms and academic demands often center around the community's mainstream language (Guardado, 2018). Multilingual adolescents frequently gravitate toward the mainstream language of their schooling and peer interactions. This tendency is especially strong when academic demands intensify, and social belonging becomes a dominant force. As a result, the heritage language, particularly if it is not used for academic purposes or among peers, can become vulnerable to attrition. A teenager who was once fluent in his heritage language might experience vocabulary stagnation, rusty grammar or a decline in confidence when speaking, as the school language increasingly dominates both the cognitive and social domains. Over time, without active and meaningful use, the heritage language may shift into a passive skill or fade entirely, especially if your teen begins to associate it more with obligation than personal relevance.

Ages 13 to 15

In the early part of adolescence, the influence of the majority language often increases as schoolwork becomes more demanding and peer relationships gain greater importance. Even if your teen continues to hear and use the heritage language at home, his daily immersion in the majority language at school and with friends can lead to reduced spontaneous use of the heritage language. He may begin to rely on the majority language for expressing more complex ideas, which can cause his heritage language vocabulary's growth to stall. In addition, grammatical accuracy and fluency may weaken if he is not receiving regular, age-appropriate input in the heritage language.

Ages 16 to 19

In the later teen years, the risk of attrition becomes even greater as your child prepares for life beyond high school. Around age 18, many leave home for college or work, often moving into environments where the majority language dominates nearly all interactions. This shift can result in a sharp decrease in heritage language use, particularly in speaking and writing. Without consistent, meaningful opportunities to use the heritage language, your teen's active skills may fade, leaving him able to understand it passively but less confident in producing it. If the heritage language becomes associated mainly with family obligation rather than personal relevance, he may disengage from it entirely. The following strategies may help with the heritage language attrition.

Try These Strategies

Ages 13 to 15

At this stage, teens are still home-centered but increasingly peer-oriented. The goal is to keep the heritage language visible, social and connected to real life so it feels like part of your teen's identity rather than a school subject.

- **Integrate the heritage language into daily routines**
  - Cook together using recipes in the heritage language, naming ingredients aloud and chatting about the day.
  - Watch a favorite show in the heritage language during dinner and discuss funny or surprising moments afterward. For example, Léandre and Dominique learned colloquial Chinese words like 溜达 (ramble) from the Chinese TV show 快乐驿站 (*Happy Post Station*).
- **Involve extended family and community**
  - Schedule casual video calls with heritage language speaking grandparents or relatives, encouraging your teen to share school updates, opinions or a recent achievement in the heritage language.
  - Attend community cultural events (e.g. heritage language film screenings, food festivals) with friends so the language is tied to social fun.
- **Use humor to build engagement**
  - Exchange jokes, watch comedic skits or share memes in the heritage language. This taps into adolescents' growing appreciation for irony, sarcasm and wordplay (Bell, 2011).

- Try tongue twisters like '四是四，十是十' ('four is four, ten is ten' in Mandarin Chinese), 'Les chaussettes de l'archiduchesse sont-elles sèches, archisèches?' ('Are the archduchess's socks dry, very dry?' in French) or 'يط حرير على حيط حديد' ('A silk thread on an iron wall' in Arabic) for playful pronunciation practice.

- **Support reading and writing for pleasure**
  - Give your child comics, magazines or novels in the heritage language that match his interests, such as sports, music or gaming.
  - Encourage your child to text you or post short social media captions in the heritage language, with proper guidance.

Ages 16 to 19

Later adolescence brings independence and preparation for adult life. The focus now is on helping your teen see the practical, personal and identity value of his heritage language, even if he is away from home.

- **Frame the language as empowerment**
  - Connect your teen's language skills to internships, part-time jobs or volunteer work where multilingual ability is an advantage (Lo Bianco, 2014).
  - Show examples of successful multilingual role models in his areas of interest.
  - Encourage metacognitive reflection about language use. Adolescents are capable of deep self-reflection. You might ask, 'How could your heritage language, such as Chinese, give you an advantage in this career or field?' This kind of question helps him think critically about the value of her language skills, making the connection between language, personal goals and future opportunities more concrete.
- **Encourage independent projects**
  - Suggest he create a podcast or vlog in the heritage language about topics he cares about (e.g. fashion, sports or social issues).
  - Have him prepare a personal statement or résumé draft in the heritage language to strengthen academic and professional vocabulary.
- **Keep extended family connections alive**
  - Set up monthly calls with relatives or community elders where he interviews them about family history, culture or traditions in the heritage language.
  - Encourage him to join student or professional groups that use the heritage language as a medium of interaction.
- **Promote metacognitive reflection**
  - Discuss how his vocabulary or grammar shifts in different contexts, such as texting friends versus talking to elders (Norton, 2013).

- Invite him to reflect on why some expressions are 'untranslatable' and what that reveals about culture.
- **Maintain reading/writing for pleasure**
  - Suggest he follow blogs, online magazines or news outlets in the heritage language that relate to his future studies.
  - Encourage him to keep a travel diary or photo captions in the heritage language when visiting new places.

When cultural identity and peer pressure collide

In the previous chapter, we examined peer pressure during middle childhood. By adolescence, this pressure often intensifies, as the influence of peers becomes pervasive and can outweigh parental encouragement in shaping linguistic choices (Brown, 1990). When a heritage language is socially devalued, teens may internalize stigma or develop ambivalent attitudes toward its use, affecting both their motivation and identity (Pavlenko & Blackledge, 2004). Research has shown that peer acceptance can influence heritage language use at this stage more strongly than parental encouragement (Phinney, 1990). Adolescence is also a natural period of self-discovery and identity formation, when questions of language and culture frequently move to the forefront, particularly for multilingual individuals (Norton, 2013).

Multilingual adolescents may need to frequently navigate the tension between maintaining a coherent sense of self and negotiating multiple cultural frameworks. This may mean feeling pressure to choose between identities or worrying they are not 'enough' of any one group. A teen might express this by saying, 'I speak the language, but I'm not really from there,' or 'I don't feel completely American or Vietnamese.' These feelings can lead to withdrawal from a heritage language or cultural community, especially when his peers fail to affirm that identity or regard it as irrelevant in daily life.

Peer pressure often intensifies this process. Adolescents naturally crave social belonging, and when heritage languages are perceived as unusual, outdated or low status, they may downplay or reject them to avoid negative attention (Hornberger, 2003a). For example, Nikol, a Croatian- and Polish-speaking teen, felt embarrassed using her home languages at school after classmates called them 'strange'. Similarly, Linjin's daughter refused to speak Chinese altogether because of perceived stigma from his peers. When teens sense that their heritage identity marks them as different in a negative way, they may experience shame, self-doubt or internal conflict, leading to reduced language use and distancing from their cultural background (Dovchin, 2025).

Ages 13 to 15

In the early to middle teen years, identity exploration is strongly tied to peer approval. Your teen may:

- Feel hesitant to use his heritage language in public, especially around peers who do not share it, for fear of standing out or being teased (Phinney, 1990).
- Avoid bringing heritage-related food, clothing or cultural references to school if they might attract unwanted attention.
- Begin compartmentalizing his language use, reserving the heritage language only for home and using the majority language exclusively in social and academic settings.
- Experience uncertainty about how to 'blend' different parts of his identity, resulting in less willingness to share cultural traditions with friends.

Ages 16 to 19

In later adolescence, identity questions may become more nuanced and self-driven, but peer and societal perceptions still matter. Your teen may:

- Consciously distance himself from the heritage language if he feels it limits his ability to assimilate into the peer environments.
- Redefine his identity in ways that prioritize the majority culture, especially when living away from home and outside the heritage language community.
- Struggle with feelings of inauthenticity, believing he is 'not a real' member of either his heritage or majority culture, particularly if his language skills weaken (Pavlenko & Blackledge, 2004).
- Question whether investing time in the heritage language is worth it, particularly if he perceives few immediate social or professional benefits.

The following strategies can help mitigate these challenges.

Try These Strategies

Ages 13 to 15: Maximizing Social Affirmation and Fun

At this stage, focus on low-stakes, high-fun social activities that normalize the heritage language and connect it to global trends.

- **Normalize Through Media and Pop Culture**

Host a multilingual media festival with films, TV shows or anime in the heritage language with subtitles. Discuss the modern slang, fashion or humor to show the culture is current and relevant, directly counteracting the feeling that the heritage culture is 'outdated' or 'irrelevant'.

- **Affirm Identity with High-Status Peers**

Facilitate a 'Cool Cousin' connection (in person or via video chat) with an older cousin or non-family mentor (ages 18 to 25) who is fluent and works in a field the teen admires (e.g. tech, music or design). This provides a visible role model who validates the language's compatibility with success and 'coolness.'

- **Integrate into Peer Activities**

Encourage joining a global gaming chat (parent-vetted group) related to your teen's interests where the heritage language is used. This shifts the language use from a 'home chore' to a tool necessary for social pleasure and performance within a peer context.

- **'Heritage Food, My Way'**

Let your teen prepare or adapt a favorite heritage dish. Encourage him to describe the recipe's origin, name the ingredients and explain each cooking step to a sibling or a relative who speaks the heritage language. You can support him by previewing the key vocabulary together. This activity allows your teen to share culture with confidence and to view the food and the language that accompanies it as a source of pride rather than embarrassment.

- **Use Humor and Creativity**

Exchange jokes, memes or funny video clips in the heritage language. This taps into your teen's growing appreciation for wordplay and irony, making the heritage language feel light and expressive.

Ages 16 to 19: Fostering Ownership and Future Value

The focus at this stage is on helping the teen see the heritage language as a key to autonomy, professional opportunity and self-definition, directly addressing feelings of inauthenticity.

- **Future Goal Alignment**

Help your teen create a draft of his résumé or college application essay. Explicitly focus on the power of the heritage language, framing it as a professional skill (e.g. 'Enhanced communication with X billion people' or 'Cross-cultural mediation experience'). This directly answers the question, 'Is this worth my time?' by linking the language to tangible, high-value professional assets.

- **Address 'Inauthenticity' Directly**

Encourage The Hybrid Identity Project. This personal, independent project (a blog, social media account or written reflection) allows the teen to explore and define his hybrid identity, such as translating song lyrics or writing photo captions into different language(s). This validates the feeling of being 'not enough of any one group' by defining the in-between space as a legitimate, unique strength.

- **Shift Public Use to a High-Status Domain**

Suggest an academic translation role. If proficient, ask him to voluntarily help translate short, official notices or school information for non-English-speaking parents in the community. This reframes public use as a form of service, expertise and leadership, elevating the language's status.

- **Deepen Cultural Nuance**

Facilitate an interview project. Have the teen interview a grandparent or community elder (in the heritage language) about a specific cultural or historical event. This strengthens family ties and provides the teen with a unique cultural depth that peers may lack.

- **Foster Autonomy and Authentic Expression**

Encourage independent engagement, allowing them to decide how and when to use the heritage language, reinforcing that the language is chosen, not imposed.
The core goal is to shift the heritage language from a source of perceived stigma to a source of pride and social capital (value within peer groups).

When development is uneven between languages

Adolescence is a period when uneven development between school and heritage languages often becomes especially visible. School languages tend to dominate in academic contexts, leading to gaps in heritage language literacy and domain-specific vocabulary (Montrul, 2023). Because the school language is consistently reinforced through textbooks, assignments, assessments and peer interactions, it quickly becomes the default medium for learning and self-expression (Guardado, 2002). In contrast, the heritage language is often confined to everyday conversation at home, which limits opportunities for advanced use such as academic writing, technical terminology or abstract reasoning (Hornberger, 2003b). Without deliberate support, expressive and receptive skills may shift rapidly toward the majority language, making it difficult for adolescents to sustain confidence in their heritage language in formal or cognitively demanding contexts.

Ages 13 to 15

For adolescents aged 13 to 15, this uneven development is compounded by heightened sensitivity to peer pressure and a strong desire for social belonging. At this stage, teens may hesitate to use their heritage language in public or may restrict it to private, home-based interactions for fear of standing out or being teased (Phinney, 1990). The result is often **compartmentalization**: Using the majority language exclusively in school and social contexts while reserving the heritage language for limited family exchanges. This split reinforces the dominance of the school language and contributes to weaker literacy development in the heritage language.

Moreover, at this stage, the challenge of asymmetrical literacy development often becomes apparent. Teens may read novels and compose essays in the school language with ease, while their heritage language literacy remains at a basic level, sometimes resembling that of a much younger child. Although oral fluency may be strong, writing and reading in the heritage language often lag behind. When Léandre and Dominique were teenagers, for example, their Chinese literacy curriculum in the Chinese school provided storybooks written for kindergartners. The mismatch between their age and the materials left them disengaged and unmotivated. This illustrates a common struggle: Literacy resources in the heritage language may not match the developmental stage or interests of adolescents, leaving them disconnected.

Ages 16 to 19

By late adolescence, identity questions become more nuanced, but the challenges of uneven development remain significant. Older teens may consciously distance themselves from the heritage language if they perceive it as limiting their integration into peer or academic environments. Some struggle with feelings of inauthenticity, worrying that weakening skills mean they are 'not a real' member of either their heritage or majority culture (Pavlenko & Blackledge, 2004). Others question whether continued investment in the heritage language is worthwhile, particularly when any immediate social or professional benefits are not evident. In both early and late adolescence, the dominance of the school language and the lack of balanced literacy opportunities make sustaining development of the heritage language particularly challenging. To help bridge the gap between your teen's heritage language and school language, you can try the following strategies.

Try These Activities

Ages 13 to 15

At this stage, peer approval matters more than ever, so the goal is helping your teen see the heritage language as natural, enjoyable and socially acceptable.

Bridge School Learning with Heritage Language Use

Encourage your teen to connect school learning with the heritage language. He might keep a brief journal explaining science concepts or summarizing history lessons in that language. If his heritage language is Polish, for example, you can help him use terms like fotosynteza (photosynthesis) or prawo Newtona (Newton's law) to reinforce classroom learning and build technical vocabulary. Linking schoolwork to family connections, such as translating a project to share with a grandparent, can also boost motivation.

Make the Language Social and Fun

Teens are more willing to use the heritage language when it feels playful and socially engaging. Share jokes, memes or TikTok clips in the heritage language, and play tongue twisters such as *'Fischers Fritz fischt frische Fische'* (German, 'Fisher's Fritz fishes fresh fish') or *'Les chaussettes de l'archiduchesse sont-elles sèches, archisèches?'* (French, 'Are the archduchess's socks dry, very dry?'). Humor and challenge reduce self-consciousness and make language use a fun, shared experience rather than a solitary task.

Encourage Peer Validation and Collaboration

Organize low-pressure, social activities where the heritage language is part of the fun, like a food festival or movie night. If your teen has cousins or friends who share the language, suggest collaborative projects such as making a short podcast, YouTube video or slideshow. The Jonson brothers, for example, co-created a German travel presentation with academic vocabulary they wouldn't normally use at home. These joint projects build both social belonging and confidence in the heritage language (Phinney, 1990).

Support Literacy through Creative Formats

Instead of limiting reading and writing to formal assignments, let your child explore comics, blogs or magazines in the heritage language that align with his interests in sports, music or gaming. Encourage texting, captions on social media or even short stories that draw on school topics; for example, writing a fictional diary entry in Spanish from the perspective of a historical figure studied in class. These formats feel authentic and keep literacy development age-appropriate.

Introduce Idioms and Expressions

Teens at this age are ready to appreciate **figurative** and **metaphorical** language (words or expressions with meanings beyond their literal sense). Teaching idioms, especially those with humor or vivid imagery, such as 炒鱿鱼 in Chinese ('to fry squid,' meaning to get fired from a job) or *avoir le cœur sur la main* in French ('to have one's heart on one's hand,' meaning to be generous), makes the heritage language more colorful and expressive. Teens often enjoy experimenting with these phrases in conversation, gaining tools to connect abstract thinking with cultural imagination.

Ages 16 to 19

By late adolescence, many begin living away from home, on college campuses or independently, which can make the heritage language feel distant or irrelevant. The goal is to show your teen that the heritage language is not just part of the past but a tool for identity, connection and future opportunities.

Connect the Language to Future Goals

Show your teen how heritage language proficiency can open doors in study abroad, internships or careers in multilingual workplaces (Hornberger, 2003b). Encourage adding the language to résumés, LinkedIn profiles or applications to highlight unique skills. Framing the language as a future asset rather than just a family obligation increases motivation.

Use Technology for Connection

If your teen lives away from home, set aside short weekly FaceTime or WhatsApp calls in the heritage language. Family group chats with jokes, memes or voice messages keep the language woven into everyday life while sustaining emotional ties (Guardado, 2002). Teens may also explore heritage language YouTube creators, podcasts or fandom forums to engage with peers beyond family.

Encourage Autonomy and Creative Expression

At this age, identity and independence matter most. Let your teen choose creative formats: Writing poems, composing music or making short films in the heritage language. Encourage projects that combine school learning with creative play, such as writing a fictional story in Chinese set in ancient Mesopotamia or translating a favorite song lyric into Hebrew. Creative ownership deepens literacy while honoring autonomy.

Deepen Cultural and Emotional Connections

Older teens often wrestle with feelings of authenticity, wondering if weakened skills mean they are 'not real' members of their heritage community (Pavlenko & Blackledge, 2004). Journaling in the heritage language, interviewing grandparents or creating a photo scrapbook with heritage language captions can help restore confidence and emotional connection. Cultural activities like these move the heritage language beyond the classroom into family life and identity.

Introduce Pragmatic and Colloquial Layers

Older teens are ready to explore nuance in tone, register and cultural context. Discuss how politeness, disagreement or humor are expressed differently across languages. Watching dramas, role-playing conversations or analyzing word choices (e.g. 您 (formal *you*) vs. 你 (informal *you*) in Mandarin) helps teens understand why social context matters. Even taboo registers, such as slang or foul language, can be discussed critically to illuminate tone, appropriateness and cultural nuance. This prepares teens to navigate real-world conversations that go beyond linguistic correctness.

Keep Literacy Authentic and Relevant

Support heritage language literacy through meaningful, age-appropriate activities. Encourage blogging, opinion pieces or **infographics** (visual summaries that combine text and images) in the heritage language on topics your teen cares about, such as politics, fashion or science. For example, your teen might create a travel blog or post captions in the heritage language on social media. These real-world projects turn literacy into a tool for communication, identity and pride.

When time management and competing priorities limit home language use

During adolescence, the overarching issue is that increasing school, extracurricular activities and social life leave little time for deliberate heritage language use. Without integration into existing routines, home language use becomes sporadic and vulnerable to decline (Wong Fillmore, 2000), and without deliberate efforts to embed practice within daily rhythms, development of the heritage language risks stalling or disappearing altogether.

Ages 13 to 15

This period is marked by significant changes in academic, social and personal life. Teens in this stage often begin encountering heavier schoolwork, more structured extracurricular activities and growing peer networks (Steinberg, 2014). As adolescents take on new responsibilities, they may experience conflicts between academic expectations and personal interests, which can leave heritage language learning marginalized. Developing literacy skills in a heritage language, especially reading and writing, requires consistent practice and cognitive effort (Cummins, 2000). However, during this period, many teens prioritize mainstream academic success, sports or social opportunities, often viewing heritage language activities as an 'extra' rather than a core commitment (Guardado, 2002).

For multilingual adolescents like my younger son Dominique, whose schedules included school, athletics and community activities, time management was an especially pressing issue. A full day of classes, followed by homework and sports practice, left little space for deliberate engagement with heritage language reading and writing. Without opportunities to use heritage languages meaningfully in everyday life, proficiency risks plateauing or declining (Wong Fillmore, 2000).

Ages 16 to 19

Late adolescence brings intensified academic and social pressures as teens prepare for life after high school. College entrance exams, advanced coursework, leadership roles, part-time jobs and social commitments all compete for time and attention (Eggles & Roeser, 2011). These years are often characterized by heightened autonomy and identity exploration, and language use may become increasingly tied to personal choices and peer influence (Norton, 2013). Development of the heritage language, requiring sustained investment, may be pushed aside as teens prioritize short-term goals such as test preparation, college applications and résumé-building activities.

For multilingual teens, the challenge is magnified: Maintaining multiple linguistic systems alongside these new responsibilities requires careful coordination and intentional parental support. The effort needed to sustain heritage language literacy, such as reading literature, writing essays or engaging in discussions on academic topics, can seem overwhelming when balanced against mainstream educational demands. Research suggests that without structured strategies, heritage language use in older adolescence often diminishes, even among highly motivated families (Montrul, 2016). The following intentional strategies may help.

Try These Strategies

Ages 13 to 15: Building Language into Daily Routines

Pair Language Practice with Existing Activities

Instead of adding more to an already full schedule, integrate the heritage language into what your teen is already doing. Listen to music, news or podcasts in the heritage language during commutes, workouts or meal prep.

Make Short Bursts of Practice Meaningful

Even 10 to 15 minutes a day can be effective if used purposefully. Encourage your teen to read a short article, text a relative or watch a brief video in the heritage language before bedtime. Regular microinteractions reinforce continuity and prevent long lapses.

Use School Assignments as Language Opportunities

Encourage your teen to explain homework concepts, presentations or creative writing ideas in the heritage language. Translating or paraphrasing helps deepen understanding while maintaining active use of the heritage vocabulary.

Leverage Technology for Quick Connections

Use messaging apps (such as WhatsApp and WeChat) to maintain heritage language chats with relatives or peers. Encourage your teen to send quick updates, voice notes or photos with captions in the heritage language. Small, consistent exchanges fit easily into busy routines.

Create Weekend Rituals

Set aside one weekend morning or meal each week for heritage language conversation, such as Sunday breakfast discussions about the week or cooking a cultural dish together. Making it a recurring ritual keeps practice consistent and meaningful without feeling forced.

Ages 16 to 19: Linking Language to Goals and Autonomy

Connect Heritage Language to Future Aspirations

Show how multilingual proficiency enhances college essays, interviews and global opportunities. Encourage your teen to include the heritage language in academic projects, volunteer work or part-time jobs that value bilingual communication.

Encourage Independent Learning through Interest-Based Media

Suggest heritage language podcasts, online magazines or documentaries related to your teen's passions, such as technology, global politics or environmental issues.

Teens are more likely to engage when the content aligns with their personal interests.

Build Language into Résumé-Building Activities

If your teen volunteers, participates in clubs or works part-time, identify ways to use the heritage language, such as translating materials, greeting customers or assisting newcomers. These authentic uses reinforce practical value and confidence.

Encourage Self-Paced Literacy Challenges

Invite your teen to set a small, personal goal, such as reading one short story per month or writing journal reflections in the heritage language. Encourage digital journaling or blog entries that integrate multimedia (photos, music or voice clips).

Reframe Heritage Language as Stress Relief, Not Obligation

Position heritage language activities as enjoyable, restorative breaks from academic pressure. Watching a favorite film, listening to songs or chatting with a relative abroad can provide emotional grounding and cultural connection amid a busy schedule.

The key is integration, not addition. Rather than carving out extra time, weave the heritage language naturally into your teen's existing world. When the language becomes a companion to their studies, interests and relationships, it thrives, even in the busiest of lives.

When there is emotional disconnection from the heritage language

Not all resistance to heritage language use stems from cognitive challenges or logistical barriers. Often, it is emotional. Teens may associate the language with feelings of embarrassment, inadequacy or past negative experiences. A rigid or unsupportive teacher at a weekend language school, teasing from peers about their accent or broader societal attitudes that devalue non-dominant languages can all contribute to this emotional distance. These encounters can leave lasting impressions, causing teens to disengage from the language and see it not as a bridge to identity or belonging, but as a source of discomfort or shame (Galmiche, 2017).

Ages 13 to 15

During the early to middle adolescent years, young people are particularly sensitive to peer evaluation and issues of social acceptance (Brown & Larson, 2009). At this stage, heritage language use may feel risky in public spaces, as speaking differently can highlight perceived differences and invite unwanted attention. Teens may worry about making mistakes or being labeled 'foreign', especially in school environments where monolingual norms dominate (He, 2006). Emotional resistance during this period often manifests as withdrawal from heritage language speaking opportunities outside the home or reluctance to engage in activities such as reading aloud or participating in cultural events.

Ages 16 to 19

In later adolescence, emotional disconnection may take on a different form. As teens prepare for transitions to college, work or independent living, they often reevaluate what aspects of their identity to prioritize (Arnett, 2014). Heritage language use may become framed less as a source of embarrassment and more as a personal choice tied to identity, belonging and future opportunities. For some, this re-evaluation may reignite interest and pride, especially when heritage language skills are linked to career prospects, travel or deepened family relationships. For others, however, lingering negative experiences, such as feeling judged for their accent or grammar, can reinforce disengagement, with language use restricted to minimal or perfunctory exchanges at home. Trying the strategies below may help.

Try These Activities

Ages 13 to 15

Rebuild Positive Associations

At this stage, your teen may feel self-conscious about speaking the heritage language. You can make it enjoyable again by weaving the language into activities you already share. Watch a Japanese anime in the original language with subtitles, cook a traditional dish and name the ingredients in Spanish, or explore a gaming community that uses Mandarin. These small, enjoyable moments help your teen associate the language with fun and belonging rather than stress (Deci & Ryan, 2000).

Praise Effort over Accuracy

Teens are often highly sensitive to mistakes, so your encouragement makes a difference. If your teen tries French liaison in a casual sentence, celebrate the attempt even if it's not perfect. If he uses Hindi honorifics but mixes them up, praise the courage to try rather than pointing out errors right away. You might say, 'I love how you're trying new words; it makes our conversation richer.' This focus on effort, not perfection, nurtures confidence and resilience (Yeager & Dweck, 2012).

Ages 16 to 19

Connect Language to Personal Goals

Connect language to personal goals. Older teens are thinking about college, work and independence, so show how the heritage language supports those plans. Your teen might add multilingual skills to a résumé, use Amharic before a family trip to Ethiopia or read travel blogs in Spanish or French when exploring study-abroad options. He might also read Hebrew texts tied to family traditions when preparing for a religious milestone. Praise effort as well as results, whether he practices a difficult phrase or drafts a résumé in the heritage language. This helps him see the language as a developing skill, strengthening confidence and long-term commitment (Yeager & Dweck, 2012).

Use Storytelling to Rekindle Bonds

Storytelling is one of the most powerful ways to bring heritage languages back into daily life because it ties language learning to memory, emotion and identity. Recording elder relatives' narratives can deepen both emotional and linguistic connection (Kouritzin, 2000). You might invite your teen to interview grandparents about their childhood in Cantonese or ask an aunt to share migration stories in Arabic. These conversations can be recorded on a phone then replayed together, pausing to discuss unfamiliar words or phrases. Teens can also turn these narratives into creative projects, such as translating them into English for younger cousins, writing a family holiday newsletter or even creating short videos with subtitles. In languages with strong oral traditions, such as Amharic proverbs or Hindi folktales, collecting and retelling these stories helps teens see themselves as cultural carriers. Storytelling not only strengthens vocabulary and grammar in authentic contexts but also affirms your teen's role in preserving family history, which can transform the heritage language from a source of discomfort into a source of pride.

When pragmatic and cultural nuances create barriers in heritage language use

For many multilingual adolescents, the challenge is not only whether they know words and structures in their heritage language, but whether they can use the language in ways that are socially, culturally and contextually appropriate. **Pragmatics** (the ability to adapt speech to the setting, relationship and purpose) develops gradually across adolescence, but in heritage languages, it often lags behind mainstream language development (Taguchi, 2019). A teen may, for instance, know how to form polite requests in Spanish but still sound abrupt when speaking with grandparents, or may be able to read Chinese characters fluently yet not follow conversational humor among peers. These gaps can limit not only communicative competence but also a sense of belonging in heritage-speaking communities.

Ages 13 to 15

At this stage, adolescents are increasingly aware of social hierarchies, peer dynamics and identity negotiations (Steinberg, 2014). Their mainstream language often reflects this shift, with flexible use of **registers** (different ways language is used depending on the social context, purpose and audience, such as formal and informal), slang and irony. In contrast, their heritage language may remain restricted to **formulaic exchanges** (a routine or fixed phrase used in familiar social situations rather than created spontaneously, such as 'How are you?'), leaving them less able to navigate everyday interactional subtleties. For example, a 14-year-old might be able to say 'Can I borrow this?' in Mandarin (我可以借这个吗?) but may not know how to soften the request with the culturally expected phrase 麻烦你了 (sorry to trouble you), which makes the interaction more polite and contextually appropriate. Similarly, a teen may translate jokes or sarcasm from the mainstream language directly into the heritage language, but fail to elicit laughter because the pragmatic cues do not transfer neatly across languages (He, 2008).

These pragmatic gaps often lead adolescents to avoid using the heritage language outside the family, reinforcing attrition in domains where nuanced social use is most critical (Wong Fillmore, 2000).

Ages 16 to 19

Older teens face even greater pragmatic demands. As they prepare for adulthood, they must navigate formal and informal registers, culturally embedded idioms and even taboo or slang language. Their mainstream language typically equips them for academic presentations, peer banter and digital communication, whereas the heritage language often lags behind in these domains (Montrul, 2016). For instance, a 17-year-old who can write a polished essay in French may still struggle to use casual expressions with cousins in France, sounding overly formal or 'bookish.' Similarly, teens may not recognize when certain words carry strong connotations in cultural context. When Léandre visited China, he often heard the common expletive '他妈的' (literally 'his mother's,' roughly equivalent to the English *mother-f****) and asked me, quite puzzled, why people were always talking about their mothers. The incident highlights how a lack of pragmatic and cultural understanding can lead to confusion or social missteps. Without exposure to informal registers, teens risk developing an incomplete communicative repertoire that does not match their peers' or relatives' lived experiences. You can try the following strategies to help your teen strengthen his understanding and use of the heritage language in socially and culturally appropriate ways.

Try These Strategies

Ages 13 to 15

Model and Practice Politeness Routines

Teach honorifics, indirect requests and culturally embedded softeners explicitly. Role-play everyday scenarios, like borrowing items, declining invitations or asking for help, so teens become more comfortable using culturally expected forms.

Encourage Intergenerational Conversations

Structure regular conversations with grandparents or older relatives. At this stage, adolescents are still shaping their sense of respect and hierarchy, so practicing culturally respectful registers in family settings can deepen awareness of honorifics and idiomatic phrases (Guardado, 2002).

Expose Teens to Humor and Informal Speech

Introduce mild slang, jokes or simple idiomatic expressions in the heritage language. Discuss why some expressions don't translate directly and help them recognize when informal speech is appropriate and when it is not.

Ages 16 to 19

Promote Peer Collaboration in the Heritage Languages

Encourage collaborative projects such as heritage language podcasts, online group chats or creative writing pieces. Older teens value peer approval and autonomy, so peer-centered activities make heritage-language use feel authentic and socially relevant.

Introduce Teens to Slang, Idioms and Everyday Informal Expressions – Even Mild Profanity-Wthin Safe and Guided Contexts

At this age, they can reflect on what is appropriate in different situations. Watching subtitled movies, listening to podcasts or exploring social media clips together can open the door to conversations about how humor, sarcasm or strong words work in real-life interactions. This not only builds their language skills but also helps them develop judgment about when and where certain expressions are acceptable (He, 2008).

Integrate Pragmatics into Academic Crossovers

Encourage debates, skits or mock interviews in the heritage language that mirror real-world social dynamics. For example, debating a current issue in Chinese or Spanish fosters both argumentative vocabulary and turn-taking strategies.

When language-specific challenges become more evident

As children enter their teenage years, the more complex features of their heritage language become increasingly evident, especially when it differs greatly from the dominant community language. These challenges may appear in phonology, vocabulary, grammar, sentence structure or pragmatic use in social settings.

Ages 13 to 15

- **Phonology:** A heritage language accent may become a visible marker for some teens. Influenced by the mainstream language, teens may exhibit non-conventional phonological features in the heritage language. For instance, heritage speakers of Mandarin can show reduced tonal contrasts or atypical neutral-tone patterns that lower intelligibility (e.g. 妈 *mā* 'mother' vs. 骂 *mà* 'to scold') (Chang & Yao, 2016). In French, bilingual children, including many heritage language learners, may show variable and sometimes omitted liaison, a well-documented locus of difficulty in acquisition (Nicoladis & Paradis, 2011). Similar cross-linguistic influence appears in Spanish, where English-dominant heritage speakers may weaken or misarticulate rhotics, especially the trilled /r/ (Amengual, 2016). In Arabic, studies report challenges with maintaining emphatic/plain contrasts among bilinguals (Al Omary, 2024).
- **Lexicon and semantics:** As teens grow, their heritage language vocabulary often reflects the settings in which they use it. Though they may communicate easily in everyday conversations, gaps can emerge in academic or specialized areas. For instance, a teen may know common Spanish words like *comida* ('food') but be unfamiliar with more subject-specific terms such as *nutrición* ('nutrition') (Montrul, 2016).
- **Morphosyntax:** Heritage language speakers may simplify complex grammatical forms in their heritage language. These patterns can vary widely across languages. For example, Russian heritage-speaking teens may say *u mama* instead of *u mamy* ('at Mom's'), Turkish heritage speakers may misapply vowel harmony (*kitap-ler* instead of *kitaplar*) and Korean speakers may omit tense consonants or honorific markers. English influence can also shape syntax: Chinese learners may rely on subject–verb–object order instead of topic-prominent structures (这个书, 我看过 'This book, I have read'), Japanese speakers may omit particles such as *wa* or *ga*, and German learners may drop verb-final order in subordinate clauses (*Ich weiß, er kommt* instead of *Ich weiß, dass er kommt*; 'I know that he is coming') (Jeon, 2008; Kupisch & Rothman, 2018; Polinsky, 2018).
- **Pragmatics:** Teens often know the right words but may miss the cultural subtleties that guide when and how to use them. For instance, a Korean heritage speaker might say 주세요 ('give me') without adding polite endings such as -요 or -세요, whereas a French speaker might skip social niceties like *s'il vous plaît* ('please') or *merci bien* ('thank you kindly'). Arabic speakers may forget to open with greetings such as السلام عليكم (*as-salāmu 'alaykum*), and Spanish speakers might use direct refusals like *no quiero* ('I don't want [it]) instead of softened forms like *quizás más tarde* ('maybe later'). These gaps make heritage-language use outside the family feel awkward.

Ages 16 to 19

- **Phonology:** Older adolescents may exhibit non-native accents, sometimes intentionally, as a marker of identity or group affiliation (Gatbonton *et al.*, 2005). Additionally, specific phonological adjustments may occur across languages; for example, Korean heritage speakers may simplify tense consonants, and Vietnamese learners may neutralize tonal contrasts (Derwing & Munro; Gatbonton *et al.*, 2005). Such patterns, though natural in multilingual development, can sometimes reduce intelligibility and affect speakers' confidence in academic or professional settings.

- **Lexicon and semantics:** Vocabulary limitations become more evident in academic and professional domains. Chinese teens may lack scientific terms like 光合作用 ('photosynthesis'), Spanish learners may struggle with idioms or figurative expressions, and Arabic speakers may use colloquial vocabulary while lacking proficiency in Modern Standard Arabic (Albirini, 2016).
- **Morphosyntax:** Fossilized simplifications persist. Russian teens may avoid genitive plurals, Turkish speakers may omit evidential markers like *-miş* and Korean speakers may rely on informal endings, avoiding socially expected honorifics. English transfer continues to affect syntax, including German subordinate clauses (*Ich weiß, er kommt* vs. *Ich weiß, dass er kommt*; 'I know that he is coming') (Kupisch & Rothman, 2018; Polinsky, 2018).
- **Pragmatics:** Late adolescents face increasing pragmatic demands across both academic and informal contexts. A French heritage speaker, for instance, may sound overly formal when addressing cousins by using *vous* instead of the more familiar *tu*, whereas others may miss culturally and linguistically appropriate cues, misunderstanding their social meaning. Similar gaps occur in other languages, for example, underusing discourse markers such as *pues* or *entonces* in Spanish can make speech sound abrupt or less natural. Though often subtle, these pragmatic limitations can shape how heritage speakers are perceived by others (Pavlenko & Blackledge, 2004).

Try These Activities

Ages 13 to 15

Phonology

- **Model pronunciation through media:** Use music, podcasts or tongue twisters that appeal to teens. For example, in Spanish, practice rolled *r* sounds with tongue twisters like '*Erre con erre cigarro, erre con erre barril*' ('R with R cigar, R with R barrel'). In German, tongue twisters such as '*Fischers Fritz fischt frische Fische*'('Fisher's Fritz fishes fresh fish') help strengthen consonant clusters. For older teens, singing along to rap or pop songs in the heritage language can sharpen rhythm, intonation and pronunciation in a fun, age-appropriate way.
- **Normalize variation:** Discuss accent differences openly. For instance, explain why Spanish heritage teens raised in the US may pronounce *pero* ('but') with an English /ɹ/ sound, and how this differs from native-like [ɾ].

Lexicon and Semantics

- **Build domain-specific vocabulary:** Connect school content to the heritage language. A Spanish-speaking teen studying biology can learn *célula* ('cell') alongside English *cell*. A Hindi-speaking teen might learn परमाणु (paramāṇu, 'atom') when taking science.
- **Use interest-based materials:** Encourage comics or blogs. A Japanese-speaking teen who likes anime can read 少年ジャンプ (*Shōnen Jump*), gaining vocabulary not covered in home conversations.
- **Teach emotional words:** Adolescents experience heightened emotional intensity. Supporting them in expressing nuanced emotions in their heritage language strengthens both linguistic and emotional competence. Teaching emotional words (e.g. *triste*, *déçu*, 불안한[*bulanhan*, *'anxious'*) helps teens navigate self-expression, empathy and social connection across languages (Pavlenko, 2008).

Morphosyntax

- **Highlight authentic structures:** Compare English and heritage syntax. A Mandarin learner can contrast *Zhège shū, wǒ kàn-guò* (这个书, 我看过, 'This book, I have read') with English 'I have read this book.' A German learner can see why *Ich weiß, dass er kommt* ('I know that he is coming') differs from English 'I know he comes.'
- **Practice through guided writing:** A Russian teen can practice writing sentences with the correct genitive plural, e.g. много столов ('many tables'), rather than the simplified много стол.

Pragmatics

- **Model and practice politeness routines:** In Korean, role-play how to ask politely using honorific endings (e.g. 주세요 instead of plain 줘 for 'give me').
- **Encourage intergenerational conversations:** Have teens ask their grandparents for stories in Spanish, practicing honorific forms like *usted* instead of *tú*.
- **Expose teens to humor and informal speech:** Share age-appropriate jokes or idioms. For example, in French, introduce *poser un lapin* ('to put a rabbit, meaning to stand someone up') and explain the cultural imagery behind it.

Ages 16 to 19

Phonology

- **Refine pronunciation through self-monitoring:** A Vietnamese teen can record themselves pronouncing tone minimal pairs (e.g. *ma, má, mả, mã, mạ*) and compare this with native models.

- **Integrate pronunciation into performance:** A Korean teen could perform in a church choir or drama group, which provides repeated exposure to formal honorific forms and tense consonants.

Lexicon and Semantics

- **Expand academic and figurative vocabulary:** Encourage older teens to read news articles. For instance, a Chinese learner might read 人民日报 (*People's Daily*) to pick up academic terms like 经济发展 ('economic development').

Promote creative expression: A French heritage learner could blog using idiomatic expressions like *avoir le cafard* ('to have the cockroach, meaning to feel down'), which deepens understanding of metaphorical language.

Morphosyntax

- **Address fossilized forms:** A Turkish learner can practice evidential markers like *-miş*. For example, compare O *gitmiş* ('He apparently left') with O *gitti* ('He left').
- **Practice authentic sentence structures:** A Japanese teen can write short essays using particles correctly (e.g. contrasting *wa* and *ga*). A German learner might deliberately construct subordinate clauses (*weil er krank ist*, 'because he is sick') to strengthen verb-final awareness.

Pragmatics

- **Promote peer collaboration:** Encourage your teen to work with peers on heritage language projects. For example, they might create a Spanish language podcast with friends, weaving in discourse markers like *pues* and *entonces* to make their conversations sound natural and connected.
- **Introduce slang, idioms and informal expressions:** Show how everyday expressions change meaning depending on context. In Mandarin, the word 厉害 (*lìhai*) can mean 'awesome' or 'terrible.' In Arabic, teens can compare colloquial greetings like شو الأخبار؟ (*shū l-akhbār?*, 'what's up?') with the formal ones used with elders.
- **Discuss foul language as pragmatics:** Older teens often hear or experiment with strong words in school or online. Rather than ignoring it, guide them in understanding when such language is inappropriate and why it carries weight in different cultures. For example, explain the social impact of French expletives like *putain* (prostitude, meaning 'damn,' 'bloody hell'), or Mandarin phrases like 他妈的 (his mother's, meaning mother f***). Help your teen analyze how peers use these words for humor, frustration or emphasis, and contrast that with respectful alternatives for family or formal settings. This helps them develop judgment rather than simply copying what they hear.

- **Integrate pragmatics into academic crossovers:** Use school-style activities to highlight register differences. In debates, for instance, encourage French learners to use formal disagreement strategies such as *Je comprends votre point, mais...* ('I understand your point, but...') and contrast them with more informal rebuttals they might use with their peers.

Monitor Your Teen's Heritage Language Progress: Parent As Researcher in Action

Continuing to monitor your teen's heritage language development is an essential part of supporting their long-term growth, especially during adolescence. This stage is particularly critical because it is often the last period when your teen will spend time at home before moving on to college, work or other independent pursuits. While early childhood is about laying the foundations and middle childhood is about consolidating linguistic skills (Lenneberg, 1967, adolescence brings new dynamics: Peer influence, identity exploration and the desire for independence (Erikson, 1968). These factors can either strengthen or weaken your teen's connection to the heritage language, which makes careful monitoring during these years even more important than in the earlier stages.

Like in the younger years, monitoring begins with an understanding of the developmental patterns typical of adolescence, followed by deeper and more targeted observation. Careful attention allows you to see which domains your teen is thriving in, where hesitation or gaps may appear and how confidence across different areas is shifting over time. For instance, you may notice that your teen is comfortable conversing with relatives but less confident in academic writing or public speaking in the heritage language. Or they may embrace slang and casual conversation with peers in one language while avoiding formal or professional use of the heritage language. These contrasts highlight both strengths and vulnerabilities.

At this stage, things can turn both ways. For some teens, adolescence brings a deeper sense of pride and confidence in their heritage language as they use it to connect with relatives, explore cultural traditions or express their individuality. For others, the pull of school pressures and peer influence may make them less inclined to use the heritage language, leading to uneven growth or hesitation in certain areas. Both patterns are natural and neither signals an endpoint. What matters most is that you continue to notice these shifts and provide encouragement, creating opportunities for your teen to experience the heritage language as relevant, meaningful and empowering.

Monitoring heritage language growth in adolescence is therefore not just about tracking progress; it is about recognizing these shifting dynamics and intentionally guiding your teen to carry the heritage language with confidence into adulthood. The support you provide now helps safeguard not only linguistic competence but also cultural connection and personal identity, ensuring that your teen leaves home with the heritage language as a source of pride and empowerment rather than uncertainty or loss.

Step 1: Understanding typical development patterns and possible multilingual variations

Table 5.1 provides a developmental overview of the language milestones in adolescence, highlights possible multilingual variations, and identifies areas that may need attention or additional support.

With this developmental understanding, you can now track your teen's heritage language growth using Table 5.2.

Step 2: Conducting deeper observations

For the adolescent years, especially once the basic language structures are mastered, it is helpful to focus assessment on **literate language** (the advanced forms of language used in reading, writing and cultural or community settings) and on the complex, abstract uses of communication. In heritage language contexts, this may include reading community newsletters or religious texts, writing letters, emails or messages to relatives, or participating in cultural storytelling and performances. These measures allow you to monitor your teen's multilingual maintenance and progress by examining her ability to structure ideas, organize information and reason effectively through language.

Ages 13 to 15

At this stage, teens begin to communicate with greater sophistication. They learn to pack more complex information into single thought units and to express ideas that are abstract, inferential and emotionally nuanced. Tracking their heritage language progress at this stage involves observing how their language grows in structure, complexity and meaning across both spoken and written forms. Several useful measures include the following.

- **Mean length of T-unit/C-unit:** A T-unit (terminable unit) consists of one main clause together with all its subordinate clauses, and is typically used in writing or formal speech (Hunt, 1970). For example, in this sentence, 'We saw the new movie that Jeremy had recommended when we went to California, ' the main clause is 'We saw the new movie,' and the subordinate clauses are 'that Jeremy had recommended' and 'when we went to California.' All three parts together form one T-unit. A **C-unit** (communication unit) includes one main clause together with its subordinate clauses, as well as elliptical responses that can stand alone in conversation (Leadholm & Miller, 1992). It is typically used to analyze spoken or informal language. For example, this exchange contains two C-units:

  A: 'Do you want to come with me?'
  B: 'Sure.'

- The response 'Sure' functions as a complete C-unit because it stands alone as a meaningful conversational reply, even though it does not contain a full clause. It would not count as a T-unit, since T-units require a complete main clause with any

Table 5.1 Characteristics of major language development and multilingual variations during adolescence

Age range	Domain	General development patterns	Possible multilingual variations (examples of linguistic interactions)	When to pay attention
13 to 15	Phonology and prosody	Speech is fully intelligible, but teens experiment with intonation, rhythm and accent to fit peer groups. May reduce or exaggerate the heritage language accent.	Accent shifting across languages; heritage language prosody may weaken without regular use. Some teens deliberately adopt or avoid 'foreign' accents to align with identity.	Strong, consistent foreign accent that limits intelligibility in any language; avoidance of speaking the heritage language because of accent insecurity.
	Vocabulary growth and precision	Rapid expansion of academic and abstract vocabulary (e.g. 'justice,' 'hypothesis'), especially in school-related domains. Increased use of discipline-specific terminology in oral and written work.	Vocabulary distribution may be uneven across languages; academic terms are often acquired in the school language while culturally bound concepts remain in the heritage language. Morphological patterns may differ (e.g. affixation vs. standalone words).	Persistent gaps in subject-specific vocabulary across all languages; inability to recall or use key terms in familiar academic contexts.
	Syntax and discourse organization	Use of more complex sentence structures (subordinate clauses, passive voice, logical connectors). Growth in cohesive devices for oral and written argumentation.	Cross-linguistic influence in clause structure (e.g. subject–verb–object vs. subject–object–verb). Switching between explicit subordination markers and implicit markers.	Frequent grammatical errors in all languages; inability to construct cohesive arguments or narratives.
	Pragmatics and social language	Improved adaptation of language to audience, tone and setting; emerging mastery of formal vs. informal registers.	Pragmatic adjustments may differ by language (e.g. honorifics vs. modal verbs). Switching politeness strategies depending on cultural expectations.	Consistently inappropriate tone or register for context; inability to adjust speech when speaking to peers vs. adults.
	Figurative and inferential language	Increased comprehension and use of idioms, metaphors, irony and sarcasm; growth in inferencing skills.	Figurative expressions may be language-specific. Teens may map, separate or creatively blend metaphors across systems.	Difficulty understanding common idioms or sarcasm in any language; over-literal interpretations that may lead to social misunderstandings.
	Identity expression	Experimentation with dialects, slang and sociolects to establish peer identity and individuality.	Code-switching for identity signaling. Emotional expression may be language-specific.	Sudden withdrawal from heritage language use; discomfort or embarrassment using certain languages in peer settings.
	Writing development	More structured essays; ability to present arguments and integrate evidence. Improved awareness of audience and purpose.	Transfer of rhetorical structures across languages. Orthographic differences may affect writing fluency.	Consistent difficulty organizing written work; inability to adapt writing style for different purposes.

(*Continued*)

Table 5.1 *Continued.*

Age range	Domain	General development patterns	Possible multilingual variations (examples of linguistic interactions)	When to pay attention
16 to 19	Phonology and prosody	Stable phonological system with near-adult control of accent and prosody. Ability to shift style, intonation and accent deliberately depending on the context.	Multilingual teens may consciously maintain or suppress accent features in different languages; exposure to peer or media input may reinforce one accent over another.	Strong heritage accent loss or rigid inability to adapt prosody/register in social or professional contexts.
	Vocabulary growth and conceptual depth	Sophisticated command of abstract, technical and discipline-specific vocabulary; nuanced lexical choices in academic and professional contexts.	Advanced concepts may be easier to express in the dominant school language; heritage language vocabulary may remain domain-specific unless reinforced through formal study.	Persistent lack of precision in the vocabulary in academic or professional communication; failure to grasp abstract concepts in any language.
	Syntax and discourse mastery	Flexible manipulation of complex syntax; skillful use of rhetorical devices (parallelism, inversion). Ability to adapt structure to persuasive, narrative or analytical purposes.	Structural adaptation across typologically different languages (e.g. gender agreement vs. no agreement).	Reliance on overly simple sentence structures; difficulty following or producing complex written or spoken arguments.
	Advanced pragmatics	Nuanced management of formality, humor and irony, culturally sensitive negotiation of meaning in diverse contexts.	High cultural-pragmatic agility, such as indirect disagreement in one language vs. direct styles in another.	Misunderstanding subtle humor or indirect language; frequent communication breakdowns in intercultural contexts.
	Figurative and metaphorical sophistication	Mastery of multilayered metaphors and intertextual references; creation of original figurative expressions in writing and speech.	Creative blending of metaphors from multiple languages and traditions.	Over-reliance on literal language; inability to interpret symbolic or metaphorical meaning in complex texts.
	Language and identity integration	Consolidation of personal and social identity through language use; stable patterns of register-shifting across settings.	Strategic identity positioning, using one language for solidarity and another for authority. Complex, deliberate code-switching.	Discomfort or lack of confidence using one or more languages central to identity; sudden heritage language loss.
	Academic and professional writing	Ability to produce extended, coherent and well-argued texts; genre-specific writing (e.g. research reports, personal statements).	Mastery of multiple rhetorical traditions. Literacy skills transfer depends on orthographic and rhetorical similarity.	Difficulty meeting academic writing expectations; inability to transfer writing skills between languages.

Table 5.2 Ways to track your teen's heritage language development

Domain	How to check (ages 13 to 15)	How to check (ages 16 to 19)	Your observation and action (example)
Phonology (pronunciation, accent, intonation)	Listen during casual conversations or when your teen records social media clips. Pay attention to accent shifts or code-switching across peer groups. Encourage reading aloud or song practice in the heritage language.	Ask your teen to record mock interviews or presentations in the heritage language. Encourage pronunciation self-assessment using apps or recordings. Discuss accent and identity – what it means to 'sound' bilingual.	**Observation:** Softens Arabic emphatics or avoids rolling *r* in Spanish. **Action:** Model pronunciation and discuss comfort vs. identity balance.
Lexicon and semantics (vocabulary, word meanings, expressions)	Track use of school and hobby-related vocabulary. Encourage bilingual glossaries for new subjects. Discuss slang or peer phrases across languages.	Encourage advanced vocabulary use: Emotional, abstract and academic terms. Integrate debates, essays or creative writing in the heritage language. Support reflective journaling on emotions and values.	**Observation:** Uses English for complex emotions. **Action:** Teach nuanced emotional vocabulary (e.g. *déçu*, *agradecido*, 불안한), and connect with real-life reflections (Pavlenko, 2008).
Morphosyntax (grammar, sentence structure)	Observe sentence complexity in messages or school assignments. Encourage storytelling that uses connectors (e.g. 'because,' 'however').	Review written or spoken essays for clause variety and correct tense usage. Encourage bilingual translation of news or academic texts.	**Observation:** Simplifies verb tenses or drops endings in heritage language writing. **Action:** Use writing prompts that elicit diverse tenses and connectors.
Pragmatics (context, politeness, humor, register)	Compare speech across contexts (home, school and online). Role-play greetings and apologies in culturally appropriate forms.	Observe register choice in formal settings (emails, interviews). Discuss how humor and sarcasm differ across languages.	**Observation:** Sounds overly formal with peers (uses *vous* instead of *tu*). **Action:** Practice role-plays for switching registers appropriately.
Text and discourse (storytelling, argumentation, organization)	Ask for oral summaries of books or shows. Encourage journaling or creative writing.	Review essays or social commentaries written in the heritage language. Discuss structure, tone and coherence in longer writing.	**Observation:** Struggles with transitions and connectors. **Action:** Create outlines together; practice linking ideas naturally.
Everyday language use (code-switching, emotional vocabulary, confidence)	Note when switching occurs (friend groups, online chats). Ask how your teen feels about each language.	Observe how confidently your teen uses the heritage language in public or professional settings. Encourage volunteering or mentoring younger heritage learners.	**Observation:** Avoids the heritage language with new peers. **Action:** Invite participation in bilingual clubs or community events.
Digital literacy (using technology to strengthen the heritage language)	Explore heritage-language podcasts, channels or forums. Encourage bilingual commentaries or reviews.	Support independent digital projects (blogs, video essays or coding tutorials) in the heritage language. Discuss online linguistic identity.	**Observation:** Consumes heritage language media passively. **Action:** Encourage weekly posts or captions in the heritage language.

subordinate clauses attached. Tracking the mean length of T-unit (MLTU) or mean length of C-unit (MLCU) goes beyond MLU, which stabilizes around age 6, offering a clearer measure of adolescent language growth in both formal and conversational contexts.

- **Clause density:** This measure captures the number of clauses (main and subordinate) per T-unit or C-unit and reflects syntactic complexity (Hunt, 1970). For example, in 'We saw the new movie that Jeremy had recommended when we went to California,' there is one main clause and two subordinate clauses, producing a clause density of 3.0. During early to middle adolescence (ages 12–15), the typical clause density ranges from 1.6 to 1.9 (Hunt, 1970). Scores below 1.6 suggest that the teen may benefit from richer language input and more opportunities for complex sentence use, while scores above 1.9 indicate syntactic skills that are above average for this developmental stage. As clause density increases, it signals your teen's growing ability to embed ideas and express complex relationships-skills that emerge strongly in expository or persuasive tasks.
- **Comprehension of figurative language:** During adolescence, teens begin to grasp that language often conveys meanings beyond its literal sense. For example, understanding that 'The exam was a piece of cake' means 'The exam was easy,' rather than something related to dessert, reflects this growing awareness. Recognizing idioms, metaphors and subtle sarcasm signals both linguistic and cognitive maturity as teens learn to interpret tone, context and implied meaning in more sophisticated ways (Nippold, 2016).
- **Narrative cohesion:** This refers to the logical linking of ideas within a story or argument through transitions and cohesive devices. For example: 'The plan failed; however, they tried a different strategy, consequently improving the results' (Scott, 2004). Strong narrative cohesion demonstrates that teens can organize and connect ideas clearly, using discourse markers and transitions to produce coherent, well-structured communication.

Ages 16 to 19

By late adolescence, teens demonstrate adultlike communication, showing mastery of abstract, persuasive and socially adaptive language across contexts. Their heritage language growth is no longer about grammatical form alone but about expressing reasoning, emotion and identity with maturity and subtlety. They now use language to argue, reflect, persuade and navigate complex social situations, skills that signal both academic advancement and emerging adulthood (Nippold, 2016).

At this stage, heritage language use becomes intentional and reflective. Teens use language as a tool for intellectual exploration and self-expression, drawing on increasingly complex structures and diverse registers. Monitoring development now involves paying attention to how language supports reasoning, persuasion and nuanced self-representation. In addition to earlier measures such as MLTU, MLCU and clause density, several deeper indicators highlight how teens use language for higher-level reasoning and cultural navigation.

- **Clausal density and sentence variety:** This measure reflects how teens pack information and relationships into complex sentences. As they engage in debates or reflective writing, they combine multiple subordinate and coordinate clauses to express layered ideas or contrasts (Berman & Nir-Sagiv, 2007). For example: 'Although I grew up speaking Spanish at home, I realize that English dominates my academic life, which sometimes makes me feel disconnected from my roots.' During late adolescence, the typical clause density range falls between 2.0 and 2.4 clauses per T-unit or C-unit (Nippold, 2016). Scores below 2.0 suggest that additional support in using complex and embedded structures may be helpful, whereas scores above 2.4 indicate advanced syntactic development. Increasing clausal density and sentence variety reflects growth in both cognitive sophistication and linguistic flexibility and are key indicators of mature academic and reflective language use.
- **Lexical sophistication and precision:** Older adolescents expand their vocabulary to include abstract, technical and emotionally nuanced terms. In the heritage language, this means mastering synonyms with subtle distinctions and culturally specific emotion words. For example, a teen who differentiates *pena* (sadness, pity) from *vergüenza* (shame, embarrassment) in Spanish, or 气愤 (*qìfèn*, anger) from 难过 (*nánguò*, upset) in Mandarin, demonstrates growing sensitivity to emotional and cultural nuance. Tracking lexical precision reveals how teens use language to express complex emotions and construct arguments with clarity and depth.
- **Comprehension of complex figurative language:** Late adolescents begin to understand layered non-literal expressions, idioms and irony, which are hallmarks of near-adult linguistic sophistication (Nippold, 2016). For example, interpreting the metaphor 'The judicial system is a vast, creaking clockwork mechanism, prone to grinding halts and unpredictable speeds,' requires grasping both the imagery and the underlying critique. This level of comprehension reflects advanced linguistic, cognitive and cultural maturity.
- **Argumentative and persuasive expression:** At this stage, teens can organize and defend arguments using logical reasoning and rhetorical skill. They are able to anticipate counterpoints and construct coherent, persuasive narratives (Nippold *et al.*, 2005). For example: 'Although some argue that technology isolates people, it actually creates new opportunities for connection by allowing instant communication across distance.' This ability reflects mastery of structure, evidence and tone, which are hallmarks of advanced language competence.
- **Metalinguistic and metacognitive verb use:** Teens increasingly use verbs that describe thought and language processes, reflect, hypothesize, infer and deduce, showing awareness of their own cognition and communication. For example, 'I hypothesize that the character acted this way because she felt excluded.' This self-referential language reveals advanced reasoning and self-awareness, foundational to academic and reflective writing.

- **Register switching and pragmatic flexibility:** As social networks widen, teens learn to adapt tone, vocabulary and formality depending on audience and purpose, such as using formal speech in a presentation ('Good evening, thank you for joining us') versus casual language with friends ('Hey, what's up?'). Appropriate register use indicates pragmatic sophistication, cultural competence and social adaptability, which are core elements of multilingual identity (Bialystok, 2021).
- **Reflective and emotional language use:** In late adolescence, multilingual teens begin using language for deeper self-expression and reflection. As they mature cognitively and socially, they communicate more abstract emotions, moral reasoning and identity-related thoughts across their languages. The dominant language often becomes the main tool for academic and social exchange, whereas the heritage language remains closely tied to emotion, memory and family connection (Pavlenko, 2005). For example, a teen might say, 'When I speak Mandarin with my grandparents, I feel closer to them, but I also realize how much I've forgotten.' Such reflections show how language mediates emotional closeness and identity formation during late adolescence (Schrauf, 2009).
- **Analysis of argumentative and persuasive text:** Analyzing essays, speeches or debates reveals the full scope of linguistic maturity. This measure evaluates how effectively teens organize ideas, support claims and respond to opposing views (Nippold, 2016). For example, reviewing an essay for a clear thesis, evidence and counterargument demonstrates executive control over reasoning and discourse. At this level, language becomes a powerful tool for critical thought, persuasion and self-representation.

Table 5.3 outlines how to apply deeper language measures during the teenage years. It is expected that a teen's heritage language will often lag behind the dominant school language, especially in syntactic complexity, academic vocabulary and figurative comprehension. This is typical and reflects natural differences in exposure and use.

Two points warrant attention. First, because this table focuses on the development of the heritage language, many adolescents will need continued support even if they already meet the benchmarks in their dominant language. Progress should be viewed within the broader context of multilingual growth, not as a deficit. Second, these measures are language-specific. For example, in assessing clause density, analytic languages such as Chinese tend to have fewer subordinating markers than English, whereas Romance languages like French or Spanish often show higher density through embedded clauses. Agglutinative languages such as Turkish or Korean may encode complex ideas within single words, and Semitic languages like Arabic or Hebrew often express subordination morphologically. These typological differences should be considered when interpreting the results.

The goal is to focus on growth over time, noting how much progress a teen has made compared with, say, a year earlier. Increased syntactic variety, more precise vocabulary or deeper reflection all signal meaningful development in the heritage language.

Table 5.3 How to use the deep measures

Age range	Focus of language growth	Key measures	How to collect samples for the deeper measures	More support needed
13 to 15 years	Consolidation of abstract thought; growth in syntactic complexity; emerging understanding of figurative language; development of cohesive and logical discourse.	MLTU/MLCU for sentence length and structure Clause density: Typical range 1.6–1.9 clauses per T-unit or C-unit Narrative cohesion: Use of transitions such as *however, therefore* and *consequently* Figurative language comprehension: recognition of idioms, proverbs and gentle sarcasm.	Collect a 5–10-minute oral narrative about a recent event. Gather a 150–200-word writing sample. Identify and count clauses; highlight transitions. Ask comprehension questions about idioms ('What does it really mean?').	Short, simple sentences with few embedded clauses. Sparse or missing transitions. Literal interpretation of figurative language. Reliance on the dominant language for academic terms. Reduced confidence using the heritage language with peers.
16 to 19 years	Mastery of adultlike communication across settings; persuasive reasoning; metalinguistic awareness; reflective and emotional expression; adaptive register use.	Clause density: Typical range 2.0–2.4 (Nippold, 2016). Sentence variety: Balance of subordination and coordination. Analysis of argumentative/ persuasive expression and text: Thesis, evidence, counterargument. Metalinguistic verb use: Examples include *infer, hypothesize, reflect* and *deduce*. Comprehension of complex figurative language: Layered metaphors and irony. Register switching: Formal vs. informal style by audience.	Collect a 300–500-word argumentative essay or 3–5-minute recorded debate. Prompt a short reflection using metacognitive verbs ('I infer…'). Identify and interpret one layered metaphor or instance of irony. Collect two samples from different contexts (teacher vs. friend) to assess register flexibility.	Clause density below 2.0 or flat sentence structure. Weak reasoning or lack of counterarguments. Limited metalinguistic vocabulary. Difficulty understanding irony or abstract figurative language. Over-formal or over-casual speech in mismatched contexts. Emotional topics are expressed mostly in the dominant language.

To make this easier, you can use AI tools to help record and analyze your teen's heritage language use.

Step 3: Pulling it all together: Documenting and reflection

Compared with early and middle childhood, monitoring a teen's heritage language progress can be more challenging, especially when they are in college or living away from home. In my own family, for example, when Léandre and Dominique were in college in different US cities and later pursued graduate studies abroad, with Léandre in Zurich and Dominique in Paris, we continued to follow their language growth through simple iPhone recordings during our weekly FaceTime conversations. These recordings revealed that Dominique's French vocabulary had expanded noticeably, whereas written samples from emails and text messages offered additional insight into their written expression, word choices and overall confidence in using the heritage language.

By contrast, Léandre's French plateaued, since he was immersed in a German-speaking environment with fewer opportunities to use or expand his French. The key point is that it is always possible to track your child's heritage-language development, regardless of their age or where they live.

The following Multilingual Development Log is designed to help you organize observations, document examples, identify strengths and recognize areas that may need additional support in your teen's heritage language growth.

Multilingual Development Log (Adolescence)

Date: ______________________

Age: ______________________

1. Language Development Journal

Observation: (e.g. new academic word, stronger debate skill, emotional expression in heritage language)

Context: (when/where it occurred; who was present) **Reflection:** (what this shows about growth or challenge)

Strategies used: (family conversation, journaling, heritage-media exposure, online discussion, etc.)

Next steps/ideas:

____

____

2. Monthly Language Snapshot

Date	Languages used	Activity/context	Examples of new words or expressions (academic, emotional, figurative)	Reflection on use/ confidence

3. Language Progress Tracker

Language	MLTU/MLCU	Clause density	Vocabulary precision	Figurative language use	Narrative/ argument cohesion	Register flexibility	Writing development
A							
B							
C							

(Use '+' for growth since the last check, '–' for regression, '=' for stable.)

4. Video/Audio Diary Log

Date of clip	Activity	Language(s)	Notable features (intonation, grammar, fluency, emotion)	Comparison with earlier clips

5. Strategy Tracker

Date	Strategy tried	Frequency	Teen's response	Observed impact	Next steps

Examples: Joining a heritage language club, journaling, discussing cultural films, practicing idioms, role-playing formal vs. informal settings.

6. Family Reflection Notes

Date	Participants	Highlights/successes	Challenges/questions	Plans for next month	Reflections

Major Takeaways of Chapter 5

The Latin root of the word *adolescence* (*adolescere*, 'to grow up') captures the essence of this transformative period. Although maintaining the heritage language may face challenges, the right support helps your teen strengthen both his language skills and identity. Several areas can make a meaningful difference as you support her through these years.

- **Autonomy matters:** Your teen thrives when engagement with the heritage language feels supportive rather than controlling. Autonomy-supportive practices foster long-term motivation and confidence (Ryan & Deci, 2000).
- **Context and relevance count:** At ages 13 to 15, playful, socially grounded activities help you and your teen keep the language alive in everyday interactions. At 16 to 19, goal-oriented and identity-affirming strategies connect the language to your teen's academic, professional and personal aspirations.
- **Your role evolves:** You move from being a manager to becoming a consultant, offering resources, encouragement and trust while respecting your teen's growing independence.

Above all, a few small but powerful practices will support both you and your teen:

- Listen with interest.
- Speak with intention.
- Value your teen's perspective.

As adolescence unfolds, your teen's world expands through friendships, academics, travel and personal passions. There will be moments when the heritage language flows effortlessly and others when it requires more effort. By weaving the language into community life, cultural traditions, shared projects and family travels, you help your teen see it as a living part of their own journey.

At this stage, you are not only helping your teen sustain their heritage language(s) but also nurturing cultural identity and enriching personal growth. In doing so, you give your teen a priceless gift: The ability to live as a multilingual individual who carries forward family stories, values and connections with pride. One day, your teen will thank you for this effort. The reflections of Léandre and Dominique in the next chapter offer a living testimony of what it means to grow up multilingual and show how this lifelong gift continues to bear fruit well beyond the years at home. This is the true art of raising multilingual children.

Notes

(1) Adolescence is the transitional stage between childhood and adulthood, typically beginning with puberty, the stage when a person becomes capable of reproduction, and continuing until a young person assumes independent roles. The exact boundaries of adolescence vary across definitions. For example, the World Health Organization defines it as the period from ages 10 to 19, whereas some researchers extend it into the early or even mid-20s. I use the range of 13 to 19 because it aligns with the widely recognized 'teen' years and reflects a distinct psychological phase.

References

Albirini, A. (2016) *Modern Arabic: Structures, Functions, and Varieties*. Routledge.

Al Omary, M. (2024) Arabic Heritage Speakers' Production and Perception of Arabic Emphatic-Plain Contrasts. Unpublished PhD dissertation, University of Wisconsin-Milwaukee. http://digital.library.wisc.edu/1793/93500

Amengual, M. (2016) Acoustic correlates of the Spanish tap-trill contrast: Heritage and L2 Spanish speakers. *Heritage Language Journal* 13 (2), 88–112. https://doi.org/10.46538/hlj.13.2.2

Arnett, J.J. (2014) *Emerging Adulthood: The Winding Road from the Late Teens through the Twenties* (2nd edn). Oxford University Press.

Bailey, B. (2000) Language and negotiation of ethnic/racial identity among Dominican Americans. *Language in Society* 29 (4), 555–582. https://doi.org/10.1017/S0047404500004036

Bell, N.D. (2011) *Humor in the Classroom: A Guide for Language Teachers and Educational Researchers*. Routledge.

Berman, R.A. and Nir-Sagiv, B. (2007) Comparing narrative and expository text construction across adolescence: A developmental paradox. *Discourse Processes* 43, 79–120. https://doi.org/10.1080/01638530709336894

Bialystok, E. (2021) Bilingualism: Pathway to cognitive reserve. *Trends in Cognitive Sciences* 25 (5), 355–364. https://doi.org/10.1016/j.tics.2021.02.003

Brown, B.B. (1990) Peer groups and peer culture. In S.S. Feldman and G.R. Elliott (eds) *At the Threshold: The Developing Adolescent* (pp. 171–196). Harvard University Press.

Brown, B.B. and Larson, J. (2009) Peer relationships in adolescence. In R.M. Lerner and L. Steinberg (eds) *Handbook of Adolescent Psychology* (3rd edn, Vol. 2) (pp. 74–103). Wiley.

Chang, C.B. and Yao, Y. (2016) Toward an understanding of heritage prosody: Acoustic and perceptual properties of tone produced by heritage, native, and second language speakers of Mandarin. *Heritage Language Journal* 13 (2), 134–160. https://doi.org/10.46538/hlj.13.2.4

Cummins, J. (2000) *Language, Power and Pedagogy: Bilingual Children in the Crossfire.* Multilingual Matters.

De Vries Guth, N. and Pratt-Fartro, T. (2011) Introduction. In T. Pratt-Fartro and N. De Vries Guth (eds) *Adolescents at School: Perspectives on Youth, Identity, and Education* (2nd edn) (pp. 1–4). Harvard Education Press.

Deci, E.L. and Ryan, R.M. (2000) The 'what' and 'why' of goal pursuits: Human needs and the self-determination of behavior. *Psychological Inquiry* 11 (4), 227–268. https://doi.org/10.1207/S15327965PLI1104_01

Derwing, T.M. and Munro, M.J. (2015) *Pronunciation Fundamentals: Evidence-Based Perspectives for L2 Teaching and Research.* John Benjamins. https://doi.org/10.1075/lllt.42

Dovchin, S. (2025) Heritage language anxiety and racialized linguistic shame. *Critical Inquiry in Language Studies*, 1–22. https://doi.org/10.1080/15427587.2025.2593820

Erikson, E.H. (1968) *Identity: Youth and Crisis.* W. W. Norton.

Galmiche, D. (2017) Shame and SLA. *Apples Journal of Applied Language Studies* 11 (2), 25–53. https://doi.org/10.17011/apples/urn.201708233538

Gatbonton, E., Trofimovich, P. and Magid, M. (2005) Learners' ethnic group affiliation and L2 pronunciation accuracy: A sociolinguistic investigation. *TESOL Quarterly* 39 (3), 489–511. https://doi.org/10.2307/3588491

Guardado, M. (2002) Loss and maintenance of first language skills: Case studies of Hispanic families in Vancouver. *Canadian Modern Language Review* 58 (3), 341–363. https://doi.org/10.3138/cmlr.58.3.341

Guardado, M. (2018) *Discourse, Ideology and Heritage Language Socialization: Micro and Macro Perspectives.* Walter de Gruyter.

He, A.W. (2006) Toward an identity theory of the development of Chinese as a heritage language. *Heritage Language Journal* 4 (1), 1–28. https://doi.org/10.46538/hlj.4.1.1

He, A.W. (2008) Heritage language learning and socialization. In D.M. Brinton, O. Kagan and S. Bauckus (eds) *Heritage Language Education: A New Field Emerging* (pp. 137–152, 189–214). Routledge.

Hornberger, N.H. (2003a) Continua of biliteracy. In N.H. Hornberger (ed.) *Encyclopedia of Language and Education* (2nd edn, Vol. 5) (pp. 275–290). Springer.

Hornberger, N.H. (2003b) *Continua of Biliteracy: An Ecological Framework for Educational Policy, Research, and Practice in Multilingual Settings.* Multilingual Matters.

Hunt, K.W. (1970) Syntactic maturity in schoolchildren and adults. *Monographs of the Society for Research in Child Development* 35 (1), 1–67. https://doi.org/10.2307/1165818

Jeon, M. (2008) Korean heritage language maintenance and language ideology. *Heritage Language Journal* 6 (2), 206–223. https://doi.org/10.46538/hlj.6.2.4

Kouritzin, S.G. (2000) Immigrant mothers redefine access to ESL classes: Contradiction and ambivalence. *Journal of Multilingual and Multicultural Development* 21 (1), 14–32. https://doi.org/10.1080/01434630008666391

Kupisch, T. and Rothman, J. (2018) Terminology matters! Why difference is not incompleteness and how early child bilinguals are heritage speakers. *International Journal of Bilingualism* 22 (5), 564–582. https://doi.org/10.1177/1367006916654355

Leadholm, B.J. and Miller, J.F. (1992) *Language Sample Analysis: The Wisconsin Guide.* Wisconsin Department of Public Instruction.

Lenneberg, E.H. (1967) *Biological Foundations of Language.* Wiley.

Lo Bianco, J. (2014) Domesticating the foreign: Global English, mobility and the future of English teaching. *English in Australia* 49 (1), 7–23.

MacWhinney, B. (2012) The logic of the Unified Model. In S. Gass and A. Mackey (eds) *The Routledge Handbook of Second Language Acquisition* (pp. 211–227). Routledge.

Montrul, S. (2016) *The Acquisition of Heritage Languages.* Cambridge University Press.

Montrul, S. (2023) Heritage languages: Language acquired, language lost, language regained. *Annual Review of Linguistics* 9 (1), 399–418. https://doi.org/10.1146/annurev-linguistics-030521-050236

Nicoladis, E. and Paradis, J. (2011) Learning to liaise and elide comme il faut: Evidence from bilingual children. *Journal of Child Language* 38 (4), 701–730. https://doi.org/10.1017/S0305000910000231

Nippold, M.A. (2016) *Later Language Development: School-Age Children, Adolescents, and Young Adults* (4th edn). Pro-Ed.

Nippold, M.A., Ward-Lonergan, J.M. and Fanning, J.L. (2005) Persuasive writing in children, adolescents and adults: A study of syntactic, semantic and pragmatic development. *Language, Speech, and Hearing Services in Schools* 36 (2), 125–138. https://doi.org/10.1044/0161-1461(2005/012)

Pavlenko, A. (2005) *Emotions and Multilingualism*. Cambridge University Press. https://doi.org/10.1017/CBO9780511584305

Pavlenko, A. (2008) Emotion and emotion-laden words in the bilingual lexicon. *Bilingualism: Language and Cognition* 11 (2), 147–164. https://doi.org/10.1017/S1366728908003283

Pavlenko, A. and Blackledge, A. (eds) (2004) *Negotiation of Identities in Multilingual Contexts*. Multilingual Matters.

Phinney, J.S. (1990) Ethnic identity in adolescents and adults: Review of research. *Psychological Bulletin* 108 (3), 499–514. https://doi.org/10.1037/0033-2909.108.3.499

Polinsky, M. (2018) *Heritage Languages and their Speakers*. Cambridge University Press.

Riera, M. (2003) *Uncommon Sense for Parents with Teenagers*. Celestial Arts.

Ryan, R.M. and Deci, E.L. (2000) Self-determination theory and the facilitation of intrinsic motivation, social development and well-being. *American Psychologist* 55 (1), 68–78. https://doi.org/10.1037//0003-066x.55.1.68

Schmid, M.S. (2011) *Language Attrition*. Cambridge University Press.

Schrauf, R.W. (2009) English use among older bilingual immigrants in linguistically concentrated neighborhoods: Social proficiency and internal speech. *Journal of Cross-Cultural Gerontology* 24 (2), 157–179. https://doi.org/10.1007/s10823-009-9091-0

Scott, C.M. (2004) Language sample analysis: Measures of syntax in school-age children and adolescents. *Perspectives on Language Learning and Education* 11 (1), 27–31.

Steinberg, L. (2014) *Age of Opportunity: Lessons from the New Science of Adolescence*. Houghton Mifflin Harcourt.

Taguchi, N. (2019) *Pragmatic Competence in L2: Theory, Research, and Practice*. Routledge.

Wong Fillmore, L. (2000) Loss of family languages: Should educators be concerned? *Theory Into Practice* 39 (4), 203–210. https://doi.org/10.1207/s15430421tip3904_3

Yeager, D.S. and Dweck, C.S. (2012) Mindsets that promote resilience: When students believe that personal characteristics can be developed. *Educational Psychologist* 47 (4), 302–314. https://doi.org/10.1080/00461520.2012.722805

6 In Their Own Words: Perspectives from Multilinguals

Up to this point, I have shared intentional strategies to support children and teens in becoming multilingual, particularly in their heritage language. Much of this insight comes from the research literature and is confirmed by my own research and practice. Although this information is informative, an important question remains: How do children such as Léandre and Dominique, who were raised in a multilingual environment shaped by intentional parenting, perceive their own multilingual upbringing now, as adults? Most importantly, how have these experiences shaped their identity, worldview and attitudes toward multilingualism? How do they reflect on the opportunities and challenges they encountered while growing up and what do they perceive as the lasting impact of their multilingual rearing?

These questions point to a significant gap in the existing literature. To my knowledge, no longitudinal studies have systematically documented the journey of multilingual childrearing from birth to adulthood by following the same individuals. This chapter serves as an initial attempt to address this gap by focusing on Léandre and Dominique, siblings who have been longitudinally documented for more than 30 years while being raised using the OPOL method. By examining their reflections as adults, this chapter provides an unprecedented glimpse into how a multilingual upbringing has shaped their self-awareness, identity and attitudes toward multilingualism, articulated in their own words.

Methods: How Information Was Collected and Analyzed

To explore how Léandre and Dominique's multilingual upbringing has shaped who they are today, I used the **phenomenological approach.**[1] That is, I looked closely at how they personally experienced growing up with several languages, how they understood those experiences and what meaning they attached to them, rather than relying on numbers or statistics. By centering on their voices and prioritizing their perspectives, I could see not only what happened but also how they felt about it and how it shaped them as multilinguals, a key goal of the phenomenological approach (van Manen, 1997).

Information collection

The information in this chapter comes from 15 open-ended questions (see Box 6.1) designed to capture Léandre and Dominique's perspectives on their multilingual upbringing as adults. Open-ended questioning allows the participants to describe their own experiences in depth and avoids constraining them to preset categories, which is central to phenomenological research (van Manen, 2016).

Box 6.1 Survey questions

Question 1: Tell me about yourself.

Question 2: Select the following words or phrases that best describe you. You are welcome to come up with your own words and phrases. Once you have chosen the words and phrases, please rank-order them (1, 2, 3, etc.). If you need clarification, please let me know.

Creative, hardworking, boring, happy, lazy, multilingual, eager to learn new things, unhappy, intelligent, sportive, spiritual, philosophical, versatile, socially conscious, adaptable, open-minded, kind, communicative, existential, goal-oriented, driven, thorough, eager to learn another language/s, detail-oriented, handy, global-minded, relaxed, easygoing, level-headed, critical, mean-spirited, petty, social, independent, self-sufficient, gossiping, humorous, suspicious, curious, thinking out of box, pushing limits, interesting, likable, prudent, thrifty, caring, narrator-minded, materialistic, artistic, stylish, leader, resilient, afraid of challenge, fickle, team player, conservative.

Question 3: How do you feel growing up as a multilingual person?

Question 4: Which language do you feel most comfortable to speak? Why? Rank-order all the languages you know.

Question 5: Do you think you behave differently when you speak different languages? If so, give some examples.

Question 6: Do you feel that you have advantages and drawbacks as a multilingual person? Why or why not?

Question 7: How did your parents raise you as a multilingual?

Question 8: Have you ever felt a sense of insecurity in using one of the languages that you grew up with (i.e. English, French and Chinese)? Why or why not? If possible, specify the age and provide some examples.

Question 9: What suggestions would you give to your parents in terms of the strategies they used to help you become multilingual? If possible, please comment on each parent separately.

Question 10: Do you let your friends, classmates, colleagues or acquaintances know that you speak more than one language? Why or why not?

Question 11: What do you think about the language mixing of multilingual people?

Question 12: What do you wish your parents had done in terms of your multilingual upbring? Do you think that they have missed anything? You can comment on each parent separately if you want.

Question 13: If you must list a few flaws about yourself, what are they? Are any of these flaws caused by being multilingual? If yes, please elaborate.

Question 14: Do you think children need to go to a heritage language school to learn a heritage language? Explain. What is your experience in Chinese school? Did it help you learn Chinese?

Question 15: Do you plan to raise your own children multilingual? Why or why not?

The questions were first sent via email to Léandre (25 years old) and Dominique (23 years old) in English, as it is the language they are most accustomed to for written surveys because of their education and primary linguistic environment. They responded in English at their convenience over a period of four weeks.

Approximately two years later, the same questions were sent to them in one of their home languages (French) when Léandre was 27 years old and Dominique was 25 years old. They returned some of their French responses promptly; however, others were returned three years later, at ages 28–29 (Léandre) and 26–27 (Dominique). Their other home language, Chinese, was used for follow-up discussions in a verbal format.

Chinese was selected for these follow-ups because it has always been my primary language of communication with Léandre and Dominique, which makes spoken exchanges natural and comfortable. In addition, their writing proficiency in Chinese is more limited than in English or French, and relying on translation tools would not have reflected the authenticity of their voices. Verbal discussions therefore provided richer and more spontaneous insights into their lived experiences.

Several important methodological considerations for collecting the information and determining the languages to use are addressed below.

- **Neutral and open-ended design:** The questions were structured to encourage free and authentic responses without leading the participants toward particular answers. This aligns with phenomenological methods that prioritize participants' lived experiences (Moustakas, 1994).
- **Timing and language:** Asking the same questions across different languages introduces both opportunities and challenges. On the one hand, responses in multiple languages can enrich an understanding of identity and voice. On the other

hand, answers in one language can be influenced by what was said previously in another. Linguistic research cautions that repeating a story within the same context can lead to abbreviated answers (Grice, 1975). Therefore, I introduced a two- to three-year gap between the responses in English, French and Chinese. This temporal distance helped reduce recall bias and allowed for more independent expressions in each language.

- **Nuance Through Repetition:** Repeating questions at different times proved valuable in uncovering subtle shifts in perspective. For example, Dominique's answers to the question 'Do you think you behave differently when you speak different languages?' changed over three rounds, each time adding depth and refining his sense of how culture and humor are tied to language. Box 6.2 illustrates how repetition can highlight the evolving and layered nature of experience.
- **Everyday realities of data collection:** Collecting information in real-life contexts is rarely neat or linear. The responses sometimes arrived years later, and the languages varied in mode (written vs. verbal). Rather than undermining the study, these irregularities reflect the very essence of qualitative inquiry: Lived experience is dynamic, shifting and deeply contextual (Emerson *et al.*, 2011). Far from being a limitation, such flexibility makes the data more authentic and closer to the realities of daily life, much like ethnographic work that grows richer with time and immersion (Hammersley & Atkinson, 2019).

Box 6.2 Sample of Dominique's response nuances through repetition

Question: Do you think you behave differently when you speak different languages? If so, give some examples.

Response in English:

Yes, but with some caveats. Assuming culture and language are intimately connected, I would say that I am a different person when speaking different languages. For example, my impression is that my sense of humor was much richer when I was in college in the US compared to when I lived in France. That is, I feel much more comfortable making jokes with people my age in English because I understand the cultural mores that surround the language I speak. It may also have to do with the construction of the language itself, but I suspect it's probably more to do with culture AND language.

Response in French (Two Years Later):

Ma personnalité en anglais est la plus développée parce que je pense que j'ai eu la majorité de mes expériences sociales « formatrices » en anglais à l'école. C'est-à-dire que je connais le mieux les coutumes culturelles associées avec l'anglais américain. Par exemple, quand je vivais en France, je me sentais comme si mon humour étais décalé de quelques décennies. Mais cela est normal car je parle le français de notre père, probablement des années 80s. Tout ça pour dire que oui, selon la langue je suis une personne différente.

My personality in English is the most developed because I believe that I had the majority of my 'formative' social experiences in English at school. That means I am most familiar with the cultural customs associated with American English. For example, when I lived in France, I felt like my sense of humor was a few decades behind. But that's normal because I speak our father's French, probably from the 80s. All of this is to say that, yes, depending on the language, I am a different person.

Response in French (Three Years Later)

Oui, je pense que je me comporte différemment selon la langue que je parle. Je trouve que mon sens de l'humour est mieux adapté aux choses adultes en anglais qu'en français ou en chinois parce que je connais mieux la culture américaine et j'ai passé plus de temps à l'école aux États-Unis. Je pense que ça a à voir avec la culture. Quand je vivais en France, j'avais l'impression de ne pas trouver aussi drôles les choses que les autres trouvaient marrantes et vice versa. Peut-être que je me sens moins adulte quand je parle français parce que j'étais entouré d'adultes sérieux en France.

(Yes, I think I behave differently depending on the language I'm speaking. I find that my sense of humor is better suited to adult things in English than in French or Chinese because I'm more familiar with American culture and spent more time in school in the United States. I think it has to do with culture. When I lived in France, I felt like I didn't find the things others found funny as amusing, and vice versa. Maybe I feel less adult when I speak French because I was surrounded by serious adults in France.)

Information analysis

After the answers to the 15 open-ended questions were collected, patterns in what Léandre and Dominique shared were examined. Instead of counting the responses or measuring scores, the answers were organized into four overarching themes: **Self-awareness and identity, multilingual experience and proficiency, parental strategies and childrearing** and **attitudes toward multilingualism** (see Box 6.3).

This process is known as **thematic analysis.** It means that each response was read carefully, repeated ideas or feelings were noted, and then the information was grouped into categories that reflected the bigger picture. A simple way to picture this process is to imagine sorting through a large box of family photos. Each photo is special on its own, yet themes begin to emerge when the photos are placed into albums: One for birthdays, another for travel, and another for everyday family life. In the same way, thematic analysis takes individual answers and brings them together into meaningful collections that show both the uniqueness of each story and the patterns that connect them.

Thematic analysis makes it possible to move beyond individual answers and to highlight the deeper meanings that connect across many experiences (Braun & Clarke, 2006). For a study of this kind, where the goal is to understand how children of multilingual families make sense of their lives, thematic analysis is particularly valuable. Each child's unique voice is respected, but common threads are also drawn out to show how family choices, language practices and personal feelings interact over time (Moustakas, 1994).

Scholars widely affirm the strength of this approach. They emphasize that thematic analysis provides a flexible yet rigorous method for identifying patterns in qualitative data (Braun & Clarke, 2006). Some also confirm that it helps researchers (a) identify themes that might not be immediately obvious, (b) provide a rich and nuanced account of the data and (c) generate new insights by making connections across different responses (Guest *et al.*, 2012).

Box 6.3 Thematic analysis of the questions

Theme 1: Self-Awareness and Identity

- **Question 1:** Tell me about yourself.
- **Question 2:** Select the following words or phrases that best describe you. You are welcome to come up with your own words and phrases. Once you have chosen the words and phrases, please rank-order them (as 1, 2, 3, etc.).
- **Question 3:** How do you feel growing up as a multilingual person?
- **Question 13:** If you must list a few flaws about yourself, what are they? Are any of these flaws caused by being multilingual? If yes, please elaborate.

Theme 2: Multilingual Experience and Proficiency

- **Question 4:** Which language do you feel most comfortable to speak? Why? Rank-order all the languages you know.
- **Question 5:** Do you think you behave differently when you speak different languages? If so, give some examples.
- **Question 6:** Do you feel that you have advantages and drawbacks as a multilingual person? Why or why not?
- **Question 8:** Have you ever felt a sense of insecurity in using one of the languages that you grew up with (i.e. English, French and Chinese)? Why or why not? If possible, specify the age and provide some examples.

Theme 3: Parental Strategies and Upbringing

- **Question 7:** How did your parents raise you as a multilingual?

- **Question 9:** What suggestions would you give to your parents in terms of the strategies they used to help you become multilingual? If possible, please comment on each parent separately.
- **Question 12:** What do you wish your parents had done in terms of your multilingual upbringing? Do you think that they have missed anything? You can comment on each parent separately if you want.
- **Question 14:** Do you think children need to go to a heritage language school to learn a heritage language? Explain. What is your experience in Chinese school? Did it help you learn Chinese?

Theme 4: Attitudes Toward Multilingualism

- **Question 10:** Do you let your friends, classmates, colleagues or acquaintances know that you speak more than one language? Why or why not?
- **Question 11:** What do you think about the language mixing of multilingual people?
- **Question 15:** Do you plan to raise your own children multilingual? Why or why not?

Responses from Léandre and Dominique to each theme and analysis

Below are Léandre and Dominique's verbatim responses in English and French across the four main themes, along with insights and analysis drawn from follow-up discussions conducted in Chinese.

Theme 1: Self-awareness and identity

Question 1: Tell me about yourself

	English	**French**
Léandre	My name is Léandre/Leander/理昂 and I am 25 years old. Growing up with 3 names and three cultures has in a way shaped who I am since I have never been limited to one frame of reference. I think one big part of my personality is not wanting to fall into a group and making that my entire identity (for example in politics or with national identity).	*Je suis moi. C'est dur de dire plus parce que je n'ai pas de contexte.* (I am me. It's hard to say more because I don't have any context.)
Dominique	I am a localized piece of the universe experiencing itself in the form of a human called Dominique. I am a little speck having a subjective conscious experience. I am also more than the list of nominal achievements, talents, predilections and physical characteristics that make up what others see, hear and hear about. So are you. In other words, I don't quite know what I am, but at least I know that I am. Someone else said it better before me.	*Je suis ton cher fils, Dominique xxxx[2], premier du nom. Cependant, je ne suis pas qu'un nom, comme l'implique la phrase précédente.* (I am your dear son, Dominique xxxx, the first of my name. However, I am not just a name, as the previous sentence implies.)

Léandre's English response was detailed and in-depth. He reflected on how growing up with three names, each representing a different culture, has significantly broadened his perspective. His rejection of exclusive belonging to a single group, whether in politics or national identity, underscores the impact of his multilingual and multicultural upbringing. His response suggests a fluid sense of self that resists categorization, allowing him to navigate different frames of reference without feeling confined to any one of them. Two years later, his French response was brief: '*Je suis moi*' ('I am me'). He explained that it was difficult for him to say more without context.

The contrast between his French and English responses highlights the evolving nature of identity expression across time and languages. Over time, as Léandre matured, his approach to answering questions became more deliberate; he no longer responded simply because he was asked but instead required more context. In terms of language, English was the medium he was accustomed to using for survey-style questions, making it feel more natural for written responses. In contrast, while he has the proficiency to write in French, responding in written form felt unnatural because French has primarily been a spoken language for him at home with his father and brother.

Dominique's English response is detailed and philosophical, reflecting an abstract understanding of identity. He describes himself as a 'localized piece of the universe' experiencing existence subjectively, demonstrating an awareness of identity's complexity and fluidity. This perspective suggests a broader, more existential view of self that transcends cultural or linguistic categories.

Two years later, his French response blends affection, humor and philosophical reflection. By calling himself *ton cher fils* (your dear son), he emphasizes relational identity, grounding his sense of self in familial connections. The term *cher* (dear) adds warmth and familiarity, reinforcing a sense of closeness. *Premier du nom* (the first of my name) playfully references historical or literary prestige, evoking the stylistic conventions of monarchy or fantasy genres (for example, 'Daenerys, first of her name'[3]). This phrasing suggests humor, theatricality or self-awareness, reflecting an appreciation for storytelling or a conscious engagement with identity as something shaped rather than simply inherited.

In the next sentence, '*Cependant, je ne suis pas qu'un nom, comme l'implique la phrase précédente*' (However, I am not just a name, as the previous sentence implies), Dominique immediately deconstructs his formal introduction, challenging the idea that identity can be reduced to a name or title. This aligns with his broader expressions of self, where he rejects simplistic labels in favor of a more nuanced understanding of existence.

Dominique's French response carries a poetic nuance, suggesting that language influences how he expresses identity. Ultimately, his reflections underscore identity as fluid, relational and consciously constructed.

As both a parent and a researcher, I was surprised that neither Léandre nor Dominique mentioned the word *multilingual* in their responses, either in English or in French. Given that they were raised in a multilingual environment, I had expected them to reference it. Yet this omission may suggest that multilingualism is so deeply embedded in their identity that they do not feel the need to explicitly acknowledge it. For them, it is natural, an inherent condition of being rather than an accomplishment requiring emphasis. This stands in contrast to individuals who acquire multiple languages later in life, for whom multilingualism often feels like a significant achievement worth noting (Pavlenko, 2005). In this sense, multilingualism for Léandre and Dominique is much like being human: we rarely introduce ourselves by saying, 'I am a human being,' because it is a fundamental part of existence that does not need to be stated. My interpretation was further confirmed in our casual conversations in Chinese.

Question 2 : Select the following words or phrases that best describe you.

	English	French
Léandre	1) Level-headed, 2) Versatile 3) Eager to learn new things 4) Happy 5) Adaptable 6) Open-minded 7) Hard-working 8) Relaxed 9) Self-sufficient 10) Handy	1) *Heureux* (happy) 2) *Polyvalent* (versatile) 3) *Détendu* (relaxed) 4) *Repousser les limites* (push the limits) 5) *Multilingue* (multilingual) 6) *Avide d'apprendre d'autres langues* (eager to learn other languages) 7) *Résilient* (resilient) 8) *Travailleur* (hard-working) 9) *Curieux* (curious) 10) *Motivé* (motivated)
Dominique	1) Creative 2) Spiritual, 3) Easygoing 4) Happy 5) Eager to learn new things 6) Philosophical 7) Sportive 8) **Empathetic** 9) **Introverted** 10) **Extroverted** 11) **Pensive** 12) **Healthy sense of humor** 13) **Healthy** 14) **Alive** 15) **Grateful** (Bolded words were added by Dominique)	1) *Créatif* (creative) 2) *Philosophique* (philosophical) 3) *Spirituel* (spiritual) 4) *Polyvalent* (versatile) 5) *Avide d'apprendre de nouvelles choses* (eager to learn new things) 6) *Ouvert d'esprit* (open-minded) 7) *Conservateur* (conservative) 8) *Doux* (gentle) 9) *Adaptable* (adaptable) 10) *Sportif* (sportive) 11) ***Dominique***

In English, Léandre did not select the word *multilingual* to describe himself, but four of the words he chose: (*versatile, eager to learn new things, adaptable* and *open-minded*) can be directly linked to the experience of being raised in multiple languages. Two years later, in his French response, Léandre did include *multilingual* as a choice to describe himself, ranking it fifth among 10 words. The inclusion of *multilingual* may reflect his working environment, where many of his colleagues come from diverse cultural and linguistic backgrounds, such as French, Chinese, Russian and Indian. Additionally, in his French response, Léandre ranked *happy* as his first choice to describe him, though in English, it was ranked fourth. This shift suggests that as Léandre has grown older, his perspective on certain aspects of identity, such as happiness, may have evolved.

Dominique's self-description in English also reflects his multilingual environment, though he did not choose the word *multilingual*. Instead, he selected words like *creative* and *eager to learn new things*, which can be linked to the broadening effects of a multilingual upbringing. In his French response two years later, Dominique did not choose *multilingual* either, but included five choices, namely *créatif* (creative), *polyvalent* (versatile), *avide d'apprendre de nouvelles choses* (eager to learn new things), *ouvert d'esprit* (open-minded) and *adaptable*, which again highlight qualities related to a multilingual background.

Although the impact of their multilingual upbringing is evident in both, Léandre and Dominique have distinct personalities. Léandre focuses on practical skills and adaptability; Dominique gravitates toward emotional depth and intellectual exploration.

Question 3: How do you feel growing up as a multilingual person?

	English	**French**
Léandre	I feel like I have more points of reference when learning new languages and can spot particularities more easily than monolingual people. However, it also makes it hard to speak completely 'authentically' since certain phrases and constructions slip between languages.	*Je me sens bien d'avoir grandi en parlent plusieurs langues. Je trouve que c'est très utile de pouvoir communiquer de plusieurs manières. En plus de l'utilité, ça a certainement contribué à mon intérêt aux langues en générale. Sans avoir grandi en tant que multilingue, je ne serais pas la même personne.* (I feel good about having grown up speaking multiple languages. I think it's very useful to be able to communicate in multiple ways. In addition to the utility, it has certainly contributed to my interest in languages in general. Without having grown up as a multilingual person, I would not be the same person.)
Dominique	Growing up multilingual, I felt I never had a fixed identity. I still don't have a fixed identity. It is in the nature of organizations/ institutions to divide according to neatly defined categories. However, this leaves out the whitespace that makes words discernible, the infinity that acts as the bridge between 0 and 1 and the gray between white and black. I have lived my entire life and my entire life has been lived somewhere in between check boxes. I am not special in this regard.	*Je me sens capable de parler en plusieurs langues... je me sens aussi capable de mieux comprendre et penser au point de vue de quelqu'un qui vient de l'étranger ou qui vit dans une autre culture. Ainsi, je trouve aussi plus intéressant les autres gens qui parlent plusieurs langues et ça me donne envie d'en apprendre plus, parce que je pense que dès qu'on en sait deux, c'est plus facile d'en apprendre une troisième, dès qu'on en sait trois, il est plus facile d'en apprendre une quatrième et ainsi de suite.* (I feel capable of speaking in several languages... I also feel capable of better understanding and thinking from the point of view of someone who comes from abroad or who lives in another culture. Therefore, I also find other people who speak several languages more interesting, and it makes me want to learn more, because I think that once you know two, it's easier to learn a third, and once you know three, it's easier to learn a fourth and so on.)

Léandre and Dominique express distinct perspectives on their multilingual upbringing, reflecting their individual experiences and thought processes.

Léandre's responses, both in English and French, emphasize the practical and cognitive benefits of multilingualism. He sees it as an advantage in language learning, enabling him to recognize linguistic nuances that monolinguals might overlook. However, he also acknowledges a challenge: Maintaining authenticity in any single language, as phrases and structures sometimes blend across them. His French response reinforces the idea that multilingualism has shaped his identity and interests, particularly his passion for languages.

Dominique, in contrast, takes a more philosophical and existential approach. His English response highlights a fluid, ever-evolving identity, shaped by existing between categories rather than fitting neatly into predefined labels. He uses metaphors to illustrate his sense of being in the 'in-between' spaces of identity, resisting rigid classification. His French response, however, is more pragmatic: He focuses on multilingualism as a tool for greater cultural understanding and connection. He sees speaking multiple languages as a gateway to learning even more, reinforcing a continuous process of growth and exploration.

Together, their responses illustrate how multilingualism can shape identity in different ways. Léandre views it through a lens of practicality and linguistic awareness; Dominique sees it as both an existential condition and a means of deepening cultural understanding.

Question 13: If you must list a few flaws about yourself, what are they? Are any of these flaws caused by being multilingual?

	English	**French**
Léandre	Sometimes I am too much of a perfectionist when it comes to speaking language. I tend to overcorrect when I speak (in a new language) and it makes it hard to stay focused on the original message I wanted to convey. Also, if I'm not sure that I can speak 100% correctly, then I am nervous about speaking and tend to remain quiet. I don't think these are caused by being multilingual.	*Non je n'associe aucun défaut avec le fait d'être multilingue.* (No, I don't associate any flaws with being multilingual.) 3 years later
Dominique	I, as a conscious observer, am perfect. So are you. However, the personality that envelops that which animates me can always use some work. As esoteric and unclear as it sounds, I believe this. In more conventional terms, however, I do have a tendency to go to extremes when trying things out, I tend to overindulge in dried mangos, I am a teetotaler (which can be a bad thing for some people), I workout too much sometimes, etc. I don't think there are many negatives that come from being multilingual (see my answer to an earlier question). Being multilingual has only ever helped in life.	*Je suis parfait; je n'ai pas de défauts. Non, je pense que mon pire défaut, c'est que je suis trop idéaliste et que je suis un peu trop têtu. Je suis aussi un mauvais perdant. Ces qualités n'ont rien à voir avec savoir plusieurs langues, je pense.* (I'm perfect; I have no flaws. No, I think my biggest flaw is that I'm too idealistic and a bit too stubborn. I'm also a sore loser. These traits have nothing to do with knowing multiple languages, I think.) 3 years later

Léandre and Dominique offer contrasting perspectives on their perceived flaws, with Léandre taking a pragmatic and self-critical approach, whereas Dominique blends philosophical reflection with a touch of humor and self-awareness.

Léandre identifies perfectionism in language learning as a personal challenge, acknowledging that his tendency to overcorrect himself and his fear of making mistakes sometimes hinder his ability to communicate freely. Although this issue is language-related, he does not attribute it directly to being multilingual, suggesting instead that it stems from personal tendencies rather than his linguistic background. His French response (three years later) is even more definitive, explicitly stating that he does not associate any personal flaws with multilingualism. This suggests that he views multilingualism primarily as a strength rather than a source of difficulty.

Dominique, on the other hand, takes a more abstract and philosophical stance. In his English response, he initially rejects the idea of flaws, asserting that all conscious beings, including himself and others, are inherently perfect. However, he then acknowledges certain personal tendencies, such as going to extremes, overindulging and being a teetotaler, framing them as quirks rather than significant flaws. In French, three years later, he humorously claims perfection before conceding that he can be overly idealistic, stubborn and a sore loser. Like Léandre, he does not see multilingualism as a source of personal shortcomings, reinforcing his belief that it has only been beneficial in his life.

Overall, both responses reflect their distinct personalities. Léandre's answer is grounded in linguistic precision and self-improvement, whereas Dominique's is more existential and playful, emphasizing personal growth and self-acceptance. Despite their different approaches, both reject the idea that multilingualism has contributed to any major flaws in their character.

Theme 2: Multilingual experience and proficiency

Question 8: Have you ever felt a sense of insecurity in using one of the languages that you grew up with? Why or why not?

	English	**French 3 years later**
Léandre	Yes. Chinese – whenever I speak with my Chinese grandmother, I never know if what I'm saying is comprehensible and I feel like I can't really express myself. French – when I was in Switzerland at XXX, speaking with people in French was a little stressful since I did not know what kind of slang to use, or what it even meant in some cases.	*0–18 en anglais* (insecure in English during these ages) *22–25 en français* (insecure in French during these ages because in xxx there are real French speakers) *18–29 en chinois* (insecure about Chinese because the recent visit in China) *C'est surtout quand de dois parler dans un nouveau contexte.* (It's mainly when I have to speak in a new context.)

Dominique	Sometimes I feel insecure with regard to Chinese because I'm illiterate and our accent may sound weird to others. Also, my vocabulary can be poor at times. When I lived in France I was insecure sometimes when trying to remember to say the silly way of saying 70 and 90 in French French 'sixty-ten' and 'four-twenty-ten' as opposed to Swiss French way of saying those numbers (literally 'sixty' and 'ninety').	*Oui. Je ne me sens pas toujours à l'aise quand je dois parler chinois avec quelqu'un qui vient de Chine parce que j'ai été encore moins exposé dans ma vie à la culture chinoise qu'à la culture francophone. J'ai « seulement » été en Chine quatre fois dans ma vie, tandis que je ne peux même pas compter les fois où j'ai été en Suisse. J'ai aussi oublié comment écrire en chinois et je ne saurais pas avoir une discussion politique en chinois.* (Yes. I don't always feel comfortable when I have to speak Chinese with someone from China because I've been even less exposed to Chinese culture in my life than to Francophone culture. I've 'only' been to China four times in my life, whereas I can't even count the number of times I've been to Switzerland. I've also forgotten how to write in Chinese, and I wouldn't know how to have a political discussion in Chinese.)

In the English response, Léandre provides concrete examples of situations where he felt insecure: Speaking Chinese with his grandmother and navigating slang in French with native French speakers from Geneva in Zurich, Switzerland. In French (three years later), he categorizes his insecurity by age groups for each language (0–18 for English, 22–25 for French and 18–29 for Chinese), emphasizing how linguistic insecurity shifts in different linguistic contexts. In my follow-up conversations with him in Chinese, Léandre also mentioned that until high school, he was more concerned with the authenticity of his English.

In his English response, Dominique describes his insecurity in Chinese in a straightforward manner, citing literacy, accent and vocabulary limitations. He also mentions feeling uneasy about the French number system in France. In French, three years later, he expands on his insecurity in Chinese by comparing his cultural exposure to China versus Switzerland. He explicitly states that he has been 'far less exposed' to Chinese culture, reinforcing the idea that linguistic confidence is tied to cultural immersion.

Though both Léandre and Dominique expressed feelings of linguistic insecurity in their home languages (Chinese and French), it was striking that Léandre also reported insecurity in his dominant language, English. Without this follow-up study, I would not have discovered this, as he had always performed strongly in academic settings in English. This finding underscores that linguistic confidence is not determined solely by external measures of proficiency but also by how speakers perceive and evaluate their own abilities.

Question 4: Which language do you feel most comfortable speaking?

	English	**French**
Léandre	English French Chinese German Russian Spanish Italian	*Anglais, français, chinois, allemand, espagnol, italien, russe. Les langues avec lesquelles j'ai grandi sont quand même les plus faciles pour moi. Apart ça, les langues qui ressemblent au français sont faciles parce que je peux penser en français en parlant.* (English, French, Chinese, German, Spanish, Italian, Russian. The languages I grew up with are still the easiest for me. Apart from that, languages that are similar to French are easy because I can think in French while speaking.)

Dominique	English French Chinese German Spanish (everything else) Italian (if speaking incorrectly is considered knowing a language) Russian (only the curse words)	1. *Je me sens le plus à l'aise en anglais parce que j'ai grandi aux États-Unis et j'ai fait l'école aux États-Unis. Cependant, je me sens aussi très à l'aise en français car j'ai grandi avec le français à la maison et j'ai vécu en France et je suis allé à l'université là-bas. Je me sense aussi à l'aise dans le chinois que je parle à la maison, mais on est limité car moi et mon frère nous ne savons plus lire et écrire.* 1) *Anglais* 2) *Français* 3) *Chinois* 4) *Allemand* 5) *Italien* 6) *Espagnol* (I feel most comfortable in English because I grew up in the United States and went to school there. However, I also feel very comfortable in French because I grew up with French at home, lived in France, and attended university there. I also feel comfortable in Chinese, which I speak at home, but it is limited because my brother and I can no longer read or write it. 1) English 2) French 3) Chinese 4) German 5) Italian 6) Spanish)

Léandre and Dominique both rank English as their most comfortable language, followed by French and Chinese. Léandre's ranking remains consistent in both his English and French responses, listing English first, followed by French, Chinese, German, Spanish, Italian and Russian. In his French response two years later, he elaborates on why some languages feel easier than others. He states that the languages he grew up with remain the easiest for him, and that languages similar to French feel accessible because he can think in French while speaking them.

Dominique's responses also align across languages, though with a more nuanced explanation in French. In both versions, he ranks English first because of his upbringing and education in the US, followed by French, which he feels very comfortable with through growing up with it at home, living in France, and attending university there. He places Chinese next, noting that while he speaks it at home, he and his brother are limited in literacy. Unlike Léandre, Dominique slightly reorders his lower-ranked languages in his French response, listing Italian ahead of Spanish, whereas in English, he humorously downplays his proficiency in Italian and Russian.

Both responses reflect how linguistic comfort is shaped by both upbringing and practical exposure. Though their rankings are similar, Léandre emphasizes linguistic similarity as a factor in ease of acquisition, whereas Dominique highlights lived experiences and literacy limitations as shaping his confidence in different languages.

Question 5: Do you think you behave differently when you speak different languages?

	English	French[4]
Léandre	Yes, I think I am more open when I speak English because I know what I say is right and I am not thinking about how to correctly structure a sentence. But it was not always like this, and only came about through practice.	*Oui. Je me sens plus à l'aise en français quand je parle de choses quotidiennes, comme à la cuisine ou dans la voiture. En anglais je me sens un peu artificiel dans ces situations. Mais je me sens plus à l'aise en anglais au travail par exemple où j'ai plus de confiance en moi.* (Yes. I feel more comfortable in French when talking about everyday things, like in the kitchen or in the car. In English, I feel a bit artificial in those situations. But I feel more comfortable in English at work, for example, where I have more confidence in myself.) (A little over one year later) *Oui, je me sens plus à l'aise quand je parle anglais ou français que d'autres langues.* (Yes, I feel more comfortable when I speak English or French than other languages.)
Dominique	Yes, but with some caveats. Assuming culture and language are intimately connected, I would say that I am a different person when speaking different languages. For example, my impression is that my sense of humor was much richer when I was in college in the US compared to when I lived in France. That is, I feel much more comfortable making jokes with people my age in English because I understand the cultural mores that surround the language I speak. It may also have to do with the construction of the language itself, but I suspect it's probably more to do with culture AND language.	*Ma personnalité en anglais est la plus développée parce que je pense que j'ai eu la majorité de mes expériences sociales « formatrices » en anglais à l'école. C'est-à-dire que je connais le mieux les coutumes culturelles associées avec l'anglais américain. Par exemple, quand je vivais en France, je me sentais comme si mon humour étais décalé de quelques décennies. Mais cela est normal car je parle le français de notre père, probablement des années 80s. Tout ça pour dire que oui, selon la langue je suis une personne différente.* (My personality in English is the most developed because I believe that I had the majority of my 'formative' social experiences in English at school. That means I am most familiar with the cultural customs associated with American English. For example, when I lived in France, I felt like my sense of humor was a few decades behind. But that's normal because I speak our father's French, probably from the 80s. All of this is to say that, yes, depending on the language, I am a different person.) (A little over one year later) *Oui, je pense que je me comporte différemment selon la langue que je parle. Je trouve que mon sens de l'humour est mieux adapté aux choses adultes en anglais qu'en français ou en chinois parce que je connais mieux la culture américaine et j'ai passé plus de temps à l'école aux États-Unis. Je pense que ça a à voir avec la culture. Quand je vivais en France, j'avais l'impression de ne pas trouver aussi drôles les choses que les autres trouvaient marrantes et vice versa. Peut-être que je me sens moins adulte quand je parle français parce que j'étais entouré d'adultes sérieux en France.* (Yes, I think I behave differently depending on the language I'm speaking. I find that my sense of humor is better suited to adult things in English than in French or Chinese because I'm more familiar with American culture and spent more time in school in the United States. I think it has to do with culture. When I lived in France, I felt like I didn't find the things others found funny as amusing, and vice versa. Maybe I feel less adult when I speak French because I was surrounded by serious adults in France.)

Léandre's English and French responses reveal an evolving perspective on language and comfort. In English, he initially emphasizes feeling more open in English because of his confidence in correctness, noting that this fluency developed over time. However, in his first French response two years later, he provides a more nuanced view, expressing greater ease in French for casual conversations (e.g. in the kitchen or car) while feeling more confident in English in professional settings. In his second French response (three years later), his answer becomes more general, simply stating that he feels more comfortable in English and French than in other languages, omitting the contextual distinctions he previously made.

Dominique's responses, both in English and French, remain consistent in emphasizing how culture and language shape his personality. In English, he describes how his humor was more developed in the US than when he lived in France, attributing this to cultural familiarity. His first French response (two years later) expands on this by suggesting that his humor felt outdated in France because he spoke a version of French influenced by his father's language from the 1980s. In his second French response (three years later), he continues this theme but adds a new layer, suggesting that speaking French makes him feel 'less adult' because his experiences in France were shaped by interactions with serious adults. This evolution in his answer shows a deepening reflection on how language use is shaped by experiences and contexts.

Question 6: Do you feel that you have advantages and drawbacks as a multilingual person?

	English	**French**[4]
Léandre	The drawback was slower development of each individual language earlier in childhood. However, the main advantage is now having a much higher capacity for learning languages since each language does not stay isolated to itself, but instead enhances the others.	*Oui certainement. C'est surtout utile pour comprendre l'étymologie des mots. J'ai l'impression que la plupart des gens ne considèrent jamais ça.* (Yes, certainly. It's especially useful for understanding the etymology of words. I feel like most people never consider that.) (Nearly one year later) *Oui quand j'étais petit je ne parlais moins bien anglais que si on parlait anglais à la maison. Mias maintenant il n'y a pas d'inconvénients.* (Yes, when I was little, I spoke English less well than if we had spoken English at home. But now there are no disadvantages.)
Dominique	I cannot think of any legitimate drawbacks to being multilingual.	*Il n'y a que des avantages en tant que personne multilingue. Ça rend la vie plus riche et beaucoup plus intéressantes de pouvoir interagir avec la culture d'un peuple qui parle une langue autre que celle du pays où l'on grandi. Pour quelqu'un qui ne sait qu'une langue, apprendre une nouvelle langue serait comme recevoir une clé qui permet à cette personne d'accéder à des millions de personnes qui parle cette nouvelle langue. Ainsi, plus on sait de langues, plus on a accès au monde (du moins au monde des humains).*

	There are only advantages like having access to more cultures and parts of the world and perhaps thinking in ways monolingual people do not have access to.	(There are only advantages to being a multilingual person. It makes life richer and much more interesting to be able to interact with the culture of a people who speak a language other than the one of the country where one grows up. For someone who knows only one language, learning a new language is like receiving a key that allows that person to access millions of people who speak this new language. Thus, the more languages one knows, the more access one has to the world (at least the human world).) (One year later) *Il n'y a que des avantages à savoir plusieurs langues. Ça nous permet de faire l'expérience d'autres mondes, d'autres cultures, d'autres peuples, qui ne seraient pas accessibles, ou peu accessibles, sans connaître leurs langues. Le monde s'épanouit en parlant.* (There are only advantages to knowing multiple languages. It allows us to experience other worlds, other cultures and other peoples that would be inaccessible, or barely accessible, without knowing their languages. The world blossoms through speaking.)

Léandre, in English, acknowledges an initial drawback in childhood, namely slower development in individual languages, but sees this as outweighed by the long-term advantage of an enhanced capacity for learning languages. His response frames multilingualism as a dynamic process where languages support and reinforce one another. In French, two years later, his response was more direct and analytical. He highlights the usefulness of multilingualism in understanding etymology, an aspect not mentioned in English. About one year after his first French response, he recalls a temporary challenge in childhood when his English proficiency was lower than it might have been in an English-speaking household, but he concludes that there are no disadvantages now. This suggests that his perception of multilingualism's impact has evolved over time, with his French response being more reflective and focused on linguistic structure, whereas his English response emphasizes cognitive flexibility.

Dominique, in both languages, takes a firm stance that multilingualism has no drawbacks, only advantages. However, the way these advantages are articulated differs slightly between languages. In English, Dominique's response is concise and conceptual, emphasizing access to cultures, the world and unique ways of thinking. The French responses two and three years later, in contrast, are more expansive and poetic, illustrating multilingualism as a key that unlocks new human connections and enriches life. The idea of 'access to the world' is present in both languages, but the French version expands on this idea with vivid imagery, suggesting that language learning allows one to 'experience other worlds' and that 'the world blossoms through speaking.' This stylistic difference between the languages may reflect a cultural or linguistic tendency for French to favor elaboration and metaphor, whereas English tends toward succinctness and directness.

Overall, both Léandre and Dominique express a strong appreciation for the benefits of multilingualism, but their responses in French appear slightly more introspective and nuanced, particularly in their choice of examples and elaboration. The English responses are clear and to the point, whereas the French responses include more philosophical and metaphorical reflections, illustrating a subtle interplay between language and thought.

Theme 3: Parental multilingual childrearing strategies

Question 7: How did your parents raise you as a multilingual?

	English	**French**
Léandre	They chose to associate one language with one parent. This surprisingly worked very well since they also spoke English between themselves as a common language. However, the drawback has been inflexibility. For example, when I want to tell a story to the entire family, I often have to say the same thing twice in French and Chinese, or just say the whole thing in French and hope that my mother understands. Neither of these situations is ideal, especially when I could just speak English and everyone would understand perfectly. In my mind though, speaking English to everyone feels out of place and it is like I have a mental block against it.	*Bien. Je suis content d'avoir la capacité de parler plusieurs langues.* (Good. I'm glad to have the ability to speak multiple languages.)
Dominique	Each parent would interact with us exclusively in his/her native language and then they would talk to each other in English	*Notre père nous parle en français et notre mère nous parle en chinois. J'ai toujours parlé français avec mon frère. Je refuse de parler anglais avec les membres de ma famille nucléaire. C'est comme ça.* (Our father speaks to us in French, and our mother speaks to us in Chinese. I've always spoken French with my brother. I refuse to speak English with members of my immediate family. That's just how it is.)

Léandre's responses in English and French differ significantly in detail, tone and depth, and the three-year gap between them suggests that age may have played a role in shaping his perspective. In his English response, Léandre provides a thorough and analytical explanation of his multilingual upbringing, explaining the OPOL method his parents used and evaluating both its advantages and drawbacks. He acknowledges that though the system worked well, it created a sense of inflexibility, particularly when addressing the whole family. He describes a mental block against speaking English with his family, even though it would be the most practical choice for mutual comprehension. This response reflects both cognitive processing and emotional awareness, as he articulates the complex interplay between linguistic habits and family communication.

By contrast, his French response three years later is strikingly brief and lacks the depth of reflection found in the English version. He simply states that he is happy to be multilingual without further elaboration. This difference could be attributed to several factors. First, age and maturity may have influenced his willingness to analyze the experience in detail; perhaps, three years later, he felt less inclined to revisit childhood language dynamics or saw multilingualism as an unquestioned part of his identity rather than something to critique. Additionally, the brevity of the French response might reflect a shift in how he expresses himself across languages. It is possible that, at the time of the English response, he was more accustomed to structuring analytical reflections in English, whereas three years later, his French expression had evolved to be more direct and concise.

Dominique's English response offers a clear depiction of how their parents raised his brother and him as multilinguals. He explained that each parent spoke to them exclusively in their native language (French for their father and Chinese for their mother). This structured approach reflects a purposeful effort by their parents to nurture multilingualism in their children. Dominique also shares that the siblings always speak French with each other, reinforcing the idea that French is central to his interactions with his father and brother. The explicit refusal to speak English within the immediate family is a crucial detail, underscoring the intentional exclusion of English in favor of the two heritage languages (French and Chinese). This decision highlights the parents' role in shaping language boundaries, ensuring that their children remain connected to their cultural roots and their native languages.

In Dominique's French response three years later, there is a deeper emotional layer added to the narrative. The phrase '*Je refuse de parler anglais*' ('I refuse to speak English') signifies more than just a preference for the family's home languages; it represents a firm stance against the intrusion of English in the familial sphere. This refusal shows how Dominique's multilingual upbringing is tied to a conscious effort to preserve the family's linguistic identity. The concluding statement, '*C'est comme ça*' ('That's just how it is'), reveals the resolve with which Dominique views this decision. It suggests that the choice to speak only French and Chinese within the family is not negotiable and is deeply embedded in the way he was raised.

The shift in tone between the two responses indicates a progression in how Dominique perceives his multilingual upbringing. The English response, written three years ago, is more neutral and factual, focusing on the linguistic structure his parents established. However, the French response three years later is more assertive, highlighting not only the linguistic choices made but also the personal significance of these choices. The change in tone may reflect a deeper understanding and appreciation of the importance of language in his identity, especially as he grow older and reflect on how his upbringing shaped his sense of self and belonging.

The time gap between these two responses points to the evolving nature of Dominique's understanding of their multilingualism. Over the years, they seem to have developed a stronger emotional attachment to the languages their parents used to raise them. The refusal to incorporate English into family life may have become not just a linguistic preference but a symbolic act of cultural preservation and identity maintenance. This evolution reflects how Dominique's multilingual upbringing has become an integral part of his personal and familial identity, tied to a sense of pride and resistance against the dominance of English in his life.

Overall, Dominique's responses reveal how his parents' multilingual approach shaped not just his language skills, but his sense of self and family connection. The intentional use of French and Chinese, coupled with a firm rejection of English in family interactions, demonstrates a strategic and deeply personal method of raising multilingual children. The emotional depth in the later response shows how these early language experiences have become a core part of Dominique's identity as he reflects on his upbringing.

Question 9: What suggestions would you give to your parents in terms of the strategies they used to help you become multilingual?

	English	**French**
Léandre	Mother: Be more consistent. It will almost always be easier to use a word in the community language (English in my case) instead of a word in the home language (Chinese). I find that when I am talking about topics that are even a little difficult, I just switch to using English words since I don't know the Chinese words. Father: Less mocking and more constructive criticism. While the mocking was somewhat effective, it also made me reluctant to use certain words or speak in a certain way because I didn't know the actual correct way. I think it would've been more effective to draw attention to the mistake, but to then point out what should've been said.	*Il faut surtout savoir la langue assez bien pour traduire et ne pas retourner à l'anglais.* (You mainly need to know the language well enough to translate and not revert to English.)
Dominique	Each parent should aggressively adhere and commit to speaking the desired language correctly. That is, there should be no room for any language but that which the parent is trying to teach the child.	*Je trouve que la stratégie de notre père marche mieux. Il faut absolument refuser de parler une langue autre que la langue qu'on essaie d'enseigner à ses enfants. Notre mère a été plus indulgente envers le chinois et le résultat est donc que nous savons moins bien le chinois que le français. Ça aurait été aussi bien de passer plus de temps parmi des Chinois, mais cela n'aurait probablement pas toujours été possible.* (I think our father's strategy works better. You absolutely have to refuse to speak any language other than the one you're trying to teach your children. Our mother was more lenient with Chinese, and as a result, we know Chinese less well than French. It would have also been good to spend more time among Chinese people, but that probably wouldn't have always been possible.)

In Léandre's English response, he suggests that his mother should have been more consistent with using Chinese, as he finds it easier to switch to English when discussing challenging topics. He also mentions that his father's approach involved mocking, which though somewhat effective, made him hesitant to speak freely out of a fear of mistakes. Léandre feels that a more constructive form of feedback would have been more helpful, where mistakes were pointed out but corrected in a supportive way.

In the French response three years later, Léandre reinforces the idea that knowing the language well enough to avoid switching to English is key. This aligns with his earlier comment about consistency, suggesting that fluency and the ability to avoid defaulting to the community language are essential to maintaining a multilingual environment.

Dominique echoes Léandre's suggestions about consistency, particularly with his mother's approach to Chinese. Dominique feels that his mother's leniency in allowing more use of English led to weaker proficiency in Chinese. In contrast, he states that his father's strategy of not allowing any language other than the target language was more effective, even though spending more time among Chinese speakers might have been beneficial but not always possible.

In their responses, both Dominique and Léandre highlight the importance of consistency and constructive feedback in language learning. Though Léandre values a balance between correction and encouragement, Dominique places more emphasis on strict adherence to the home language, especially for their father, as a more effective strategy for multilingual development.

Question 12: What do you wish your parents had done in terms of your multilingual upbringing?

	English	**French**
Léandre	Mother: I wish for consistency in using Chinese instead of English words. There is still a lot of relatively basic vocabulary I don't know. Father: Less rigidity in using English (kind of contradictory to the point above). I'm not sure if there is a better way in between the two, so this suggestion might not be useful.	*Je pense que c'est bien comme ça. C'est déjà pas mal.* (I think it's good as it is. It's already not bad.)
Dominique	Although I disliked the severity and commitment of our father's approach to teaching French, I now appreciate it because of its results. I wish our mother had been a little more hard-nosed when it came to learning to read and write in Chinese from an early age. However, it is difficult to compare because French has the advantage of using an alphabet-based writing system, so it is easier to learn and retain.	*J'aurais préféré que notre mère insiste plus pour qu'on parle un chinois pur et qu'on apprenne mieux à lire et à écrire, pas forcément avec la force avec laquelle on a été « encouragés » à apprendre le piano, mais avec une douceur ferme et avec des incitations de jouets. Cela dit, notre enfance a été bonne et j'ai beaucoup aimé grandir dans notre famille. Donc, ce n'est pas vraiment un problème.* (I would have preferred if our mother had insisted more on us speaking pure Chinese and learning to read and write better—not necessarily with the same force as how we were 'encouraged' to learn the piano, but with firm gentleness and incentives like toys. That said, our childhood was good, and I really enjoyed growing up in our family. So, it's not really an issue.)

In Léandre's English response, he points out the inconsistency in his mother's use of Chinese, wishing that she had stuck more to Chinese words instead of switching to English. He also expresses some ambivalence about his father's strict approach to speaking French, suggesting that though it may have been effective, he is uncertain about whether a middle ground would have been better. This reflects a nuanced view, where Léandre sees room for improvement but also acknowledges the effectiveness of both parents' methods. His reflections are relatively balanced, suggesting that though he could have benefited from more consistency in language use, the overall approach wasn't necessarily wrong.

In contrast, Léandre's French response three years later reveals a more resigned and reflective attitude. His statement, '*C'est bien comme ça. C'est déjà pas mal*' (It's fine like that. It's already not bad) suggests acceptance of the multilingual approach his parents used, recognizing that, despite any past wishes for improvement, it was largely successful. This shift may reflect maturity and a more positive view of his upbringing, as age and experience often bring a broader perspective. It indicates that Léandre has moved past any dissatisfaction, appreciating his upbringing as a whole rather than focusing on what could have been different.

Dominique's English response reflects a critical view of their father's approach, acknowledging that though he initially disliked his strict insistence on speaking French, he now understands and appreciates its effectiveness in promoting fluency. They also express a wish that their mother had been more 'hard-nosed' in teaching Chinese, particularly when it came to reading and writing. However, Dominique makes a point of recognizing that French, with its alphabet-based writing system, was naturally easier to learn and retain, which added an element of complexity to comparing the two languages.

In the French response three years after, Dominique's reflection expands on his earlier thoughts, stating that he would have preferred his mother to be more insistent on pure Chinese and more focused on literacy, but with a gentler, yet firm, approach. The mention of incentives like toys and a softer approach indicates a recognition of the balance required in language learning. This suggests a deeper appreciation for the process as they reflect on it with age. Despite these wishes, Dominique also emphasizes that his childhood was positive, expressing gratitude for the family environment and reiterating that these were not significant problems.

Overall, the shift from the English to the French response shows a maturation in both siblings' perspectives. Léandre's earlier response, though critical, leans more towards a desire for balance, whereas his later reflection in French suggests a sense of contentment with their upbringing. Dominique's evolution is more evident in his reflections, where he initially expressed dissatisfaction with the lack of rigor in Chinese literacy, but later softened his stance, recognizing the value of his upbringing while still identifying areas for improvement. The French responses, three years later, demonstrate a more thoughtful and measured reflection on his multilingual upbringing, shaped by the passage of time and increased maturity.

Question 14: Do you think children need to go to a heritage language school to learn a heritage language?

	English	French
Léandre	I don't think that children need to go to a heritage school to learn the spoken language. But it does help (in theory) to learn the written language. My experience with Chinese school was not that positive. I was about 4 years older than everyone else, so I never took it seriously. Also, the setting in a run down community college with dirty and broken desks was not inspiring to me. In the end though, I think I still remember how to write some of the characters I learned there.	*Il faut utiliser la langue souvent. Si la seule manière de le faire c'est à l'école, c'est mieux que rien. L'école chinoise était inutile pour moi parce que c'était seulement une fois par semaine et en plus on parlait anglais avec les autres camarades.* (You need to use the language often. If the only way to do that is at school, it's better than nothing. Chinese school was useless for me because it was only once a week, and on top of that, we spoke English with the other classmates.)
Dominique	Ideally, rather than immersing children in an environment with other learners of a language, I think the most effective way of having a young child learn a language is prolonged exposure to the language in a native setting. Thus, the child will not be able to fall back on a favored tongue and will have to learn the desired language. It will likely be uncomfortable in the short-run and the child may also suffer socially, but the child will benefit the most linguistically. In this sense, I think Chinese school was actually quite detrimental because my classmates and my brother would invariably fall back on English when we were not in class or on a quick break.	*Je pense que pour que les enfants apprennent bien une langue, n'importe quelle langue, il faut qu'ils soient exposés à une éducation dans cette langue. Quand il s'agit d'une éducation, ça ne veut pas forcément dire qu'ils doivent suivre des cours, mais ils doivent apprendre des choses dans les langues qu'ils apprennent. Une bonne analogie serait d'apprendre à jouer d'un instrument : je pense que le cerveau est comme l'instrument lui-même et une pièce de musique est comme une langue. En apprenant de nouvelles pièces, on raffine notre maîtrise de l'instrument. Ainsi, en apprenant plus de langues et d'autres choses en général, on apprend mieux à maîtriser le cerveau. Mon expérience à l'école chinoise n'était pas mal, dans les quelques années où on y a été.* (I think that for children to learn a language well, any language, they need to be exposed to education in that language. When it comes to education, this doesn't necessarily mean they must take formal classes, but they should learn things in the languages they are learning. A good analogy would be learning to play an instrument: I think the brain is like the instrument itself, and a piece of music is like a language. By learning new pieces, we refine our mastery of the instrument. Similarly, by learning more languages and other things in general, we learn to better master the brain. My experience at the Chinese school wasn't bad, during the few years we attended).

Léandre's English and French responses express the same core message but differ in form and emphasis. In both, he questions the effectiveness of heritage language school and stresses that frequent use, rather than occasional instruction, is essential for language development. However, the French response was written three years after the English one, which helps explain the shift in style.

His earlier English response is detailed and experience-based. He describes contextual factors that affected his motivation, such as being older than his classmates and learning in an uninspiring environment. He also makes a nuanced distinction, noting that heritage school may be less important for spoken language but can support literacy.

In contrast, the later French response is concise and principle-oriented. Rather than recounting specific experiences, he summarizes his conclusion: Once a week instruction has limited value, especially when peers use English, though it may still be helpful if no other exposure is available. The shift from narrative detail to conceptual summary reflects developmental consolidation and a more streamlined interpretation of earlier experiences.

Dominique's responses also show continuity alongside developmental change, with the French version written several years later.

Several years later, his French response presents a broader and more integrative view. He emphasizes learning meaningful content through the language rather than simply studying it and uses a cognitive analogy comparing the brain to a musical instrument. His evaluation of Chinese school became more moderate, describing the experience as 'not bad.'

Taken together, the differences reflect not only language choice but also developmental perspective. With time, both Léandre and Dominique moved from experience-based judgments toward more generalized and balanced interpretations, illustrating how multilingual individuals refine their understanding of language learning as they mature.

Theme 4: Attitudes toward multilingualism

Question 10: Do you let your friends, classmates, colleagues or acquaintances know that you speak more than one language?

	English	**French**
Léandre	Only if it's relevant. I don't think it's good to volunteer this information without being asked since it feels like bragging.	*Oui, pourquoi pas?* (Yes, why not?)
Dominique	I only let them know if it comes up in conversation. Unless it's directly relevant to the matter at hand, I don't see why it would appropriate to mention it. If I were to meet someone and then that person, immediately and without context, told me, 'yeah, I speak about twelve languages', I would be impressed but I would also assume that person is insecure about something.	*En général, je parle surtout la langue dominante du pays dans lequel je me trouve avec mes amis. J'ai seulement vraiment passé du temps en Amérique, où les gens parlent surtout anglais. En France, je parlais anglais avec beaucoup de gens, mais je parlais seulement français avec les gens dont le français était la langue maternelle.* (In general, I mostly speak the dominant language of the country I'm in with my friends. I've only really spent time in America, where people mainly speak English. In France, I spoke English with many people, but I only spoke French with those whose native language was French.)

Léandre's responses show a subtle shift in attitude between the English and French versions. In his English response, he expresses hesitation about mentioning his multilingualism unless it is directly relevant, as he perceives it as potentially boastful. His French response three years later, however, is much more casual and open: '*Oui, pourquoi pas?*' ('Yes, why not?'). This brief and nonchalant answer suggests a greater ease in acknowledging his multilingualism when speaking in French, in contrast to his more cautious tone in English. This difference could indicate a shift in confidence or a change in how he perceives the social implications of revealing his language abilities over time. Additionally, in his workplace, where many of his colleagues are multilingual, he frequently switches among French, Chinese and Russian. In this context, multilingualism is the norm rather than something exceptional and therefore does not carry the same suggestion of boasting.

Dominique's responses also show a notable difference in focus. In English, Dominique strongly expresses a reluctance to disclose his multilingualism unless it is directly relevant, emphasizing that unsolicited disclosure could come across as insecurity. The response suggests a critical view of people who announce their language abilities without context. However, in the French response three years later, Dominique does not directly address whether he lets others know about his multilingualism. Instead, he describes his language use patterns, explaining that he primarily speaks the dominant language of the country he is in. He notes that in France, he speaks English with many people but reserves French for native speakers. This shift in focus suggests that Dominique's perspective may have evolved, moving from a concern about how multilingualism is perceived socially to a more pragmatic approach centered on functional language use in different environments.

Question 11: What do you think about the language mixing of multilingual people?

	English	**French**
Léandre	I think it is inevitable. It is impossible to completely isolate the languages you know since you are still the same person. In English, my friends have commented that I have a particular and unique vocabulary, probably because I am influenced by French.	*C'est inévitable, mais probablement mieux à éviter si possible.* (It's inevitable, but probably better to avoid if possible.)
Dominique	I think language mixing provides a richer experience of life than would be the case when only knowing one language. However, I would not limit this to languages as knowing more and more things and making connections between ostensibly unrelated matters would also enrich life experience.	*Je pense que n'importe quel mélange de langues chez les personnes multilingues, c'est bien. Plus on sait de langues, plus on est intéressant. Cependant, il y a des mélanges plus intéressants que d'autres. Par exemple, si quelqu'un savait le serbe et puis un dialecte africain, je trouverais cela plus intéressant que quelqu'un qui sait l'italien et l'espagnol. Mais, en général, savoir plusieurs langues, ce n'est qu'une bonne chose.*

		(I think any mix of languages in multilingual people is great. The more languages you know, the more interesting you are. However, some combinations are more interesting than others. For example, if someone knew Serbian and then an African dialect, I would find that more interesting than someone who knows Italian and Spanish. But in general, knowing multiple languages is only a good thing.)

Léandre's English response emphasizes the inevitability of language mixing, noting that it is impossible to fully separate the languages one speaks, since they all belong to the same individual. He also shares that his English vocabulary is influenced by French, as observed by his friends. However, in his French response three years later, he maintains that language mixing is inevitable but adds that it is 'probably better to avoid if possible.' This subtle shift suggests a more cautious stance toward language mixing, possibly reflecting changes in his environment, experiences or personal views over time. While he originally accepted language mixing as a natural phenomenon, his later comment hints at a preference for maintaining linguistic boundaries when feasible.

Dominique's English response presents language mixing as enriching, not only in terms of multilingualism but also as part of a broader intellectual experience, connecting different areas of knowledge enhances life. In his French response three years later, Dominique still views language mixing positively but introduces a new perspective: Some language combinations are more interesting than others. He suggests that less common pairings, such as Serbian and an African dialect, are more intriguing than more closely related languages like Italian and Spanish. This evolution in thought may reflect greater exposure to multilingual environments, a refined appreciation for linguistic diversity or an increased awareness of how certain language combinations might stand out in different social or cultural contexts.

The time gap between responses reveals subtle shifts in both siblings' perspectives. Léandre moves from an acceptance of language mixing to a more reserved stance, possibly because of professional or social factors. Dominique, on the other hand, expands his reasoning, not just affirming multilingualism's value but also adding a nuanced view on how certain linguistic pairings might be perceived. These differences highlight how multilingual individuals' attitudes toward language use can evolve over time depending on their experiences and changing contexts.

Question 15: Do you plan to raise your own children multilingual?

	English	French
Léandre	Yes – I think knowing multiple languages natively is a very useful skill that cannot be acquired in any other way.	*Oui, mais probablement seulement en français parce que je pense que je ne sais pas assez bien le chinois.* (Yes, very probably only in French because I don't know Chinese well enough.)

Dominique	Ideally I would like to raise my hypothetical children multilingual. However, this depends on my future wife and the languages she does or does not speak. In any case, I cannot see how this will not benefit them. Also, I'm assuming getting into college will become harder and harder with easy online applications making for a larger pool of applicants, so they'll need any advantage they can get.	*J'ai absolument l'intention d'élever des enfants multilingues. Ça serait aussi stylé qu'ils sachent la langue de ma future femme si elle parle une autre langue couramment. Comme j'ai dit avant, il n'y a que des avantages à savoir plusieurs langues.* (I absolutely intend to raise multilingual children. It would also be cool if they knew my future wife's language, if she speaks another language fluently. As I said before, there are only advantages to knowing multiple languages.)

Léandre's English response expresses a clear intention to raise his children multilingual, emphasizing that native language acquisition is an invaluable skill that cannot be replicated through other means. However, his French response three years later presents a shift in perspective. Though he still affirms his intention to raise multilingual children, he limits this to French, stating that he does not believe his Chinese proficiency is strong enough. This suggests a more pragmatic approach, where his confidence in his own language abilities now plays a role in shaping his decision. The change may reflect an increased awareness of the challenges of transmitting a language that he does not feel fully proficient in, or it may indicate a shift in priorities based on his experiences over the three-year period.

Dominique's responses, in contrast, show an evolution toward greater certainty and enthusiasm. In the English response, Dominique expresses a preference for raising multilingual children but acknowledges that it would depend on their future spouse's language abilities. He also brings in a practical perspective, suggesting that multilingualism could serve as an advantage for his children in an increasingly competitive academic landscape. In the French response three years later, Dominique is much more definitive, stating outright that he 'absolutely' intends to raise multilingual children. The response also conveys a sense of excitement, particularly in the comment that it would be '*stylé*' (cool) if his children could learn his future spouse's language. This response reinforces his longstanding belief in the advantages of multilingualism while showing a shift toward a more personal and even playful appreciation of the idea.

Overall, the time gap between responses reveals different trajectories for the two siblings. Léandre moved from a general belief in the benefits of multilingualism to a more constrained, self-aware perspective based on his own linguistic confidence. Dominique, on the other hand, transitioned from a practical and somewhat conditional stance to an enthusiastic and fully committed one. These differences highlight how personal experiences, self-perception and external factors influence attitudes toward language transmission over time.

Key Takeaways from the Survey

Having read Léandre and Dominique's responses firsthand, along with my interpretation through my conversation with them (in Chinese), you can now gain a deeper understanding of how they perceive themselves, assess their linguistic competence in their heritage languages, reflect on their parents' approach to home languages and express their attitudes toward multilingualism. Their perspectives offer valuable insights for parents raising multilingual children, particularly in heritage languages. These reflections help evaluate the long-term impact of a multilingual upbringing and the effects of the OPOL method on children's linguistic and personal development. Below are the key takeaways.

Positive experience with multilingualism

Léandre and Dominique have thrived in a multilingual environment, particularly within a OPOL framework. Their upbringing has fostered a strong sense of identity and belonging to multiple cultural and linguistic communities, underscoring the profound benefits of multilingualism. Research (Little & Zhou, 2024) aligns with their experiences, demonstrating that multilingualism can enrich children's sense of self and strengthen their connection to their heritage. Both siblings credit their multilingual background with shaping their identities in meaningful ways. Léandre, for instance, describes how growing up with three names and cultures has cultivated a fluid sense of self, enabling him to resist rigid categorization. Such navigation across languages can support a multifaceted sense of self, as multilinguals often experience shifts in persona across languages (Dewaele, 2016). Similarly, Dominique reflects on the existential and relational dimensions of identity, highlighting how multilingualism has empowered him to navigate diverse cultural and linguistic spaces with ease. These experiences illustrate that multilingualism not only enhances linguistic abilities but also fosters a more nuanced, adaptable and multifaceted sense of self.

Long-term impact of multilingual upbringing

As adults, both Léandre and Dominique view their multilingual upbringing as a significant advantage, despite some challenges. They recognize that their ability to speak multiple languages has opened doors to personal, academic and professional opportunities. Their experiences highlight the long-term benefits of multilingualism, including cognitive flexibility, cultural awareness and enhanced communication skills.

Multilingualism as a gateway to cultural understanding

Both Léandre and Dominique emphasize how multilingualism has enriched their understanding of different cultures. Dominique, in particular, noted that speaking multiple languages allows for deeper connections with people from diverse backgrounds and provides access to new ways of thinking. This cultural flexibility is a significant advantage of multilingualism, enabling individuals to engage more meaningfully with the world.

Confidence in language proficiency grows over time

Multilingual confidence is not fixed. It often shifts as children, adolescents and young adults move across new social and cultural environments. Feelings of linguistic insecurity, the sense that one's language ability is 'not enough' compared with 'native' speakers or monolingual peers, are common, especially when one language is used in a new or demanding context. With continued exposure and meaningful use, confidence and proficiency tend to reinforce each other over time, allowing individuals to move from a focus on correctness toward functional communication and a more secure multilingual identity (Kramsch, 2009).

The experiences of Léandre and Dominique illustrate this developmental process. In his English response, Léandre described feeling insecure when speaking Chinese with his grandmother and when navigating slang with native French speakers during his studies in Switzerland. In a French reflection written three years later, he reframed these experiences developmentally, identifying periods of insecurity across languages and concluding that such feelings arise mainly when speaking in a new context. Follow-up conversations also revealed that during his school years, he was concerned about sounding authentic even in English, his dominant language.

Dominique's responses show a similar shift. In English, he attributed his insecurity in Chinese to limited literacy, accent and vocabulary. Three years later, his French reflection linked confidence more explicitly to cultural exposure, noting that his limited contact with Chinese society, compared with extensive experience in the French-speaking environment in Switzerland, affected his comfort level and ability to discuss complex topics.

These accounts highlight an important insight: Linguistic confidence is shaped not only by proficiency but also by context, cultural familiarity and self-perception. Temporary insecurity is a normal part of multilingual development, but with time, experience and continued use, confidence typically grows.

Consistency with sensitivity: Balancing structure and flexibility in language input

Language input and output are closely related, and both siblings emphasized the importance of consistent language exposure in their reflections. They noted that their father's firm commitment to speaking French at home, although it sometimes felt restrictive at the time, ultimately contributed to their strong French proficiency. In contrast, they perceived their Chinese development as less robust. In their view, their mother's occasional use of English to facilitate communication during Chinese interactions may have reduced the need to remain fully within the language.

At the same time, this interpretation needs to be understood within a broader context. The mother's flexibility was not simply inconsistency but a responsive approach grounded in attention to the children's social and emotional needs, helping conversations flow, reducing frustration and maintaining a positive relational climate. From a developmental perspective, such responsiveness can support motivation and willingness to communicate. However, children do not always perceive the intentions behind parental adjustments in the same way. In Léandre's and Dominique's retrospective accounts, the contrast between their father's firm language boundary and their mother's more flexible approach led them to associate greater effectiveness with the former. Whether strict consistency is always the optimal strategy remains debatable, as language development unfolds within complex emotional and relational dynamics. In this case, however, their outcomes and perceptions suggest that sustained, clearly bounded input was more effective for long-term proficiency.

It is also important to consider linguistic distance and structural complexity. Chinese differs substantially from English and French in its phonology, writing system and grammar. Unlike alphabetic French, written Chinese is logographic and requires the memorization of a large number of characters, a process that typically demands extensive and sustained exposure. Chinese also relies on tonal distinctions and has fewer cognates or shared vocabulary with English than French does. In contrast, French and English share many lexical, morphological and syntactic similarities resulting from their historical contact, allowing for greater cross-linguistic transfer and facilitating learning (Odlin, 1989). Research has shown that languages that are typologically closer support faster acquisition through positive transfer, whereas typologically distant languages require more intensive input and practice (Ellis, 2008).

From this perspective, the siblings' comparatively weaker Chinese proficiency cannot be attributed solely to differences in parental language practices. The greater linguistic distance between Chinese and both English and French, combined with the higher demands of character literacy and tone mastery, likely amplified the effects of reduced input consistency. Their experience illustrates an important principle for multilingual families: When a heritage language is typologically distant from the dominant societal language, both the quantity and the consistency of exposure become even more critical.

Taken together, their reflections highlight three interacting factors in multilingual outcomes: the consistency of language boundaries, the emotional climate of interaction, and the structural distance between languages. Children may later attribute success primarily to strict consistency, yet their development reflects a more complex interplay of relational responsiveness and linguistic realities.

Adapting heritage language education to children's needs

Both siblings shared negative experiences with their Chinese school, highlighting the need for a thoughtful reconsideration of heritage language teaching methods. Although learning the language was valuable, the negative experiences left a lasting impact. This suggests that teaching methods should be engaging, culturally relevant and sensitive to children's emotional experiences to foster a positive learning environment.

Balance of parental strategies

Both siblings reflected on the effectiveness of their parents' strategies in raising them multilingual. Though they appreciated the OPOL approach, they also noted areas for improvement, such as greater consistency in language use and more constructive feedback. Their reflections underscore the importance of balancing strict language boundaries with flexibility and encouragement, especially when children face challenges in language acquisition.

Future plans for multilingual parenting

Their multilingual upbringing has clearly left a positive and lasting impression, as both Léandre and Dominique expressed a strong desire to raise their own children multilingual, albeit with slightly different approaches. Léandre plans to prioritize French, given his confidence in the language, whereas Dominique is eager to pass on multiple languages, including any languages spoken by a future spouse. Their intentions highlight a deep belief in the value of multilingualism and a commitment to offering their children the same linguistic and cultural advantages they themselves benefited from.

Reflection

After reading and analyzing Léandre and Dominique's surveys, several themes emerged that invite reflection on what we would keep and what we would do differently if we were to do it all again.

What we would do again

Both Léandre and Dominique spoke with gratitude about growing up in a multilingual home. They agreed that the OPOL approach gave them a strong foundation in their home languages, French and Chinese. This structure provided clarity, creating boundaries that helped them see each language as distinct and purposeful. However, its impact went beyond communication. It gave them a sense of belonging, allowing each language to carry its own emotional meaning and rightful place in their lives.

Over the years, the OPOL practice at home and beyond became so natural that it shaped how they think and interact to this day. Both children still refuse to speak English within the family, a reminder that what began as a language strategy has grown into our family's enduring way of relating to one another.

Here is a telling example. When they were in high school, I gave both children permission to write to me in English if writing in Chinese felt too demanding. They never did. Instead, they continued trying to write in Chinese, often with great effort, checking words online to find the right expressions. Later, they found playful ways to communicate with me by writing in Spanish, Italian or Russian, the languages they were learning at the time, simply to avoid writing in English. At some point, they occasionally and reluctantly wrote to me in English, and only when a thought felt too complex to translate. In the end, they cleverly found a clever way by writing to the entire family in French, avoiding English altogether. These choices reveal how deeply the OPOL communication pattern has been woven into their being. Because they were raised speaking only Chinese with me, they simply cannot bring themselves to use English when communicating with me. Instead, when Chinese writing feels difficult, they turn to other languages such as Spanish, Italian or Russian rather than switching to English. Even using another language feels more natural to them than breaking the long-established bond of writing to me in Chinese.

What we would do differently

Léandre's and Dominique's reflections prompted us to think carefully about what we might change if we were starting again. Both felt that they would have benefited if I had remained more consistently within Chinese, particularly as they grew older. When conversations became abstract or required specialized vocabulary, I sometimes shifted into English to keep communication smooth and to avoid frustration. At the time, this flexibility reflected my effort to support their emotional comfort and maintain a positive interaction.

In retrospect, however, this approach may have reduced the intensity of Chinese input at a stage when it was becoming especially important. Given the structural distance between Chinese and English and French, and the additional demands of tone and character literacy, Chinese required not only exposure but sustained use at increasingly higher levels of complexity. If we were to begin again, I would make a more deliberate effort to maintain Chinese as the primary medium, even during cognitively demanding conversations, while providing support through paraphrasing, repetition or scaffolding rather than switching languages. Their experience suggests that when a heritage language is typologically distant and cognitively demanding, both the consistency and the depth of input become critical for long-term development.

At the same time, this reflection does not diminish the value of relational flexibility. Multilingual parenting often involves a delicate balance between preserving emotional connection and maintaining language boundaries. The challenge is not to eliminate responsiveness, but to sustain the target language while supporting the child's understanding and confidence within it.

My husband's approach to French also became a point of reflection. He was steady and consistent, and his corrections, sometimes delivered with humor that bordered on sarcasm, captured the children's attention, though they occasionally made them more cautious. Dominique later observed that my gentler stance in Chinese, compared with their father's firmer expectations in French, partly explains why his French became stronger, especially in reading and writing. Looking back, a combination of clear expectations with warm encouragement, which Dominique later described as 'firm gentleness,' might have strengthened their Chinese while preserving their willingness to take risks. Notably, both children now recall their father's corrections with affection and often laugh about them.

Ultimately, we must acknowledge the outcomes. My flexible, child-centered approach supported emotional ease but may have contributed to weaker competence in written Chinese. In contrast, my husband's consistent language boundaries supported stronger proficiency in French. The contrast between our styles reminded us that language development is shaped not only by good intentions but also by the quality, consistency and cognitive level of input. At the same time, it reinforced an equally important lesson: There is no single formula for raising multilingual children. What matters most is finding a thoughtful balance between structure and responsiveness, guided by love, patience and a long-term commitment to growth.

What we have learned

Perhaps the most revealing part of their reflections is what they left unsaid. Neither Léandre nor Dominique highlighted themselves as multilingual. For them, this way of being was so natural that it required no label. Multilingualism was not something they acquired; it was something they lived. This realization reminded us that language learning is never just about proficiency. It shapes how children see themselves, how they relate to others, and how they find their place in the world.

If we were to do it again, we would keep the structure that nurtured this effortless multilingual identity. We would be more deliberate in maintaining Chinese across every domain and more mindful in giving feedback that invites curiosity and experimentation. Parenting, we have learned, is less about perfection and more about presence and the willingness to keep trying, adapting and learning alongside our children.

Through this journey, we came to see that raising multilingual children is an unfolding process of persistence, creativity and love. Every conversation, every story and every shared moment becomes part of the invisible tapestry of identity. Its impact deepens quietly over time, shaping how our children think, feel and connect across languages and cultures.

We also learned that multilingualism extends far beyond words. It cultivates flexibility, empathy and a sense of belonging in more than one world. It has taught our children how to adapt without losing themselves and it has taught us, as parents, how to listen and grow. Their desire to raise their own children multilingually speaks to their understanding that language is not only a means of communication but a way of expanding the heart and mind.

Looking back, we realize that the art of raising multilingual children is, at its core, the art of growing together. It is a lifelong exchange between parents and children, where every word, every effort, and every moment of connection continues to unfold long after childhood ends.

Notes

(1) Phenomenology was developed by the German philosopher Edmund Husserl (1859–1938) and later expanded by another German philosopher, Martin Heidegger (1889–1976). Husserl focused on how individuals experience and make sense of the world from a first-person perspective, whereas Heidegger emphasized how people's understanding of themselves is shaped by history, society, and language.
(2) Dominique's two middle names and his last name were deleted to protect his identity.
(3) The phrase 'Daenerys, first of her name' comes from *Game of Thrones* and refers to Daenerys Targaryen. It is part of her formal royal title, used to emphasize her lineage and claim to the throne. The phrasing evokes the ceremonial, monarchic language used to introduce rulers.
(4) The siblings answered this question twice in French over a year apart because I initially thought they hadn't responded.

References

Braun, V. and Clarke, V. (2006) Using thematic analysis in psychology. *Qualitative Research in Psychology* 3 (2), 77–101. https://doi.org/10.1191/1478088706qp063oa

Dewaele, J.-M. (2016) 'Why do so many bi- and multilinguals feel different when switching languages?'. *International Journal of Multilingualism* 13 (1), 92–105. https://doi.org/10.1080/14790718.2015.1040406

Ellis, R. (2008) *The Study of Second Language Acquisition* (2nd edn). Oxford University Press.

Emerson, R.M., Fretz, R.I. and Shaw, L.L. (2011) *Writing Ethnographic Fieldnotes* (2nd edn). University of Chicago Press.

Grice, H.P. (1975) Logic and conversation. In P. Cole and J.L. Morgan (eds) *Syntax and Semantics, Vol. 3: Speech Acts* (pp. 41–58). Academic Press.

Guest, G., MacQueen, K.M. and Namey, E.E. (2012) *Applied Thematic Analysis*. Sage.

Hammersley, M. and Atkinson, P. (2019) *Ethnography: Principles in Practice* (4th edn). Routledge.

Kramsch, C. (2009) *The Multilingual Subject*. Oxford University Press.

Little, S. and Zhou, Y. (2024) Beyond roots and wings: co-constructing a framework for heritage language children's liminal and limbotic identities. *Journal of Multilingual and Multicultural Development* 46 (6), 1555–1568. https://doi.org/10.1080/01434632.2024.2421437

Moustakas, C. (1994) *Phenomenological Research Methods*. Sage.

Odlin, T. (1989) *Language Transfer: Cross-Linguistic Influence in Language Learning*. Cambridge University Press.

Pavlenko, A. (2005) *Emotions and Multilingualism*. Cambridge University Press.

Ringbom, H. (2007) *Cross-Linguistic Similarity in Foreign Language Learning*. Multilingual Matters.

van Manen, M. (1997) *Researching Lived Experience: Human Science for an Action Sensitive Pedagogy* (2nd edn). Routledge.

7 All Things Considered: Closing Thoughts

In this book, I have shared intentional strategies for raising multilingual children, from pre-journey preparation to adolescence and young adulthood, along with the perspectives of our adult children who have grown up multilingual from birth. I hope these suggestions and reflections have offered you both insight and encouragement to embark on or continue your own multilingual childrearing journey with greater confidence and joy.

In this concluding chapter, I bring together the broader insights that have emerged by introducing a conceptual framework drawn from a grammatical term known as the **middle voice**, which I will explain shortly. This framework illuminates the process of raising multilingual children as a shared journey of becoming, in which parents and children co-create language, identity, and belonging rather than one side acting or achieving alone.

In addition to synthesizing these ideas, this chapter also turns to areas often overlooked in the daily work of raising multilingual children. I refer to these as 'lessons between the lines', insights that may seem subtle but are vital to the multilingual childrearing journey. Some of these lessons invite deeper reflection on topics rarely discussed in the literature, whereas others touch on aspects that may even be seen as controversial. Bringing these issues into view offers a more textured and authentic understanding of what it means to live, learn and grow together through multiple languages.

The Middle Voice as the Heart of Multilingual Parenting

Raising multilingual children is not something parents do *for* their kids, nor something children accomplish alone. It is a shared journey shaped by daily conversations, routines and experiences. The grammatical term 'middle voice' offers a helpful way to understand this shared process. In Ancient Greek, the **middle voice** shows that a person is both performing an action and experiencing its effects simultaneously. For example, *paideuō* means 'I teach,' while *paideuomai* means 'I learn.' Heritage language learning works in a similar way: Parents and children continually shape and are shaped by what unfolds between them.

This mutual shaping is precisely what gives rise to what Claire Kramsch (2009) calls a **'third space,'** where languages, cultures and identities are co-created. Because language is mutually experienced (the middle voice), interactions generate something new: Shared expressions, hybrid practices unique ways of belonging. Our children did not simply alternate among their languages. Through family life, they formed a flexible space where their identities shifted and expanded, preventing them from being confined to a single frame of reference.

Entering this third space is an act of co-creation that happens through everyday middle voice moments: Listening, responding and sharing your own stories. As Wittgenstein (1961: 149) wrote, 'The limits of my language mean the limits of my world.' Raising your child in more than one language expands that world for both of you.

With this middle voice perspective in mind, we can now explore the following areas in a more integrated way.

Situating heritage language development in a whole-person approach

Raising a multilingual child is not simply about transmitting vocabulary or maintaining a family language. It is an integral part of raising a whole person. Through heritage language, children build emotional connection, social understanding, cultural awareness and a strong sense of identity. Language becomes a way for them to understand themselves and to feel rooted in their many communities.

The middle voice offers insight into how this development unfolds. Rather than seeing the parents as instructors and the children as recipients, the middle voice reminds us that both participate in a shared, evolving process. Parents respond to a child's curiosity or hesitation, and children grow within this responsive environment. Every interaction (whether a toddler naming objects or a teenager choosing language use) shows how the development of language and personal development move forward together, mutually influencing one another.

Situating heritage language in holistic development means understanding it as a living, relational process. You are not simply helping your child acquire a language. You are nurturing their confidence, empathy, cultural grounding and emerging sense of self. The goal is not a fixed level of proficiency but an ongoing dialogue between your child's whole growth and the many worlds they inhabit, linguistic, social, emotional and cultural alike.

Setting co-constructed goals

The middle voice also reminds us that goals in heritage language learning emerge through interaction, rather than being defined by the parents alone or achieved by the children independently. They emerge through a process of negotiation, shaped by both guidance and response. Goals work best when they are flexible, realistic and responsive to your child's abilities, developmental stage and your family's context. The aim is not perfection or replicating the proficiency of native speakers raised in a heritage environment. Instead, it is about building a solid foundation together, knowing that learning a heritage language outside its natural environment will follow its own rhythm.

In our family, we often had to revisit the goals we had set when our children were younger. As teenagers, their demanding schedules left little time for literacy in both French and Chinese. Expecting them to reach native-level proficiency in reading and writing was no longer realistic, especially in Chinese. Rather than holding onto those earlier benchmarks, we adjusted. As long as a foundation was built, there would be opportunities to deepen literacy later. This shift, made with the children and in recognition of their reality, reduced stress for everyone and kept our multilingual journey alive. The process itself became an achievement, as our goals were continually shaped in the space between our guidance and their lived experience.

Resistance as middle voice dialogue

No multilingual journey is free of resistance. At certain points, children may refuse to attend heritage school, resist parental expectations or favor the dominant peer language rather than the heritage language. Such moments can feel discouraging. Yet when viewed through a middle voice lens, resistance is not rejection but an opportunity for dialogue, a moment when children are expressing their emerging agency and inviting conversation about meaning, purpose and ownership. When approached this way, resistance often becomes the starting point for renewed engagement rather than the end of the effort.

One good example of how resistance can transform over time comes from my older son, Léandre. As a child, he dreaded attending Chinese school every weekend and often questioned why he had to go. Rather than viewing his resistance simply as defiance, I tried to keep the conversation open, acknowledging his feelings while explaining our long-term hopes for him. Years later, when in college, he chose to enroll in a Chinese course for heritage speakers, this time out of his own motivation. What had once been external pressure gradually became an internal choice.

A similar pattern appeared with my younger son, Dominique. When he was little, I took him to piano lessons, but his resistance was so strong that I used to joke each session felt like a heart attack for me. Instead of forcing him to continue or abandoning the activity entirely, we shifted the approach. We kept the dialogue open and moved toward gentle, playful exposure by listening to music together and keeping the piano within reach without pressure. Years later, he returned to the instrument on his own terms, and it has since become a daily joy and creative outlet.

The development of heritage language often unfolds in the same way: Resistance in one season, renewed interest in another. When resistance is treated as a signal for conversation rather than confrontation, parents can adjust expectations while maintaining continuity and positive emotional connections. Seeds planted with patience and care may lie dormant for years only to sprout later in the most unexpected and rewarding ways. From a middle voice perspective, resistance is not a barrier but a space for negotiation and co-construction, where parental intention and the child's growing autonomy come together to shape the long-term journey.

Family wellbeing is a process of family communication

Research shows that heritage language use is closely tied to family relationships and overall wellbeing. When children develop both their community and heritage languages, they gain a stronger sense of resilience and connectedness (Toppelberg & Collins, 2010), whereas losing a shared language weakens communication across generations (Fillmore, 2000).

The middle voice reminds us that heritage language maintenance is created not by the parents or children alone but through shared communication. Everyday conversations at dinner, bedtime or during routines become acts of co-creation that build trust, intimacy and belonging. Wellbeing grows from this mutual exchange rather than from one-sided instruction.

This is especially important in OPOL families, where one parent may not understand the other's communication with the children. Retelling or repeating messages so everyone is included can turn these moments into opportunities for connection. Children learn flexibility, the parents feel acknowledged and family bonds grow stronger.

Family wellbeing also involves navigating cultural and individual communication styles. Cultural norms shape interaction, yet parents bring their own temperaments as well. In our family, my husband's emphasis on precise French and my more flexible use of Chinese offered distinct communicative voices that our children wove into their own.

Navigating differences: Individual and cultural communication styles

Cultural norms shape how parents and children interact, yet each parent also brings a personal way of speaking. Across cultures, parents differ in how they guide interaction. Japanese parents, for example, often value subtlety and non-verbal cues, whereas American parents may prioritize direct expression and frequent praise (Clancy, 1986). Yet families rarely follow cultural templates rigidly. Individual temperaments lead parents to blend or adapt these norms in daily life, creating unique patterns of communication.

Seen through the middle voice, such differences are not contradictions but forms of co-construction. Each parent contributes a linguistic style shaped by culture and personality, and their children draw from both to build their own communicative repertoires. What matters most is genuine, responsive interaction that nurtures confidence, competence and connection in the heritage language.

Feedback as a dialogic process

During development of the heritage language, mistakes are inevitable. Research shows that parents who provide correction indirectly through repetition, reformulation or clarification requests, rather than overt criticism, are more effective in supporting children's growth (Chouinard & Clark, 2003). The middle voice indicates that feedback is not a top-down act of fixing but a shared process in which parents offer gentle correction and children internalize new forms. Errors are not failures but stepping stones that invite dialogue. Because this correction occurs within loving and responsive interaction, it strengthens both the child's learning and the family bond. In this way, feedback and internalization function as a co-constructed process that keeps heritage languages alive. As discussed later in the chapter under the heading 'Balancing Gentle Demand with Responsive Interaction,' feedback works best when it is not only dialogic but also paired with the gentle demand needed to create lasting change.

Translanguaging as negotiation

Translanguaging (using more than one language within a single conversation) is a middle voice practice because it keeps communication moving through shared negotiation rather than strict rules. When Dominique struggled to express ideas from an English essay in Chinese, I let him insert the English terms so he could continue speaking. This kept the dialogue alive and gave me natural openings to revisit the Chinese vocabulary later. In this way, translanguaging supported communication and connection rather than replacing the heritage language. For multilingual children, the ability to translanguage is a powerful tool for expression and identity.

However, in the early years, using each parent's heritage language consistently can help children build a strong foundation and clear associations. Once this foundation is in place, translanguaging often emerges naturally, allowing children to draw on their full linguistic repertoire in ways that both facilitate and enrich communication.

Syncretic communication as co-creation

A powerful expression of the middle voice in multilingual development appears in syncretic communication, the creative blending of linguistic and cultural elements from a child's full repertoire to achieve nuanced goals. This practice reflects not confusion but cognitive flexibility, as children weave their languages together in a collaborative meaning-making process shaped by both their agency and their environment.

My observation of our two multilingual sons shows how immersion in multiple languages nurtures this syncretic discourse. Drawing on their linguistic **funds of knowledge** (the multilingual experiences and cultural insights children draw from everyday practice), they could mix languages, play with sounds and meanings and invent words that reflect their identities. For example, when both children were young, Léandre coined *fromage criminel* ('criminal cheese') to describe a cheese so delicious it felt illicit, while Dominique created *violonisateur* for someone who plays the violin so badly that it violates the listener's ears, words they invented with their father (Wang, 2008). These are not errors but imaginative expressions born in a family environment that encouraged experimentation and enjoyment.

Syncretic communication is the middle voice in action, showing how multilingual children become co-creators of language. They are neither passive followers of parental rules nor isolated linguistic inventors, but active participants who continually reshape language within the dialogic space of the family and its intersecting cultural worlds.

Heritage language competence: A practice of shared engagement

When looking at multilingual competence, the middle voice offers a realistic perspective. It reminds us that competence is not a fixed skill but a dynamic capacity that is lived and shaped through the continual, shared engagement of parents and children.

Research confirms that input matters (Goodman *et al.*, 2008), but the middle voice clarifies how input is made powerful within a multilingual context. Exposure is most effective when it is dialogic and relational, neither as one-sided teaching nor passive listening but as a shared experience such as singing together, reading aloud or inventing a joke at the dinner table. This relational practice is key, as studies show that a strong home language foundation can support growth in other languages (Mitits *et al.*, 2018).

What matters is not only the amount of input a child receives but the extent to which families and children co-inhabit the heritage language, making it a living part of their shared life. By focusing on this mutual practice, we see that multilingual competence is not just something the child possesses but something the family practices collectively. This shared linguistic life nurtures the child's ability to draw flexibly on their full, diverse language repertoire.

Assessing heritage language

Heritage language assessment looks different through the lens of the middle voice. Because heritage speakers grow up with multiple languages and uneven exposure, they rarely match monolingual norms (Polinsky, 2018). The question shifts from '*How nativelike is my child?*'to '*What can we do together in this language?*'

Assessment becomes relational. Proficiency appears not only in reading and writing but in shared practices such as a bedtime story, a family joke or a conversation with grandparents. These everyday moments reveal how language fosters belonging and connection, even if they do not align with standardized benchmarks.

Research shows that heritage speakers often have strengths traditional tests miss, including contextual awareness and cross-linguistic creativity (Hornberger, 2003). In a middle voice approach, parents and children co-participate: The parents create opportunities and scaffolding, and the children expand their repertoire through inventive use of language.

At home, assessment can be playful and interactive. Reading together becomes assessment when a child retells a story or invents new phrases. Cooking can serve the same function when a child explains each step in the heritage language. These practices highlight what families can do together rather than imposing external judgment.

Ultimately, heritage language assessment reflects family language life more than individual mastery. Multilingualism exists on a spectrum, and there is no 'perfect' multilingual child. Proficiency naturally fluctuates across languages, contexts and stages. Supporting a child's multilingual journey means valuing progress over perfection and recognizing that every multilingual profile is unique.

Technology, media and resources alone will not raise a multilingual child

The middle voice framework guides us to view technology and media as helpful for heritage language only when paired with interaction. Watching television alone is passive; watching together, laughing, asking questions and discussing characters turns it into a shared, meaning-making activity. For example, children learn phonetic distinctions through live, responsive interactions, not from television or audio alone (Zimmerman *et al.*, 2009).

This principle applies equally to learning materials. When my sons dismissed their Chinese textbooks as 'for babies,' the issue was not their ability but a mismatch between the materials and their identities. Resources work best when chosen collaboratively, balancing levels, interests and family context. A comic book, favorite song or video game can engage a child more authentically than a workbook because it reflects a shared choice.

Parent as researcher

When you take on the role of researcher, observing and documenting your child's multilingual journey, you engage in a middle voice practice. This is neither detached research nor simple parental involvement but a process in which you both guide and are guided by your child. Keeping journals, recording conversations or reflecting on daily interactions becomes a dialogic act in which noticing and revisiting moments reshapes how you and your child experience language together. Scholars of family language policy show that parents continually adjust their strategies according to their children's responses, making them both participants and analysts (King *et al.*, 2008).

For instance, recording Léandre's playful word experiments or Dominique's creative coinages was not simply preservation but shared meaning-making. Writing these moments down allowed me to re-hear my children and let their voices shape my own. Research on multilingual families highlights the same dynamic: Parents are not just teaching but continually interpreting their children's practices, much like ethnographers of their own homes (Gregory *et al.*, 2004; Okita, 2002). Studies on multiliteracy show that shared reading and writing become powerful tools when reflected on together (Kenner, 2004) In this sense, the parent as researcher principle is co-creation, where documentation and interpretation evolve alongside the child's actions. Over time, these reflective habits strengthen language development and family cohesion, creating a shared multilingual record that becomes part of your family's legacy.

Growing together

Multilingual parenting is best understood through the familiar metaphor of a marathon, not a sprint. The middle-voice lens helps us see this long journey as one in which parents and children grow up together. For example, teaching my sons Chinese not only guided their learning; it also reshaped mine. I rediscovered aspects of my heritage, deepened my understanding of the language and broadened my cultural awareness. Through the middle voice, I came to see that my children's multilingual growth and my own were intertwined. As they expanded their identities, I expanded with them in patience, resilience and openness.

A marathon also calls for flexibility. As children's interests rise and fall and life shifts around them, families adjust the pace together, reintroducing a favorite book, seeking support, planning a trip or simply adding a few more minutes of conversation. Each small step strengthens the shared path.

This is the priceless gift you give and receive: A family identity that endures. You are giving your child the ability to see the world through multiple lenses and to carry your family's voice into the future. And in walking beside them, you grow as well. As your child's world expands, so does yours.

Together, you are not simply managing languages; you are practicing an art, the art of shaping a living, evolving family culture. With patience, intention and care, you weave a tapestry of love and language, with each conversation, story and shared moment adding a new thread. Over time, this quiet artistry nurtures resilience, joy and a deep sense of connection that will continue to unfold across generations.

Lessons Between the Lines

Having explored the broader dimensions of raising multilingual children through the lens of the middle voice, I now turn to a few aspects that often go unnoticed in everyday family life but still carry deep meaning. These lessons reveal themselves in small details, in the in-between moments of parenting, when language and family life quietly weave together and shape one another.

Building a strong foundation in at least one language

For multilingual children, achieving equal proficiency in all their languages is often difficult. Although this book supports multilingual development, it can be practical to help children build strong competence in one primary language while allowing their other languages, especially heritage ones, to grow through meaningful use and sustained exposure.

Because our children grew up in the United States and attended English-speaking schools, we emphasized developing English as their strongest language for literacy and academic learning. They completed their education from pre-kindergarten through college in English, establishing a secure foundation before moving to Europe for graduate studies, where they continued expanding their multilingual abilities.

This approach allowed them to develop deep proficiency in English, which is essential for critical reading, writing and communication in an information-driven world. A solid foundation in one language equips multilingual children to navigate academic, social and professional contexts with confidence, and these skills often transfer across languages.

This practice aims to mitigate the risk of what is sometimes termed **semilingualism**, a state in which individuals perceive their command across their linguistic repertoire as less than nativelike (Baker & Wright, 2021). An acquaintance of mine expressed this feeling when reflecting on her own language abilities. After moving from South Korea to the United States during high school and later to Germany, she shared that she did not feel fully strong in any of her languages. She noted that her Korean literacy had plateaued at a secondary level and described a persistent sense of insecurity about her grammar in both English and German.

Her experience suggests that when a strong academic foundation is not fully consolidated in at least one language, individuals may develop a fragmented sense of communicative competence (Cummins, 2000). At the same time, it is important to recognize that such perceptions often reflect **domain-specific development**, where different languages are used for different life stages and purposes, rather than a true lack of ability (Pavlenko, 2014). Supporting sustained literacy and academic skills in at least one threshold language remains a vital foundation for confident multilingual development.

Building heritage language intuition through early exposure

Early exposure to a heritage language does more than provide additional hours of input. It helps children internalize the rhythm, structure and feel of the language in ways that later learners rarely achieve. Children who are exposed early often develop a reliable linguistic intuition, a sense for what sounds right or wrong, even when they cannot fully explain the grammar or spelling rules.

Take the example in Box 7.1: A friend of mine, a non-native Chinese speaker, once sent me a message using an earlier version of Google Translate that was filled with awkward phrasing and nonsensical expressions. Because he lacked an internalized sense of the language, the text sounded clearly unnatural. In contrast, children like Léandre and Dominique, who were exposed to Chinese from birth, may not always write every character correctly or use every tone perfectly, but they can immediately sense when a sentence does not sound right. I once did a small experiment with Léandre and asked him to write the same message as my friend in Chinese using Google Translate as support. His version, however, came out natural and authentic. Over the years, both Léandre and Dominique have occasionally used Google Translate or other translation tools as references, yet they consistently revise or reject translations that sound unnatural, guided by their intuitive sense of Chinese.

Even if a heritage language never reaches the same level of proficiency as a dominant mainstream language, early exposure still builds sensitivity to rhythm, phrasing and nuance. This intuition becomes especially valuable in translation, creative expression or self-correction, giving heritage language speakers an awareness that late learners often lack.

Studies of heritage language speakers support this notion of metalinguistic intuition. For example, research on Spanish heritage language speakers shows that they display nativelike intuition about sound patterns and word structures, even when their formal grammatical knowledge is less developed (Shelton *et al.*, 2017). The advantage of early heritage language exposure, therefore, is not only about acquiring vocabulary or grammar but about cultivating a deeper linguistic sensibility, a kind of natural ear that supports confident, authentic and nuanced communication across languages.

Box 7.1 Writing example of a non-heritage language speaker

Original Message in Chinese (through Google Translate)

亲爱的小雷,

你好吗? 我希望一切都受到惩罚, 这是这么长时间我都没有听你的。 我接受选举委员会 的xxxx是不是从至少看到自己盎司每年剥离的唯一理由! 看你来了, 如果不及早比晚。 谢谢。

Literal Translation in English
Dear Little Thunder (My name in Chinese, 蕾, actually means "early morning flower bud," but my friend used a different character, 雷, which has a similar pronunciation but means "thunder"). How are you? I hope everything is punished, this has been so long time I have not heard you. I accept the election committee's xxxx is it not the only reason to at least see one's own ounces peeled off every year! See you came, if not early compared to late.
Thanks.

Intended Message
Dear Friend Xiao-lei,
The only reason I accepted the nomination for xxxx committee is that I don't want to miss the opportunity to see you at least once a year. Look forward to seeing you.
Thank you.

Examples from Wang (2016: 7).

Balancing gentle demand with responsive interaction

Parenting in multilingual families often involves walking a fine line between being responsive to your children's needs and maintaining firm expectations. I always tried to be responsive to my children's feelings, ensuring that language learning remained positive and connected. My instinct was to encourage communication in any form, even if it meant mixing languages or overlooking small errors, so that they would continue to engage comfortably. However, over time, I came to realize that responsiveness alone may not be enough to sustain steady progress in the heritage language.

My husband's approach offered a valuable contrast. He tended to be steady and structured, speaking to our children in full French sentences and consistently correcting their errors, even when they resisted. His gentle persistence provided the predictability and clarity that helped them internalize grammatical accuracy and develop stronger competence in French. By contrast, my hesitation to correct their Chinese, out of concern for preserving comfort and harmony, sometimes allowed small inaccuracies to persist. For example, they still occasionally say 放袜子 ('put down socks') instead of 穿袜子 ('put on socks').

In their reflections in Chapter 6, Léandre and Dominique both noted that they wished I had been a little more insistent about using Chinese at home. They compared this with their father's approach to French. Even though they sometimes found his corrections irritating, his steady reformulations helped them internalize grammatical precision and strengthen their competence in French. Their reflections confirmed what I had gradually come to understand: That gentle insistence, when paired with warmth and patience, can make a lasting difference in children's language development.

Such balance does not contradict the principle of dialogic interaction but complements it. Responsiveness keeps communication meaningful, whereas gentle demand adds structure and continuity. As psycholinguist Annick De Houwer (2007) observes, persistence offered with affection supports stronger multilingual growth. Children thrive when love and structure coexist, finding both comfort and motivation in the steady rhythm of their parents' guidance.

Focusing on the small wins

Raising multilingual children is rarely a straight path. It is a winding journey filled with adjustments, pauses and renewed beginnings. Life changes, routines shift and children's interest in one language may rise and fall over time. This ebb and flow are not a sign of failure but part of the natural rhythm of multilingual development.

Progress often happens quietly, in small steps that are easy to overlook. A child may begin to answer a simple question in the heritage language after months of silence, choose a favorite song in that language or mix fewer words from another tongue than before. These moments may seem minor, yet they signal deep, gradual growth. Research on family language interaction shows that small, consistent efforts such as brief conversations, shared stories and gentle persistence can accumulate over time to sustain multilingual development (Grosjean, 2010).

Celebrating these small wins helps maintain motivation for both parents and children. Even passive understanding represents a strong foundation on which active skills can later be built. The key is to stay flexible, to keep experimenting with new ways to engage, and to recognize that every authentic interaction counts. Multilingualism is not achieved in leaps but in layers, through many moments of connection that, over time, create something lasting and deeply meaningful.

Maintaining consistency in your chosen language

Though many factors influence multilingual development, few are as powerful as consistency in parental language use. When parents maintain steady and predictable language patterns, they create the stable environment children need to acquire and sustain multiple languages effectively. Research has shown that parental consistency is one of the strongest predictors of successful multilingual development (De Houwer, 2007). In contrast, inconsistent input can blur linguistic boundaries, reduce the quality of exposure and contribute to the language shifting toward the majority language. Studies have found that when children receive inconsistent or mixed input, they have greater difficulty detecting stable grammatical patterns and forming clear associations between words and contexts (Savarino *et al.*, 2025). Similarly, research on multilingual families indicates that frequent parental language mixing can weaken their children's commitment to the heritage language and increase reliance on the dominant community language (Cox *et al.*, 2021).

In many multilingual families, inconsistency often arises from good intentions. Parents may switch into the other parent's language to be inclusive or to make communication easier. However, when this occurs frequently, children may perceive one language as more accessible or socially valued; over time, they may default to the dominant community language, even in situations where the heritage language is intended to be used.

Consistency does not mean rigidity. Occasional flexibility can strengthen connection, especially in emotionally charged moments or when clarification is needed. What matters most is a reliable pattern that helps children associate each language with meaningful relationships and contexts. A steady approach builds both structure and trust: Children know what to expect, and this predictability enhances their sense of linguistic security.

Ultimately, maintaining consistency is not about enforcing a rule but about creating stable conditions for growth. When parents model confidence and continuity in their language use, they send a clear message that both languages are valued and worth sustaining.

Shifting parental roles: From manager to consultant

The role of parents in multilingual childrearing is dynamic and evolves with their children's developmental stages. In the early years, parents function primarily as managers. They provide structure, make decisions about language strategies and ensure consistent exposure to each language. This managerial role involves establishing routines such as bedtime stories in the heritage language, arranging playdates or classes that reinforce language use and maintaining regular contact with relatives who speak the heritage language. During this period, children depend heavily on their parents' organization and direction, and consistent parental management lays the groundwork for successful multilingual development (King *et al.*, 2008).

As children grow older, however, their social worlds expand. School, peers and personal interests increasingly influence their language use and identity. At this stage, parents are most effective when they shift from being managers to consultants. Instead of setting every routine, they guide and support their children's growing autonomy by offering encouragement, resources and authentic opportunities to use their languages. Research on family language policy shows that older children and adolescents respond more positively when they have agency in how they use and develop their languages (Luykx, 2005). A consultant-like stance recognizes children as active agents in their multilingual journey who are capable of negotiating meaning and identity through their own choices and experiences.

This gradual shift from manager to consultant reflects the broader process of parenting itself (Riera, 2003). Early childhood requires structure and direct involvement, whereas adolescence benefits from dialogue, trust and partnership. Embracing this evolution helps families sustain both the heritage language and family harmony, supporting not only linguistic growth but also mutual respect across generations.

Aligning your approach to your child's heritage language level

When raising multilingual children, it's essential to align your approach with each child's age and stage of heritage language development. What works for a 6-year-old won't necessarily work for a 14-year-old, even if both have similar language skills. For instance, although a 14-year-old's heritage language ability may be at the level of a native-speaking 6-year-old, their interests, cognitive maturity and learning preferences call for different strategies. For example, when my two sons were in high school, they often grew frustrated with the textbooks at their Chinese heritage language school, calling them 'for babies'. These materials, though effective for younger children, didn't engage older learners who needed content that respected their maturity and interests.

Therefore, it is essential to use age-appropriate resources, such as stories, cultural topics or conversational topics that align with your children's age and interests, which can help keep them motivated and improve heritage language learning.

Cultivating agency

Supporting a child's language learning journey involves empowering her to take ownership of the process. Cultivating agency (the capacity for a child to act independently and make their own choices) in multilingual development means encouraging active engagement with their heritage language(s) and making decisions that shape their learning experience (Benson, 2011).

This can include providing constructive feedback and allowing the child to explore the language in ways that resonate with them. For example, letting them choose conversation topics, engage in storytelling or use the language creatively reinforces their sense of autonomy. By encouraging the child to take the initiative and make decisions in their language journey, you help build their confidence and foster a proactive attitude toward multilingualism.

This approach not only strengthens their connection to the language but also promotes lifelong language engagement.

Connecting language and culture

Cultural Celebrations: During holidays and special occasions, multilingual children may blend traditions from different cultures to create unique celebrations. For example, a child who celebrates both Diwali and Thanksgiving may incorporate elements like Indian spices in traditional Thanksgiving dishes, adding a multicultural twist to the festivities.
Multilingual Storytime: When reading or telling stories, multilingual children may introduce characters or settings from different cultures, seamlessly weaving together diverse cultural backgrounds. This expands their understanding of the world and exposes them to a broader range of storytelling traditions.
Multilingual Fashion: Multilingual children may incorporate elements of different cultures into their personal style and fashion choices. They might blend traditional clothing or accessories from various cultural backgrounds, creating unique and fashionable ensembles that celebrate their multicultural identity.
Language Fusion in Cooking: Multilingual children may experiment with blending ingredients, flavors and cooking techniques from different culinary traditions. They might create innovative recipes that combine the best of multiple cultures, resulting in a fusion cuisine that reflects their diverse background and culinary creativity.

Appreciating accent and focusing on the articulation of clarity

One can strive to improve pronunciation and clarity, but attaining a completely nativelike accent, especially in a heritage language, is rare (Polinsky & Scontras, 2020). Simultaneous multilinguals, who acquire several languages from birth, often speak them without a noticeable accent. However, phonetic research shows that even highly proficient speakers may retain subtle traces of one language in another (Sancier & Fowler, 1997). Because linguistic systems remain interconnected in the brain, frequent use of one language can influence the production of sounds in the others. This means that even advanced multilinguals may sound slightly different from monolingual speakers of any given language. For multilingual children, an accent in their heritage language is not a sign of deficiency but a reflection of their lived linguistic environment and experience.

Accent variation is natural and widespread, even within a single language. English, for instance, is spoken with American, British, Australian and South African accents, each being distinct and equally valid. Heritage languages are no different. A child growing up in the United States who speaks Chinese, French, Arabic or another heritage language will naturally carry phonetic influences from

English or the local speech community into that language. This convergence of sounds reflects real-life interaction, not imperfection. It is a record of relationships, experiences and identity.

Although I deeply appreciate the beauty of diverse accents, I have also learned how unclear articulation can interfere with understanding. Once, I was trying to change a plane ticket over the phone, and the person assisting me spoke with such a heavy accent in English that I could not understand her at all. That experience reminded me that clarity in speech is not about erasing accent but about ensuring comprehension. For multilingual children, focusing on articulation helps them express themselves clearly and confidently, allowing their voices to be heard and understood.

Variation in accent is part of the beauty of multilingualism. Accents tell stories about where we have been, who we speak with and how we connect across cultures. Instead of correcting every deviation, it is far more helpful to celebrate the meaning and effort behind communication. What matters most is intelligibility, clarity and confidence. When children feel accepted for how they sound, they are more likely to speak their heritage language freely and continue developing it over time.

Some multilingual individuals even intentionally retain their distinctive accent, even when they are capable of adopting a more standard or prestige form. They may view their accent as an expression of authenticity and identity, a conscious choice not to blend in completely (Giles & Johnson, 1987). This resistance to accent convergence is in itself a form of self-definition (Pavlenko, 2003). It aligns with communication models that value intelligibility over nativeness, affirming that speaking clearly and confidently in one's own voice is a powerful expression of multilingual identity (Galloway & Jenkins, 2009).

Being mindful of communication contexts for first-born and only children

Children acquire language within a social environment where the people around them provide essential references for the relationships linking words, objects and actions. However, first-born or only children in a OPOL household often rely exclusively on their parent(s) for input. Without a range of conversational models, their early language development may reflect the limited perspectives available to them.

In our own family, this became evident during the first two years of our older son Léandre's life. He initially struggled with the French first-person pronoun *je* (I) when expressing ideas such as 'I sit.' Instead of saying '*Je veux m'asseoir*' (I want to sit down), he would say '*Veux t'asseoir*' (you want to sit). This mirrored his father's phrasing, '*Tu veux t'asseoir?*' ('Do you want to sit?'), which he frequently heard directed at him. With no other French-speaking references, Léandre adopted the pattern he observed, misinterpreting the pronoun's intended perspective. Similarly, he sometimes used *merci* ('thank you') in place of 'here you are,' again reflecting his interpretation of how his father used the phrase. Interestingly, this pattern disappeared once his younger brother Dominique was born. From the beginning, Dominique had another linguistic reference – his sibling – and did not experience the same confusion.

Parents of first-born or only children can gently broaden their child's linguistic environment in creative ways. One approach is to simulate conversational variety at home. Parents can encourage their child to 'speak' with dolls, stuffed animals or imaginary friends, creating additional voices and perspectives. Another useful strategy is role-play: Reversing roles so that the child pretends to be the parent and uses expressions such as 'I want' or 'You need' in context. Parents can also expand real-life exposure by arranging opportunities for the child to interact with multiple speakers of the heritage language, such as relatives, playgroups or community events.

These experiences enrich children's linguistic input, helping them develop a more balanced understanding of pronouns, phrases and conversational norms. Even in homes where one parent is the sole speaker of a heritage language, small creative adjustments can help simulate a broader language community, supporting children's overall communicative competence and confidence.

Recognizing gendered-language input

Since you and your spouse are the primary sources of heritage language input for your child, your way of speaking, including intonation, mannerisms, vocabulary and gender-influenced speech styles, is likely to influence their language development. Men and women often have distinct speech patterns (Tannen, 1990), and children tend to model the language of those they interact with most frequently (Anderson *et al.*, 2021; Bandura, 1977). For example, Léandre's early exposure to English came primarily from two college students majoring in communication sciences who practiced their skills with him. I had volunteered Léandre to provide him with additional English input. As a result, when he began speaking English, his voice often carried a higher pitch that mirrored theirs. This example illustrates how children's speech patterns are shaped by the linguistic and paralinguistic features of their language models.

Similarly, sociolinguist Una Cunningham-Andersson observed that her children, growing up in Sweden, developed what she described as a 'sissified' English because she was their sole English-speaking model (Cunningham-Andersson & Andersson, 2004). In a similar vein, linguist Madalena Cruz-Ferreira (2006) recounted a Portuguese friend's comment that her 3-year-old son spoke Portuguese in a manner perceived as effeminate. I noticed a comparable pattern in my own family. As the primary Chinese language model for my sons, both Léandre and Dominique initially adopted my intonation and word choices, which tended to reflect feminine speech patterns not typically associated with Chinese men.

To minimize gendered influence in children's heritage language input, parents can take intentional steps to broaden exposure. One effective approach is to provide opportunities for children to interact with speakers of different genders. For instance, a mother raising a son might arrange for him to spend time with male speakers of the heritage language, whereas a father raising a daughter can do the reverse. Exposure to a wider range of voices helps children hear multiple registers and styles. Parents can also incorporate diverse media such as stories, films, songs or audiobooks featuring speakers of different genders to enrich the linguistic environment.

Ultimately, children will adopt the speech styles they find comfortable and authentic. Variation in pitch, intonation or expression is not inherently right or wrong; it reflects the richness of human communication. Parents can offer variety and guidance, but their children's individual choices in how they express themselves are part of their growing sense of identity and belonging within each of their languages.

Being aware of the 'secret' language

When children are raised in a home language that is not widely spoken in the broader community, that language can sometimes take on the role of a 'secret' language. This dynamic often allows parents and children to exchange comments in front of others without being understood, which can feel empowering and even playful (Piller, 2002). When Léandre and Dominique were young children, for example, they sometimes whispered in French about people's appearances while we were out in public. Yet in today's globalized world, your 'secret' language may not be so secret after all. It is important to model for your child respectful and appropriate language use in public to avoid possible embarrassment or misunderstandings.

In families following a OPOL approach, children typically associate one language with each parent. Sometimes, the parents may not understand each other's languages. In such cases, children may learn to play one parent against the other by 'tattling' in different languages. This strategic use of language to manage family dynamics and relationships, often referred to as **triangulation** (Bowen, 1978) or **strategic codeswitching** (Gumperz, 1982; Rahmadani, 2023). For example, when Dominique was little and unhappy with me, such as when I nagged him to brush his teeth, he would complain to his father in French: '*Maman m'agace*' (Mother is annoying me). Conversely, when frustrated with his father, he would complain to me in Chinese: '爸爸不好' (Father is bad to me). Even today, similar moments still occur in our family. For instance, not long ago, Léandre complained to his father in French, '*Je sais pourquoi je suis fatigué, parce que maman me fatigue tout le temps*' (I know why I'm tired, because my mother is nagging all the time).

These moments reveal how multilingual environments shape children's interactions, sometimes in unexpected ways. Though playful, this 'tattletale' habit can unintentionally encourage gossip or division. Parents can gently address it by fostering open family communication, modeling mutual respect across languages and reminding children that language is a bridge to understanding, not a tool for creating distance.

Leveraging sibling influence

In multilingual families, it is common for siblings to default to the dominant societal language in their everyday interactions (Bridges & Hoff, 2014). This pattern reflects the strong influence of peers and school environments, where the dominant language is reinforced most consistently. However, siblings can also play an important role in sustaining heritage language practices when their parents provide intentional guidance and modeling.

In my own family, for example, my children, Léandre and Dominique, speak French with each other, which helped reinforce consistent communication in that language. My husband, Philippe, spent more time with the children during their early formative years, especially in their heritage language development. As a result, when Philippe and the two children converse together, they do so in French. As a result, Léandre and Dominique developed stronger skills in French than in their other heritage language, Chinese. This pattern illustrates how parental involvement and sibling dynamics can intersect to support heritage language use.

Research highlights that when siblings choose to communicate in a heritage language, the language gains an additional layer of reinforcement within the family domain (Schwartz, 2010). Shared routines, sibling play and collaborative tasks conducted in the heritage language provide rich opportunities for practice that feel natural and enjoyable. By contrast, when siblings shift to the dominant language, the heritage language may weaken if their parents do not actively create contexts where it feels meaningful and useful (Bridges & Hoff, 2014).

Ultimately, parents play a crucial role in guiding sibling language practices. Encouraging siblings to use the heritage language together – whether through games, storytelling or shared traditions – can significantly increase its vitality. Siblings are often children's longest-lasting conversation partners, and their language choices can influence family linguistic patterns well into adulthood (Barron-Hauwaert, 2011).

Defining success within your own situation

Success in raising multilingual children does not follow a single definition. It varies according to each family's circumstances, resources and goals. For some families, success may mean a child becoming fully fluent in speaking, reading and writing multiple languages. For others, it may mean a child understanding the heritage language even if they respond in the dominant community language. Circumstances such as parents' work schedules, community support, school environments and the extended family's involvement all shape what is realistic and meaningful. What matters most is not measuring your child against an external standard but recognizing the progress made within your own family context. Every shared word, every attempt to connect across languages and every effort to keep the heritage alive is a form of success worth celebrating.

Persisting through challenges

Raising multilingual children is rarely a smooth or predictable process. Life circumstances change, routines shift and children's interest in one language may fluctuate over time. When progress feels slower than expected, it can be easy to lose confidence or question your approach. Yet patience and persistence are among the most valuable qualities a parent can cultivate.

Research consistently shows that language learning develops unevenly, with plateaus and spurts that vary across time and context (De Houwer, 2009). What matters most is sustained engagement rather than early perfection. Even when your child appears to resist the heritage language or mix languages more frequently, those moments still reflect active processing and gradual growth. Continuing to speak, read and interact in your heritage language, no matter how imperfectly, is far more effective than stopping altogether.

The key is to remember that your efforts are never wasted. Every story shared, every song sung every conversation held in your language contributes to your child's foundation for future growth. As the linguist Patricia Kuhl (2010) notes, children's brains remain remarkably adaptable, constantly tuning to the sounds and patterns of the languages they hear. Progress may come slowly, but it does come. Staying patient, rather than giving up too quickly, ensures that multilingualism remains a living, evolving part of your family life.

Catching the train late

Parents sometimes worry that if they did not start early with heritage language exposure, the opportunity has passed. Although early beginnings offer advantages, especially for pronunciation and grammar, research makes clear that later starts can also lead to successful multilingual and multicultural development (Birdsong, 2006).

Older children and adolescents bring their own unique strengths to the process. They often possess greater memory capacity, more advanced metalinguistic awareness and a clearer sense of purpose in learning. When they understand that their heritage language connects them to family, culture or identity, motivation becomes a powerful ally (Jia & Fuse, 2007). In fact, studies show that older learners can sometimes match or even surpass younger ones in areas such as vocabulary, syntax and learning strategies (Long, 1990).

Even early exposure that seems to be forgotten can leave lasting traces. Research on internationally adopted children reveals that sounds from a language once spoken in infancy can later be reactivated. For example, children adopted from China into French-speaking families, though no longer using Chinese, were able to distinguish Chinese tones as accurately as bilingual peers who had continuous exposure from birth (Pierce, 2014).

These findings offer an encouraging reminder that it is never too late to begin. Starting later may require creativity, patience and sustained practice, but the rewards of multilingualism, including stronger cognition, deeper cultural connection and richer communication, remain within reach. What matters most is not when you start but that you start and keep going.

Supporting neurodivergent children in multilingual development

Raising a multilingual child with **neurodivergence**[1] or developmental disabilities is not only possible but often beneficial. Research consistently shows that multilingual exposure does not hinder the language development of children with intellectual or linguistic differences. On the contrary, it can enhance social communication (Uljarević, *et al.*, 2016), cognitive flexibility (Bialystok, 2015), and family connection (Tannenbaum & Howie, 2002). For example, studies with children who have Down syndrome and autism spectrum disorder have found that multilingual exposure does not delay language milestones (Hambly & Fombonne, 2012; Ward & Sanoudaki, 2021). In many cases, these children demonstrate similar progress to their monolingual peers in terms of vocabulary, comprehension, and social interaction. Multilingualism can also promote greater perspective-taking and emotional expression, which are especially valuable for children who face communicative challenges (González-Barrero & Nadig, 2019).

Equally important, multilingual exposure allows children with disabilities to participate more fully in family and cultural life. When families share their heritage language, they create stronger emotional bonds and preserve vital connections to extended relatives, traditions and identity (Yu, 2013). Parents sometimes fear that speaking more than one language will confuse their child or slow their progress, but evidence overwhelmingly shows that this concern is unfounded (Paradis *et al.*, 2011).

The key is to provide intentional, supportive and meaningful input across languages. Families can adjust their expectations, use visual supports or simplified structures and collaborate closely with educators or speech language specialists who understand multilingual development. With patience and consistency, neurodivergent children can thrive as multilinguals, gaining both communicative competence and a stronger sense of belonging in their linguistic communities. The gift of multilingualism, encompassing connection to family, identity and culture, belongs to every child.

Spending quality time with your child

When all is said and done, the heart of heritage language learning is not found in a method alone but in time spent together. Talking, playing and exploring in your heritage language is more than practice; it is how your child learns to express, to connect and to become. Every conversation and every shared moment in your heritage language becomes part of who your child is becoming.

Research reminds us that children's strongest language growth arises from meaningful, responsive interaction with parents, not from passive exposure or instruction alone (Hart & Risley, 1995). Studies of multilingual families show that when heritage language input is limited, it often falls behind the community language. In one study, Polish trilingual children in the United Kingdom had English vocabularies equal to their monolingual peers, yet their Polish vocabulary was smaller, largely because their home exposure was limited (Mieszkowska *et al.*, 2017). Heritage languages do not sustain themselves automatically; they flourish through time, presence and shared experience. The quantity and quality of time parents spend with their children remain among the strongest predictors of both vocabulary growth and overall language development (Hoff, 2003).

In our own family, this lesson became a way of life. My husband and I spent as much time as possible with our sons, Léandre and Dominique. We did not believe in 'parent time away'. This may sound unconventional, but those years of constant togetherness became the heartbeat of our family life. We took them everywhere: To cultural events, on family trips and on daily errands. We spoke, listened and laughed in our heritage languages, letting them flow naturally through every experience. Looking back, what moves me most is not only their ability to live comfortably in three languages, but also the kind of people they have become: Compassionate, curious, grounded and connected to their roots. Their languages grew from the same soil that nurtured their humanity, time, presence and care.

Spending quality time with your child means offering your full attention, not merely being nearby but being truly present. It means listening, responding and discovering together. It is creating spaces where words and affection grow side by side, where language is not taught but lived. This is where the heritage language takes root and where your child learns not only how to speak but how to belong. When you give your time, you give more than language; you give memory, connection and the gentle rhythm of shared life. In those moments, you begin to practice what this book celebrates: The art of raising multilingual children and giving a priceless gift.

Closing Remarks

I hope this book has affirmed for you that raising your child with your heritage language is not only worthwhile but profoundly meaningful. Along the way, there will be imperfections. Your child may speak with an accent, choose the wrong word or struggle to read and write in the heritage language. Progress may be uneven, and moments of resistance or fatigue may arise. But what matters most is not perfection but participation. Every effort, every word and every shared moment in your heritage language adds to a living story of connection, care and love that continues to grow with your family.

Raising a multilingual child is not something you do to your child, nor something your child accomplishes alone. It is something you create together. Each exchange, whether it is a playful conversation, a shared story, a moment of discovery or even an occasional argument, becomes part of a larger tapestry that intertwines language, identity and connection in everyday life. Some seeds blossom early and others rest quietly until the time is right, but all take root in the soil you nurture with intention and patience.

As you walk beside your child in the journey, your own world expands. You rediscover forgotten words, hear familiar ones in new ways and reconnect with the cultural threads that shaped you. Through this process, you are not simply passing on a language but also cultivating a legacy. You are practicing an art that requires mindfulness, flexibility and faith, trusting that your efforts, even when invisible, are shaping something enduring and beautiful.

The gift of multilingualism is more than the mastery of words. It is a bridge across generations, a mirror of identity and a voice that carries love across time and place. May you continue to perfect the art of raising multilingual children, cherishing the small moments and quiet victories that give life to this priceless gift, as language becomes love made visible. With my heartfelt wishes as you pass on your heritage language to your child.

Note

(1) Neurodivergence refers to natural differences in how people's brains develop and function, including conditions such as autism, ADHD, dyslexia, or intellectual disabilities. It highlights diversity rather than deficit, recognizing that children learn and communicate in varied but equally valuable ways (Singer, 2017; Walker, 2021).

References

Anderson, N.J., Graham, S.A., Prime, H., Jenkins, J.M. and Madigan, S. (2021) Linking quality and quantity of parental linguistic input to child language skills: A meta-analysis. *Child Development* 92 (2), 484–501. https://doi.org/10.1111/cdev.13508

Baker, C. and Wright, W.E. (2021) *Foundations of Bilingual Education and Bilingualism* (7th edn). Multilingual Matters.

Bandura, A. (1977) *Social Learning Theory*. Prentice Hall.

Barron-Hauwaert, S. (2011) *Bilingual Siblings: Language Use in Families*. Multilingual Matters.

Benson, P. (2011) *Teaching and Researching Autonomy in Language Learning* (2nd edn). Longman.

Bialystok, E. (2015) Bilingualism and the development of executive function: The role of attention. *Child Development Perspectives* 9 (2), 117–121. https://doi.org/10.1111/cdep.12116

Birdsong, D. (2006) Age and second language acquisition and processing: A selective overview. *Language Learning* 56 (S1), 9–49. https://doi.org/10.1111/j.1467-9922.2006.00353.x

Bowen, M. (1978) *Family Therapy in Clinical Practice*. Jason Aronson.

Bridges, K. and Hoff, E. (2014) Older sibling influences on the language environment and language development of toddlers in bilingual homes. *Applied Psycholinguistics* 35 (2), 225–241. https://doi.org/10.1017/S0142716412000379

Chouinard, M.M. and Clark, E.V. (2003) Adult reformulations of child errors as negative evidence. *Journal of Child Language* 30 (3), 637–669. https://doi.org/10.1017/S0305000903005701

Clancy, P.M. (1986) The acquisition of communicative style in Japanese. In B. Schieffelin and E. Ochs (eds) *Language Socialization across Cultures* (pp. 213–250). Cambridge University Press.

Cox Jr, R.B., deSouza, D.K., Bao, J., Lin, H., Sahbaz, S., Greder, K.A., Larzelere, R.E., Washburn, I.J., Leon-Cartagena, M. and Arredondo-Lopez, A. (2021) Shared language erosion: Rethinking immigrant family communication and impacts on youth development. *Children* 8 (4), 256. https://doi.org/10.3390/children8040256

Cruz-Ferreira, M. (2006) *Three is a Crowd? Acquiring Portuguese in a Trilingual Environment*. Multilingual Matters.

Cummins, J. (2000) *Language, Power and Pedagogy: Bilingual Children in the Crossfire*. Multilingual Matters.

Cunningham-Andersson, U. and Andersson, S. (2004) *Growing Up with Two Languages: A Practical Guide for the Bilingual Family* (2nd edn). Routledge.

De Houwer, A. (2007) Parental language input patterns and children's bilingual use. *Applied Psycholinguistics* 28 (3), 411–424. https://doi.org/10.1017/S0142716407070221

De Houwer, A. (2009) *Bilingual First Language Acquisition*. Multilingual Matters.

Fillmore, L.W. (2000) Loss of language, loss of culture, loss of self. *Early Childhood Today* 15 (2), 52–53.

Galloway, N. and Jenkins, J. (2009) Intelligibility in English as a Lingua Franca. *ELT Journal* 63 (4), 303–315.

Giles, H. and Johnson, P. (1987) Ethnolinguistic identity theory: A social psychological approach to language maintenance. *International Journal of the Sociology of Language* 68, 69–99. https://doi.org/10.1515/ijsl.1987.68.69

González-Barrero, A.M. and Nadig, A.S. (2019) Can bilingualism mitigate set-shifting difficulties in children With autism spectrum disorders? *Child Development* 90 (4), 1043–1060. https://doi.org/10.1111/cdev.12979

Goodman, J.C., Dale, P.S. and Li, P. (2008) Does frequency count? Parental input and the acquisition of vocabulary. *Journal of Child Language* 35 (3), 515–531. https://doi.org/10.1017/S0305000907008641

Grosjean, F. (2010) *Bilingual: Life and Reality*. Harvard University Press.

Gumperz, J.J. (1982) *Discourse Strategies*. Cambridge University Press.

Hart, B. and Risley, T.R. (1995) *Meaningful Differences in the Everyday Experience of Young American Children*. Paul H. Brookes.

Hoff, E. (2003) The specificity of environmental influence: Socioeconomic status affects early vocabulary development via maternal speech. *Child Development* 74 (5), 1368–1378. https://doi.org/10.1111/1467-8624.00612

Hornberger, N.H. (2003) *Continua of Biliteracy: An Ecological Framework for Educational Policy, Research, and Practice in Multilingual Settings*. Multilingual Matters.

Jia, G. and Fuse, A. (2007) Acquisition of English grammatical morphology by native Mandarin-speaking children and adolescents: Age-related differences. *Journal of Speech, Language, and Hearing Research* 50 (5), 1280–1299. https://doi.org/10.1044/1092-4388(2007/090)

Kenner, C. (2004) *Becoming Biliterate: Young Children Learning Different Writing Systems* (pp. 23–120). Trentham Books.

King, K.A., Fogle, L. and Logan-Terry, A. (2008) Family language policy. *Language and Linguistics Compass* 2 (5), 907–922.

Kramsch, C. (2009) *The Multilingual Subject*. Oxford University Press.

Kuhl, P.K. (2010) Brain mechanisms in early language acquisition. *Neuron* 67 (5), 713–727.

Long, M.H. (1990) Maturational constraints on language development. *Studies in Second Language Acquisition* 12 (3), 251–285. https://doi.org/10.1017/S0272263100009165

Luykx, A. (2005) Children as socializing agents: Family language policy in bilingual families. *International Journal of Bilingual Education and Bilingualism* 8 (2–3), 181–206.

Mieszkowska, K., Łuniewska, M., Kołak, J., Kacprzak, A., Wodniecka, Z. and Haman, E. (2017) Home language will not take care of itself: Vocabulary knowledge in trilingual children in the United Kingdom. *Frontiers in Psychology* 8, 1358. https://doi.org/10.3389/fpsyg.2017.01358

Mitits, L., Alexiou, T. and Milton, J. (2018) Cross-linguistic influence in multilingual children's vocabulary: The role of the home language. *International Journal of Multilingualism* 15 (3), 243–259.

Okita, T. (2002) *Invisible Work: Bilingualism, Language Choice and Childrearing in Intermarried Families* (pp. 109–149). John Benjamins. https://doi.org/10.1075/impact.12

Paradis, J., Genesee, F. and Crago, M. (2011) *Dual Language Development and Disorders: A Handbook on Bilingualism and Second Language Learning* (2nd edn). *Brookes*.

Pavlenko, A. (2003) 'I was a fluent speaker twenty years ago': Acquiring a new self in a new language. In A. Pavlenko, A. Blackledge, I. Piller and M. Teutsch-Dwyer (eds) *Multilingualism, Second Language Learning, and Gender* (pp. 165–194). Mouton de Gruyter.

Pavlenko, A. (2014) *The Bilingual Mind: And What it Tells us about Language and Thought*. Cambridge University Press.

Pierce, L.J., Klein, D., Chen, J.K., Delcenserie, A. and Genesee, F. (2014) Mapping the unconscious maintenance of a lost first language. *Proceedings of the National Academy of Sciences* 111 (48), 17314–17319. https://doi.org/10.1073/pnas.1409411111

Piller, I. (2002) *Invisible Ink: The Use of a 'Secret' Language in Bilingual and Monolingual Contexts.* Multilingual Matters.
Polinsky, M. (2018) *Heritage Languages and Their Speakers.* Cambridge University Press.
Polinsky, M. and Scontras, G. (2020) Understanding heritage languages. *Bilingualism: Language and Cognition* 23 (1), 4–20. https://doi.org/10.1017/S1366728919000245
Rahmadani, A. (2023) Navigating multiple languages: The use and effect of code-switching in children from mixed marriage families. *Indonesian Journal of Applied Linguistics* 13 (1), 13–25. https://doi.org/10.17509/ijal.v13i1.58252
Riera, M. (2003) *Uncommon Sense for Parents with Teenagers.* Celestial Arts.
Sancier, M.L. and Fowler, C.A. (1997) Gestural drift in a bilingual speaker of Portuguese and English. *Journal of Phonetics* 25 (4), 421–436. https://doi.org/10.1006/jpho.1997.0051
Savarino, M., van Witteloostuijn, M., Verhagen, J., Rispens, J. and Lammertink, I. (2025) Effects of input consistency on children's cross-situational statistical learning of words and morphophonological rules. *Languages* 10 (3), 52. https://doi.org/10.3390/languages10030052
Schwartz, M. (2010) Family language policy: Core issues of an emerging field. *Applied Linguistics* 31 (2), 171–192.
Shelton, M., Counselman, D. and Gutiérrez Palma, N. (2017) Metalinguistic intuitions and dominant language transfer in heritage Spanish syllabification. *Heritage Language Journal* 14 (3), 288–306.
Singer, J. (2017) 'Neurodiversity: The birth of an idea'. In H. Bertilsdotter Rosqvist, N. Chown and A. Stenning (eds) *Neurodiversity Studies: A New Critical Paradigm.* Routledge.
Tannen, D. (1990) *You Just Don't Understand: Women and Men in Conversation.* William Morrow.
Tannenbaum, M. and Howie, P. (2002) The association between language maintenance and family relations: Chinese immigrant children in Australia. *Journal of Multilingual and Multicultural Development* 23 (5), 408–424. https://doi.org/10.1080/01434630208666477
Toppelberg, C.O. and Collins, B.A. (2010) Language, culture, and adaptation in immigrant children. *Child and Adolescent Psychiatric Clinics of North America* 19 (4), 697–717. https://doi.org/10.1016/j.chc.2010.07.003
Uljarević, M., Katsos, N., Hudry, K. and Gibson, J.L. (2016) Practitioner review: Multilingualism and neurodevelopmental disorders - an overview of recent research and discussion of clinical implications. *Journal of Child Psychology and Psychiatry* 57 (11), 1205–1217. https://doi.org/10.1111/jcpp.12596
Walker, N. (2021) Neurodiversity: Some basic terms and definitions. In N. Walker, *Neuroqueer Heresies.* Autonomous Press.
Wang, X.L. (2008) *Growing up with Three Languages: Birth to Eleven.* Multilingual Matters.
Wang, X.L. (2016) *Maintaining Three Languages: The Teenage Years.* Multilingual Matters.
Ward, R. and Sanoudaki, E. (2021) Bilingualism in children with a dual diagnosis of Down syndrome and Autism Spectrum Disorder. *Clinical Linguistics & Phonetics* 35 (7), 663–689. https://doi.org/10.1080/02699206.2020.1818288
Wittgenstein, L. (1922) *Tractatus Logico-Philosophicus. Translated by C.K. Ogden.* Routledge & Kegan Paul, p. 149.
Yu, B. (2013) Issues in bilingualism and heritage language maintenance: Perspectives of minority-language mothers of children with autism spectrum disorders. *American Journal of Speech-Language Pathology* 22 (1), 10–24.
Zimmerman, F.J., Christakis, D.A. and Meltzoff, A.N. (2007) Associations between media viewing and language development in children under age 2 years. *The Journal of Pediatrics* 151 (4), 364–368. https://doi.org/10.1016/j.jpeds.2007.04.071

Index

www.ingramcontent.com/pod-product-compliance
Lightning Source LLC
Chambersburg PA
CBHW080334090826
49567CB00029B/351
* 9 7 8 1 8 3 6 6 8 4 4 7 3 *